CIVIL STRIFE IN THE MIDLANDS

1642-1651

CIVIL STRIFE IN THE MIDLANDS

1642-1651

The most Illustrious and High borne PRINCE RUPERT,
PRINCE ELECTOR, Second Son to FREDERICK
KING of BOHEMIA, GENERALL of the HORSE
of Hs MAJESTIES ARMY, KNIGHT of the Noble
Order of the GARTER.

Woodcut depicting Prince Rupert and the 'Birmingham Butcheries' from a
pamphlet entitled *The Bloody Prince, or a Declaration of the Most Cruell
Practices of Prince Rupert and the rest of the Cavaliers . . .*, dated 1643.
(See Chapter Six.)
Reproduced by permission of the Syndics of the University Library, Cambridge.

CIVIL STRIFE
in the
MIDLANDS
1642 – 1651

R. E. SHERWOOD

PHILLIMORE

1974

Published by
PHILLIMORE & CO. LTD.
London and Chichester

Head Office: Shopwyke Hall,
Chichester, Sussex, England.

ISBN 0 85033 027 0

PRINTED IN GREAT BRITAIN
by W & J Mackay Limited, Chatham

FOR   DOREEN

And revolution brought upon the
Cities of the Hellas many terrible
Calamities, such as have and always
Will be while human nature remains
The same. . .

THUCYDIDES

CONTENTS

ILLUSTRATIONS

MAPS

PREFACE

This is an attempt at a connected account of the part played by, and the military events that took place in, the Midlands during the English Civil War. More important, it is also an attempt to describe some of the burdens that the war laid on the backs of the inhabitants of this region which, because of its divided allegiance and strategic position, probably suffered more, and certainly for longer, than the rest of the country during the great struggle.

Certain incidents of minor military significance may appear to have received treatment disproportionate to their importance to the general conduct of the war. This has been done purposely in order to emphasise the effects of the war on the community, the bulk of which was totally indifferent to the cause of either party and wished only to be left in peace.

Naturally the war in the Midlands cannot be completely isolated for separate treatment without distortion or the omission of relevant and supremely important facts. I have, therefore, endeavoured throughout to keep local occurrences linked up with the main stream of events.

The Midlands is a singularly anomalous region, possessing, as it does, no fixed boundaries. For my Midlands I have chosen those counties that I believe are most generally regarded as belonging to this region. They are, Derbyshire, Gloucestershire, Herefordshire, Leicestershire, Northamptonshire, Nottinghamshire, Oxfordshire, Rutlandshire, Shropshire, Staffordshire, Warwickshire and Worcestershire.

I have quoted extensively from contemporary material believing, as I do, that only by relating events in the words of those whose story it is can a living picture of this remarkable epoch in our annals be evoked. The original spelling and punctuation of the period, which tended to be arbitrary, have been largely retained. Only where their peculiarities obscure the meaning of the text have they been modernised. Editorial insertions appear within square brackets. The dates indicated are in the contemporary reckoning except that the year is

11

given as beginning on 1 January and not 25 March.

At the risk of sounding repetitious I have called the two contending parties by their correct names only, those of Royalist and Parliamentarian, and not by any of the appellations afforded to them by their respective enemies, or by later generations, except, of course, when I have quoted from contemporary material.

The main sources which I have used are listed in the bibliography, and references to quotations from these are given in each chapter. In addition to those works listed various local histories and guide books have also been consulted. These often valuable sources of information I have not enumerated principally because many of them make only slight or indirect reference to the Civil War. Nevertheless, my acknowledgement of their usefulness is nonetheless genuine for the general form in which I give expression to it.

I wish to thank the Principals and particularly the staffs of the following Libraries and Record Offices for the assistance afforded to me in consulting their works and original sources of information on the period, and for responding so readily and courteously to my enquiries for information: The University Library, Cambridge, The British Museum and Public Record Office, London, The City of Birmingham Reference Library, Gloucester City Library, Worcester City Libraries, Museum and Art Gallery, Staffordshire Record Office, County Borough of Northampton Central Public Library, and the National Library of Wales, Aberystwyth, together with the Town Clerk of the Borough of Wolverhampton and the Town Clerk's Department of Stourbridge Corporation.

This book owes much to the advice of others. In particular I am indebted to Mr. Roy May who first drew my attention to the subject, and also to Dr. R.C. Smail, M.B.E., M.A. (Cantab.), Fellow of Sidney Sussex College, Cambridge, and Professor C.A. Holmes, M.A., Ph.D. (Cantab.) of Cornell University and sometime Fellow of Christ's College, Cambridge, both of whom gave me considerable encouragement and practical assistance.

I have also to thank my wife to whom I owe a debt which can never be fully repaid.

Cambridge   R.E. Sherwood

CHAPTER ONE

THE KING THROWS DOWN THE GAGE

On 22 August 1642, at Nottingham, Charles, King of England, raised his royal standard. This was the time honoured signal for assembling feudatories and retainers for military service and as such was a declaration of war. This was not, however, to be a war against the foreigner, but against the King's own subjects to determine whether the will of the monarch or the will of Parliament should be supreme in the land.

It had been evident for some time that the monarchy and much of the nation were moving in opposite directions; on the one hand the King was preparing to establish himself as an absolute, albeit paternal, ruler while on the other certain of his subjects were drifting towards revolution. In his attempts to secure a more centralised and autocratic form of government Charles was simply reflecting the absolutist theory of Divine Right, common to rulers of the age. But mid-17th century English society contained elements that were determined to resist the King's policies. The most powerful of these elements were the commercial and gentry classes whose interests were represented in Parliament, the institution in which their resistance to princely autocracy became crystallised. Among the merchants were many who considered that they should command a share in the government of the country commensurate with their not inconsiderable economic power. At the same time, sections of the gentry class, who in the exercise of local power enjoyed a degree of autonomy, resented the encroachment upon their political and judicial liberties by the government, which was the logical outcome of the King's centralising policies.

These were, of course, the middle class groups of English society; middle class, that is, in the sense that on the social scale they were interposed between the nobility and the so-called labouring poor. But Charles's religious policies determined that these groups would secure the support of both the as yet disenfranchised masses and some of the nobility. This was because many Englishmen from peer to ploughman had been directly affected by the strong strain of apocalyptic revivalism which ran through 17th century religion, and which had taken on varieties of expression that Charles, in his insistence on uniform religious practice, and submission to his state church, which many thought was being 'squared' to the Church of Rome, refused to tolerate.

Also, with the possibility of the old order being overthrown, potential revolutionary movements of all shades, some fighting for abstract doctrines, others for more tangible things, attached themselves to the Parliamentary cause. Thus, under the umbrella title of 'Parliament', elements of all classes were united against Charles's autocratic rule, even though these elements were not moved by the same grievances or desired the same ends.

The translation of these feelings into physical opposition to the King, and for that matter the feelings themselves, were, however, mainly confined to the southern and eastern counties of England. The relatively isolated northern and western districts of the country, excepting the large commercial centres, remained unaffected by the political, social and theological speculation which had stirred up men's minds elsewhere. Here, and in 'other dark corners of the land'[1] that had been held in a similar anachronistic state of social suspense, the sentiment of unceasing loyalty to an established monarch as a religious and moral duty was still strong. It was, therefore, to these areas that Charles looked for support when Parliament finally resolved to fight for the maintenance of their civil liberties as men, and their religious liberties as Christians.

Between the districts in which one party was practically supreme lay a debatable land formed by the Midland counties. This debatable land was not only the scene of numerous struggles between Royalist and Parliamentarian for local supremacy, but was also the ground on which the main armies of the contending parties clashed in the struggle for national supremacy.

While most of England suffered considerable damage, this particular area, because of its divided allegiance and strategic importance, suffered more, and for longer, than the rest of the country. Thus, the Midlands, described somewhat ungraciously by Hilaire Belloc as 'sodden and unkind', can justifiably be called the Belgium of the English Civil War.

Charles had chosen Nottingham as the opening scene of the coming tragedy for purely strategic reasons. Lying as it did on the Trent, which was conterminous with the southern-most confines of the Royalists' northern territory and the debatable Midland plain, it represented the nearest safe point to the King's objective, London. Nottingham also commanded a vital bridge in the national highway system, such as it was, thus providing a convenient rallying point for Royalists from all parts of England.

Englishmen did not, however, respond with particular alacrity to the King's call to arms. The Royalists' attempt to enlist the support of the trained bands by a Commission of Array met with little success. This was hardly surprising for although, by contemporary definition, the trained bands or county militia 'accounted the main support of the realme, and bulworks against unexpected invasions', they were, with the exception of the trained bands of London, 'effeminate in courage and incapable of discipline, because their whole course of life was alienated from warlike imployment'.[2] Furthermore, they held it their chief privilege not to be compelled to fight outside their own county and as often as not would not fight even inside it. Charles therefore disarmed the trained bands of Nottinghamshire and the adjacent counties of Derby and Leicester and used their weapons to arm his volunteers, such as they were.

The lack of volunteers from among private individuals, especially from those living in Nottinghamshire and the adjacent counties, is also explicable, for the Royalists daily pillaged men's houses, drove away their cattle, took their arms and money, spoiled their goods, and in consequence robbed them of all means of living and subsistence.[3]   In particular the persistent malfeasance of the King's nephew, Prince Rupert, during his foraging expeditions, did little to win support for the Royalist cause. On one such expedition the Prince demanded from the Mayor of Leicester the sum of £2,000, 'for the safeguard of his Royall person, against the rebellious insurrections of the true Malignant Party', adding that 'If any disaffected persons with you shall refuse themselves or perswade you to neglect this command, I shall tomorrow appear before your towne in such a posture with horse, foote and cannon as shall make you knowe tis more safe to obey than resist his Maiesties Commands'.[4]   Pecuniary demands as the price of immunity from plunder may have been standard practice in Europe where the Prince had gained his military experience, but to peace-loving Englishmen, who knew nothing of 'the liberty of wars', although they were soon to learn, it was an infringement upon their personal liberties. Charles did, however, remonstrate with Rupert concerning his actions at Leicester, but kept the money, about £500, which was all that the citizens felt disposed to give.

Many potential Royalists may also have felt that the King was weakening in his resolve when he attempted to come to terms with Parliament after the standard had been raised, and that their immediate support might well be answerable if a compromise peace was made, as at one time seemed likely. In addition, the number who desired to sit still was greater than those who desired to engage in either party, until 'prompted' by one side or the other.

Although the King's strength increased after it became evident that there could be no agreement between himself and Parliament, the measure of support was still far less than he had anticipated. As a result of this he became disenchanted with Nottingham where he had received so many mortifications; not the least of which was a rather cynical petition submitted by some Midland bowyers and fletchers begging him to fight the war with bows and arrows and so support their declining business. Charles therefore turned his gaze towards the Welsh border 'where', according to the contemporary historian, the Earl of Clarendon, 'the power of the Parliament had been least prevalent, and where some regiments of foot were levying for his service'.[5]

The would be warrior-king, accompanied by 500 horse, five regiments of infantry, which included some 'very good recruits of foot' from Staffordshire,[6] and 12 pieces of artillery, quitted Nottingham on 13 September for what was to be the first of his marches through the Midland shires. He arrived at Derby on the same day where 'he received clear information from the well affected party in Shrewsbury that that town was at his devotion'.[7] Shrewsbury offered other inducements too. It was on the borders of North Wales where, as has already been stated, the Royalists could count on considerable support, and it commanded the River Severn which might prove useful.

After resting for three nights at Derby, Charles set out for Shrewsbury. He spent a night at his own royal castle at Tutbury, which a century earlier had been one of the many prisons of his grandmother, Mary Queen of Scots, and travelled thence to Uttoxeter, Stafford and Wellington.

At Uttoxeter the King found 'a little army of knights and gentlemen rallied in a warlike posture'. But they assured him that they came 'rather as petitioners than opposers' and asked him to abandon his evil counsellors and his arms.[8] On the 17th Charles arrived at Stafford where he received a more encouraging reception and where Rupert is reported to have entertained the local populace with a display of marksmanship by picking off the weathercock on St. Mary's steeple.

Wellington was reached by the King and his small but now growing army on 19 September. Here the first concentration of Royalist forces took place. Here also the King caused his military orders for the discipline and government of the army to be read at the head of each regiment, after which Charles himself spoke, with some volubility we are told, to the whole army:

Gentlemen,

You have heard these orders read. It is your part in your severall places to observe them exactly. The time cannot be long before we come into action. Therefore, you have the more reason to be careful. And I must tell you, I shall be very severe in the punishing of those, of what condition soever, who transgresse these instructions. I cannot suspect your courage and resolution; your conscience and your loyaltie hath brought you hither, to fight for your religion, your King, and the laws of the land. You shall meet with no enemies but traitours, most of them Brownists, Anabaptists and atheists; such who desire to destroy both Church and State, and who have already condemned you to ruin for being loyall to us.

And by way of a peroration Charles made his declaration of intent in the form of a protestation, indicating to all the stand he was making in the ensuing struggle:

I desire to govern by the known laws of the land, and that the liberty and property of the subject may be by them preserved with the same care as my own just rights. And if it please God, by his blessing upon this armie raised for my necessary defence, to preserve me from this rebellion, I do solemnly and faithfully promise in the sight of God to maintain the just priviledges and freedom of Parliament, and to govern by the known laws of the land to the utmost of my power; and particularly to observe inviolably the laws consented to me by this Parliament. [9]

According to Clarendon, 'a more general and passionate expression of affection cannot be imagined than he [the King] received by the people of those counties of Derby, Stafford, and Shropshire, as he passed, or a better reception than he found at Shrewsbury, into which town he entered on Tuesday the 20th of September'.[10] But then the presence of such armed might was guaranteed to strike a decent love into the hearts of the King's fearful subjects. This was probably as true of Shrewsbury as anywhere else and was no doubt the reason for the enthusiastic welcome that Charles received from the inhabitants of that town.

The King's continuance at Shrewsbury soon caused considerable inconvenience and hardship to the inhabitants of the town and surrounding districts. The soldiers who had been billeted upon them often conducted themselves with great swagger and would resort to acts of violence whenever their exaggerated demands were not complied with. The situation was exacerbated by the large influx of new recruits into the town who were compelled to live by plundering their 'hosts', as the Royal coffers were insufficient to pay them.

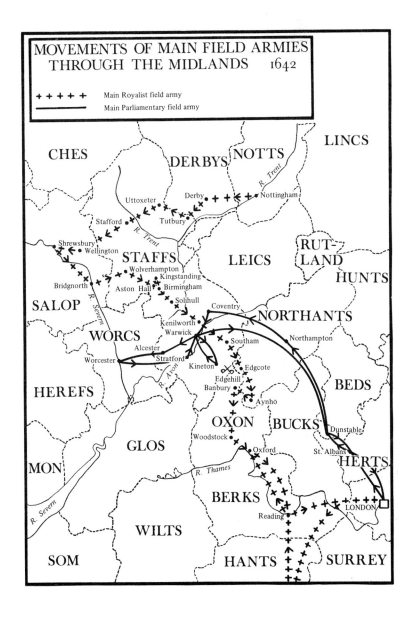

MOVEMENTS OF MAIN FIELD ARMIES
THROUGH THE MIDLANDS   1642

+ + + + + Main Royalist field army
───────── Main Parliamentary field army

It was for the express purpose of paying the soldiery that the Royal mint at Aberystwyth was removed to Shrewsbury and re-established in a building at the bottom of Pride Hill. The mint, which was under the superintendence of Thomas Bushell, a prominent Midland tycoon from Cleeve Prior in the Vale of Evesham, coined a great part of the plate sent to the King by the colleges of Oxford and Cambridge and private individuals. The obverse of the pieces struck at Shrewsbury were similar to, and sometimes from the same dies as, those struck at Aberystwyth, but with the words RELIG.PROT.,LEG.ANG.,LIBER.PAR., [the Protestant religion, the laws of England, the liberties of Parliament] on the reverse, which represented in abbreviated form Charles's Wellington declaration.[11]   But the mint was 'more for reputation than for use', as 'for want of workmen and instruments they could not coin a thousand pound a week',[12] and was therefore unable to assuage 'the incurable disease of want of money'.[13]

Further attempts to ameliorate the King's chronic financial condition included the sale of titles. Sir Richard Newport, a wealthy Shropshire knight, bought a peerage for a figure variously reported at something between £2,000 and £10,000, but the mayor of Shrewsbury was less forthcoming and refused the King's request to purchase a knighthood. These short-term measures did very little to improve matters and most of the soldiers remained unpaid. The result was that the swaggering soldiery added to their insatiable lust for plunder the need to vent their spleen at not receiving pecuniary reward for their service. The recipients of the soldiers' attentions were naturally the long suffering townsfolk, which must have dampened the enthusiasm of many a would-be Royalist among them, especially as their complaints to the King had little effect in alleviating their misery. Even people living miles away from Shrewsbury in the outlying districts of the county were raided by the looting soldiers, as the following letter[14] from John Weever of Drayton in Hales to Sir Francis Ottley, military governor of Shrewsbury, testifies:

> May it please your worship to bee advertized, that divers persons have had their houses plundered by some northern persons (as is conceyved that followe the campe) and especyallie the house of

John Weever dwellinge in the parishe of Drayton in Hales in the Countye of Saloppe who is his majesties most obedyent and dutyfull subject whose house the sayd persons Intended to have plundered uppon Monday night last and this last night beinge Tewseday they endeavored to plunder it but were prevented by reason hee did suspecte them then cominge thyther, and that same night they did hurte and did much vyolence to a poore man & to two of his sonnes that had lyttle or nothinge to loose, whereof his majesties most obedyent & faythfull subjects humblye pray Redresse in that behalfe

At your worships service to bee
commanded

September the 28th   Jo: Weever
   1642
Divers other persons have Receyved
the lyke revenge in these parts
that are noe Roundheades but
moste duitefull subjects to his majestie.

CHAPTER ONE

[1] John Corbet, *A true and impartiall History of the Military Government of the Citie of Gloucester* (London, 1647), p.10.

[2] Corbet, *History of the Military Government of Gloucester,* p.11

[3] *The Resolution of the County of Nottingham presented to the Earle of Essex, 12 Sept. 1642.* Thomason Tracts, E.117 (British Museum).

[4] *Records of the Borough of Leicester 1603-1688,* ed. Helen Stocks (Cambridge, 1923), p.318.

[5] Edward, Earl of· Clarendon, *The History of the Rebellion and Civil Wars in England,* ed. W. Dunn Macray (Oxford, 1888), Book VI, 21.

[6] *Ibid.*

[7] *Ibid.,* Bk. VI, 23

[8] *The King's Majesty's Demands and Propositions ... at Uxeter, (1642),* Thomason Tracts E.118.

[9] *His Majesties Speech and Protestation made in the Head of his Armie between Stafford and Wellington, 19th September, 1642.* (London, 1642)

[10] Clarendon, Bk.VI, 29.

[11] 'History of the Shrewsbury Mint, with an account of the coins struck there', by R. Lloyd Kenyon, *Shropshire Archaeological Society Transactions*, 2nd Series, Vol.X (1898), p.251.

[12] Clarendon, Bk.VI, 69.

[13] *Ibid.*, Bk. VI, 64

[14] 'The Ottley Papers Relating to the Civil War', ed. William Phillips, *Shropshire Archaeological Society's Transactions*, 2nd Series, Vol.VII (1895), p.249.

CHAPTER TWO

PARLIAMENT ACCEPTS THE CHALLENGE

While Charles was still at Nottingham the sardonic, pipe-smoking Earl of Essex had occupied Northampton with the main Parliamentarian army. There exists a very clear description of mid-17th century Northampton in the letters of Sergeant Nehemiah Wharton, a merchant apprentice serving in the Parliamentary Army. 'Our place of rendezvous is Northampton', he writes, 'which, for situation, circuit, and stateliness of building, exceeds Coventry; but the walls are miserably ruined, though the county abounds in mines of stones'.[1]

If Wharton's letters, which were addressed to his master in London, appear reminiscent of those written by someone serving abroad it is because the war had given Wharton what was probably his first opportunity of stepping over the border of his home county or 'country', for under normal circumstances the vast majority of the population in 17th century England rarely, if ever, ventured further than a few miles from their native village or town.

Essex's object was not to effect an outright military victory over the King but to put sufficient pressure upon him to bring about a compromise favourable to Parliament, and for this the earl did not lack resources. Parliament did not experience the manifold difficulties which beset the King, chiefly because the Parliamentary party held London. As the nucleus of its army Parliament could command the services of the London-trained bands which, apart from being reasonably well drilled and well officered, were a little more inclined to fight outside their own locality than the trained bands in other parts of the country, although they naturally preferred to remain at home defending the capital. The remainder of the Parliamentary army was made up of volunteers. John Vicars, the Parliamentary chronicler, records that 'about 5,000 able young Citizens in one day offered their service to the parliament',[2] most of whom were fired with emotional zeal for the cause. But the prospect of licensed brutality and looting also attracted the sweepings of humanity from the streets of the metropolis, cut-throats, cut-purses, and the like, into the army.

Control of London also gave the Parliamentarians immediate, if not permanent, pecuniary advantages as it was the economic and commercial hub of the nation. According to Vicars, 'an £100,000 worth of plate [was] ordered to be forthwith coyned into money, to prepare an army, and necessaries thereto'.[3] Thus, on 6 August 1642 the Committee of Lords and Commons for the Safety of the Kingdom was able to command that the soldiers should have delivered unto them, at their first marching, coats, shoes, shirts, and caps to the total value of 17s. for every man.

Added to the obvious advantages that London could provide in terms of the provision of money, men and materials, was a less obvious advantage in the field of propaganda. As there were few presses outside London Parliament possessed a virtual monopoly in this new and potent aspect of warfare. The population was bombarded with innumerable tracts and news-sheets which did, as the poet John Hall remarked, 'like hailstones fly'. Some were vehicles for the political and religious speculation which swept England at the outbreak of the Civil War. Others, which resembled penny dreadfuls and shilling shockers, gave publicity to matters which were calculated to instil in the mind of the reader a deadly hatred towards the King and his party. From 'correspondents' came reports that the King's soldiers had crucifixes hanging around their necks, and worse, that when the King and his army occupied Shrewsbury 'Cavaliers' had 'ravished the wife of a very discreet, moderate, able, and godly minister in Shropshire'. And it was not unusual for some prominent Royalist to die many times over in gory 'reports' of 'Great and Cruell Battles'.

The Royalists were eventually able to reply to the outpourings of the Parliamentarian presses with their news-sheet *Mercurius Aulicus, A Diurnal, Communicating the intelligence, and affaires of the Court to the rest of the Kingdom.*

In this unembellished statements were also rare and Parliamentary reports of great victories became reversals in which the 'Rebels' were 'extremely well cudgelled', or received 'a handsome bashing' from the King's forces. Thus the reports of both sides, official, or otherwise, would tend, at first sight, to be lacking in veracity. But beneath the crude propoganda, the party venom, the vituperation, prurience, and sheer wishful thinking, there often lay a kernel of truth capable of extraction and decoction.

Essex, when he learned of the King's move in the direction of Shrewsbury, also decided to move west. He crossed Warwickshire and on 23 September entered Worcestershire, the beauty and bounteous fruitfulness of which county inspired Wharton to wield again his prolific pen:

> Briefly Worcestershire is a pleasant county, abounding in corn, woods, pastures, hills, and valleys; every hedge and highway beset with fruit, especially pears, whereof they make that pleasant drink called perry, which they sell for 1d. a quart, though better than ever you tasted at London. [4]

The Parliamentary army arrived at Worcester, which in Wharton's estimation was 'the largest city I have seen since leaving London',[5] on 24 September. This same city, whose motto was CIVITAS IN BELLO IN PACE FIDELIS, had but a few days earlier harboured a convoy of bullion on its way from Oxford to the King. A detachment of troops from Essex's army, under Colonel John Brown, attempted to ambush the convoy at Powick Bridge, just outside the city. But Prince Rupert, who had detached himself from the main Royalist army at Stafford, was also trying to make contact with the convoy. The result was a sudden and unexpected meeting between the two parties on the bridge. In the skirmish that followed, which was the first real contact between the main field armies, the Parliamentarians fared rather badly for 'the Prince charged and routed them and sent them packing in great confusion and disorder'.

This ignominious defeat had a marked psychological effect on Essex's troops, which was not improved upon by the fact that a continuous down-pour had rendered them bedraggled and mud-stained. It was understandable therefore that the soldiers needed an outlet for their anger and frustration,

and where better than on Worcester, which was, according to
Wharton, 'so base, so papistical, and atheistical, and abomin-
able, that it resembles Sodom, and is the very emblem of
Gomorrah, and doubtless it would have been worse than
either Algiers or Malta, - a very den of thieves, and a
receptacle and refuge for all the hell-hounds in the country,
- I should have said in the land'.[6]

The cathedral suffered most, in anticipation, it would seem,
of the Solemn League and Covenant that Parliament and
many of its supporters were to take in September 1643, to
extirpate 'Popery . . . superstition, heresy, schism, profane-
ness, and whatsoever shall be found to be contrary to sound
doctrine and the power of godliness'.[7] Thus, by destroying
the cathedral organ, vestments, images and other visible
tokens of the old religion, the Parliamentary soldiers were
able to prove their zeal for the purity of the Protestant faith
and satisfy their predatory instincts at the same time. Their
enthusiasm for sacrilege was further stimulated by the dis-
covery of a Royalist arms cache in the crypt, for which it was
felt that reprisals were in order.

In the city itself everything of value was confiscated and
despatched to London as booty, including the mayor and one
of the city aldermen. This was in spite of the fact that the
city had paid Essex the sum of £5,000 for immunity from
plunder. For good measure the earl also hanged in the market
place some citizens whom he suspected of being Royalist
spies.

Looting was not, it seems, confined to the city. According
to a Royalist source Mr. Rowland Bartlett of Castlemorton,
a village some 13 miles from Worcester, received the unwel-
come attentions of some of Essex's men during which it was
reported:

> They take away good store of bacon from his roofe, and beefe
> out of the powdering tubs; they steale his pots, pannes, and kettles,
> together with his pewter to a great value, they seize on all his
> provisions for hospitality and house-keeping, and then breake his
> spits, as unnecessary utensells, they expose his bedding to sale, and
> presse carts to carry away his chairs, stooles, couches, and trunks. [8]

Apparently this was not the first visit that Bartlett had
received from Parliamentary soldiers in search of loot. Earlier,

on 21 September 1642, some soldiers from Gloucester, commanded by Captain Scriven, the son of an ironmonger of that city, had surrounded Mr. Bartlett's house and after Scriven had confiscated the family's more valuable possessions he allowed his men to take away what they liked.

... in a confused tumult they rush into the house; and as eager hounds at a losse offer here and there, and know not well where to fasten, so these hunt from the parlour to the kitchen, from thence by the chambers, to the garrats ... besides Master Bartlet's, his wives, and childrens wearing apparell, they rob their servants of their clothes: with the but ends of musquets they breake open the hanging presses, cupboards, and chests: no place was free from this ragged-regiment ... they met with Mistress Bartlets sweet-meats, these they scatter on the ground: not daring to tast of them for feare of poyson ... except bedding, pewter, and lumber, they left nothing behind them, for besides two horses laden with the best things (Scrivens owne plunder) there being an hundred and fifty rebells, each rebell returned with a pack at his back. As for his beere, and perry, what they could not devoure, they spoyle, the earth drinking what the rebells could not. [9]

Another instance of plundering, this time in Strensham, was recorded by Sergeant Wharton, in another of his letters:

Tuesday our soildiers, by commission from his Excellency [Essex], marched seven miles to Sir William Russell's house, and pillaged it unto the bare walls. [10]

Some time was, however, devoted to constructive activities whilst the Parliamentary army was at Worcester. Essex attempted to instil some training and military discipline into his men, 'to bring them to use their arms readily and expertly' so that they would 'be well instructed in the necessary rudiments of war, that they may know to fall on with discretion, and retreat with care'. Essex also spoke at the head of his army as Charles had done at Wellington: 'I do promise', harangued the earl in a speech that echoed almost exactly the sentiments of the King, '... that I shall undertake nothing but what shall tend to the advancement of the true Protestant Religion, the securing of his Majesty's person, the maintenance of the just privilege of Parliament, and the liberty and property of the subject'.[11] The reference to his Majesty's person avers Parliament's official policy of sedulously avoiding attacks on Charles in person and attributing all their woes to the King's 'evil counsellors' from whose hold Parliament hoped to secure the release of the King. This rather naive attitude did not, however, survive the war.

CHAPTER TWO

[1] *The Calendar of State Papers: Domestic Series* 1641-1643, p.385.

[2] John Vicars, *God in the Mount, Or, England's remembrancer* (London, 1642), p.126.

[3] *Ibid.*, p.127

[4] *Cal. S.P. Dom.* 1641-1643, p.395.

[5] *Ibid.*

[6] *Ibid.*, p.397

[7] John Rushworth, *Historical collections abridged and improved* (London 1703-1708), Vol.5, p.212.

[8] B. Ryves, *Mercurius Rusticus: or, the countries complaint of the barbarous out-rages committed by the sectaries of the late flourishing kingdome* (Oxford, 1646), part I, p.164.

[9] *Ibid.*, pp.162-164

[10] Letters from a Subaltern Officer in the Earl of Essex's Army, written in the summer and autumn of 1642, *Archaeologia, or, Miscellaneous Tracts relating to Antiquity*, published by the Society of Antiquaries of London, Vol.XXXV (1853), p.330.

[11] *A Worthy Speech spoken by the Earle of Essex in the Head of his Armie, 24th September, 1642*, Thomason Tracts, E.200.

CHAPTER THREE

THE ROAD TO EDGEHILL

Encouraged by the preoccupation of Essex's army at Worcester, and eager to afford employment to his soldiers, whose dissatisfaction was growing daily, Charles finally resolved to advance towards the centre of disaffection, London, as the only hope of a sure victory depended on him wresting the control of the administrative and financial centre of the country from the Parliamentary party. The King and his army therefore moved out of Shrewsbury on 12 October, to the immense relief, no doubt, of the ill-used Salopians. A small garrison was, however, left behind to ensure that the town remained in Royalist hands.

Rupert again detached himself from the main army, taking a small body of men with him to scour the countryside in search of arms, money and recruits. His foraging took him to Shifnall, Wolverhampton, and Enville where he spent a night as the guest of Walter Moseley of the Mere. He travelled thence to Stourbridge where he lodged at the house of Richard 'the Fiddler' Foley, the site of which is now occupied by the *Talbot Hotel*. Foley was the son of a Dudley nail maker and had done rather well for himself by marrying the daughter of William Brindley, of the Hyde, Kinver. Brindley had been responsible for the introduction of the German method of making iron to Kinver Mill, the first to be erected in England for the rolling and slitting of iron. By using techniques learned on visits to Sweden, Foley developed his father-in-law's process still further, and became one of the prominent industrialists of his day. It is therefore likely that the purpose of Rupert's visit was to open the preliminary negotiations of the agreement which Foley later entered into with the King to supply the Royal army with iron ordnance, grenades, shot, pike-heads and nails.

The following extract from the accounts for October 1642

of the mayor of Walsall, John Walton, shows that Walsall too
received a visit from the Prince.

	£	s.	d.
Payd for Wyne and Bottles presented to Prince Roberte and otherwise for beere in all		17.	0.
Give Prince Roberte Secretarie	2.	0.	0.
Given Prince Roberte in Gould, And a Purse with it	20.	0.	0.

From Stourbridge Rupert was able to observe the activities
of the Parliamentary army at Worcester from a safe distance.
There was, however, a small Parliamentary force, commanded
by a Lord Wharton, quite near to Stourbridge, at Kidderminster. The appearance on 14 October of some of Rupert's
scouts on Kinver Edge, which is a great bluff of sandstone
just outside Stourbridge, led Wharton to believe that the
whole body of the King's army was marching towards
Worcester and would be passing through Kidderminster.
His lordship quite naturally 'made a soldier-like retreat from
Kidderminster, excusing his not fighting with Prince Rupert
in regard of the inequality of numbers; but it is commonly
and confidently reported by others that for haste or fear he
left some wagons and 3 or 4 pieces of ordnance behind him'.[1]
Haste and fear were probably responsible for this entry,
dated 14 October 1642, in the Kidderminster parish register:

> ... buried, one Thomas Kinge a pliament souldier that brake his
> necke, fallinge downe the rocke towards Curstfield into the
> hollowway that leads to Beawdley .

The abandoned ordnance, 'requisitioned' by Rupert, was
of considerable value, for at this time guns, by gross weight,
were valued at between £20 and £30 a ton. It was these
pecuniary considerations that prompted one Royalist, the
Earl of Denbigh, to remark: 'I had rather lose ten lives than
one piece of my artillerie'.
The same day on which he left Shrewsbury Charles entered
Bridgnorth where, we are told, people cheered him through
the streets and the bells were pealed to welcome him. · But
joy was no doubt tempered with anxiety as preparations for
the evil days to come were carried out. The gates were

strengthened with chains and posts, and chains had been placed at the ends of several streets.

The King remained at Bridgnorth for three days and stayed at the castle as the guest of Sir Thomas Whitmore of Apley, while the army, which with the arrival of the last of the Welsh levies had grown to 14,000, was billeted on the inhabitants of the town and the surrounding countryside.

On 15 October the King arrived at Wolverhampton where he occupied a house the site of which is now part of the Mander Centre shopping area. The townspeople, we are told, responded generously to an appeal by the King for money; Mr. Gough, who was reputed to be the town's wealthiest merchant contributing £1,200.

Charles also despatched a summons, signed and 'Given att Our Court att Wolverhampton this 17th day of October, 1642', addressed to his 'trusty and wellbeloved' inhabitants of Lichfield to send all their arms and contributions of money and plate, 'to our Royall Standard', in order to relieve the King's 'extraordinary visible necessity'. It is not known whether the response by the 'trusty and wellbeloved' inhabitants of Lichfield to the King's summons was as enthusiastic as that of the townsfolk of Wolverhampton, who had 16,000 good reasons (the number of soldiers now in Charles' army) for their display of loyalty.

The soldiery occupied themselves in their idle moments at Wolverhampton in the usual manner, by plundering the inhabitants of the town and the surrounding districts. They afforded to the Church of St. Peter the sort of attention that is normally attributed to soldiers of the Parliamentary army, who, it might be said, could at least claim valid theological reasons for their actions. The church chest was broken open and rifled and many records and papers are known to have disappeared or been tampered with, among them the title deeds of Thomas Bradney, a Wolverhampton man in the King's army, who took advantage of his being billeted in the church to prosecute a private quarrel he had with his landlord by disarranging his title deeds. Also, many tombs were destroyed, the brasses being ripped from their matrices, and the bronze statue of Admiral Leveson, a local dignitary of Elizabethan times, was taken away to be cast into a gun.

The statue was, however, rescued by the family whose Royalism obviously had its limitations.

The King rested three nights at Wolverhampton, and then moved on to Sir Thomas Holte's residence. This was Aston Hall, then a few miles outside Birmingham, but now well within the city boundary. Here Charles spent the night of Tuesday 18 October. The following morning he addressed new recruits at a place now called Kingstanding, before proceeding on his journey through Birmingham to Kenilworth Castle.

While the King was travelling through Birmingham the townspeople successfully plundered the Royal baggage train, captured some of the guards, and despatched prisoners and loot to the Parliamentary garrisons at Warwick and Coventry. It was at this time that the phrase 'sent to Coventry' is thought to have originated, for although the Royalist prisoners-of-war at Coventry were allowed a certain amount of freedom within the city, the citizens were so strong for Parliament, that they refused to fraternise or even to speak to the incarcerated 'Cavaliers'.

For its 'peremptory malice to his majesty'[2] of which there was more, according to the same source, than at any other place, Birmingham was to pay a heavy price. It should, however, be noted that the Royalists did, on their passage through, plunder the town, although this was in defiance of the King's orders.

It was near Birmingham, at Solihull, that Charles was rejoined by his nephew, Rupert, after the latter's three days' stay at Stourbridge. He had travelled with the precious ordnance captured at Kidderminster through Hagley and over Clent. *En route,* at Kings Norton, then 'a praty uplandyshe towne', but now one of Birmingham's southern suburbs, the Prince had a brush with a Parliamentary force on its way to join Essex. According to a contemporary pamphlet, the Parliamentarians, under the command of Lord Willoughby, scored a decisive victory, 'killing about 50 of the Cavaleers, and taking 20 prisoners, with the losse of 20 men'. If this account is credible then the Parliamentarians more than redressed the Kidderminster *débâcle.*

As the King was now on the move for London, Essex was

forced to move his army out of Worcester in order to get between the Royal army and its objective. Very soon both armies were marching in the same direction and drawing closer together every mile, although neither the King nor Essex was aware of the situation. This was caused by a breakdown in military intelligence, for which there were two main reasons. In the first place the roads at this time were in desperate need of repair. This is exemplified by a contemporary complaint by the Vicar of Alvechurch that 'diverse enormities redounded from the ill and negligently repaired highways', and that he himself had been 'twice fast set in the mire when riding about my lawful and necessary occasion of tythes'. Also, both armies had to pass through areas which were either completely unaware of, or uninterested in, the quarrel between Parliament and the King. The inhabitants of these areas would see no purpose in imparting valuable information to military spies of either side.

By 22 October the Royal army had reached the village of Edgcote˙ on the Northamptonshire/Warwickshire border, whence it was resolved that an attack on the Parliamentary garrison at Banbury would be launched the next day in order to obtain new clothing and victuals for the men.

While the King's army was thus camped at Edgcote and in the surrounding villages of Wormleighton, Culworth, Wardington, Cropredy and Ratley, Essex was at Kineton, which is barely a dozen miles from Edgcote and only three miles from the nearest Royalist billet at Ratley. But it was not until the morning of the 23rd that the Parliamentarians received their first intimation of the close proximity of the two armies; a fact only ascertained by the Royalists themselves at about 11 o'clock the previous evening.

The reports as to how the presence of the Royalist forces was first detected vary. One says that a scouting party riding out of Kineton on that Sunday morning perceived a fair body of horse 'upon Edge-hill in Warwickshire',[3] while another claims that a 'Worthy Devine', the Reverend Adoniram Bifield, caught sight of Rupert's cavalry quite by chance 'by the help of a perspective glass, from the top of a hill'.[4] Either way the result was the same.

Charles decided to join battle that day partly because the

Parliamentary forces might increase, but chiefly because in this particular part of the country the population was so devoted to the Parliamentary party that 'they had all provisions brought to them without the least trouble; whereas on the other side, the people were so disaffected to the King's party that they had carried away or hid all their provisions, insomuch as there was neither meat for man or horse; and the very smiths hid themselves, that they might not be compelled to shoe horses ... This proceeded not from any radical malice, or disaffection to the King's cause or his person', but from the belief 'that the cavaliers were of a fierce, bloody, and licentious disposition, and that they committed all manner of cruelty upon the inhabitants of those places where they came, of which robbery was the least'. In consequence many companies of the private soldiers in the Royal army had 'scarse eaten bread in forty and eight hours' before the battle .[5]

The King drew his infantry up six deep and the cavalry three deep on the ridge of Edgehill. The infantry comprised pikemen and musketeers. The pikemen were placed in the centre and were armed with a sword and a pike, some 16 to 18 feet long, with which they defended the musketeers from cavalry attacks. The musketeers, who were positioned on the wings of the pikemen, were armed, as their name suggests, with a musket. This was fired by means of a fuse or lighted match, which was a small cord made of twisted strands of tow, prepared by boiling in vinegar or the sediment of wine. After firing the front rank was supposed to fall back so that the second row could fire, and so on, until, by the time all six ranks had let fly, the original front rank was ready to fire again. Unfortunately, because it was impossible to time a fuse accurately, the second file would sometimes fire before the front rank had time to get out of the way. As often as not, the musket would not go off at all. Because of the ineffectiveness of the match-lock musket it is very probable that more died from wounds received by the use of the musket as a bludgeon (the technical term was 'clubbing them down'), than were actually shot.

The cavalry formed the wings of the army and was armed with a carbine and a sword. Its function was to advance at a trot to within firing range of the enemy, halt, discharge pistols and then close, exchanging sword thrusts until the enemy gave ground.

As the technique of ordnance-casting had not yet advanced far beyond the primitive skill of the bell-founder, the artillery drawn up at Edgehill was naturally crude. Any gun, however inaccurate, was deemed fit for service as long as it would stand a charge, and considerable skill and resource was required on the part of the gunners, who were unlikely to possess the knowledge of trigonometry and logarithm deemed necessary by the official manual at the time - Robert Norton's *The Gunner.*

The Parliamentarians took up position on a slight swell mid-way between the village of Kineton and the foot of Edgehill escarpment, which is a marlestone eminence running from Sun Rising Hill to Knowle End; both infantry and cavalry being drawn up in six ranks. Essex had with him some 14,870 men, a somewhat larger army than the King, who now had a total of about 14,300 men. This was in spite of the depletion of the Parliamentary forces to garrison Northampton, Warwick, Hereford, Worcester, Banbury and Coventry.

The Parliamentarians were also far better armed than the Royalists. This was, as already suggested, due to the Parliament's control of money and its possession of the magazines of Hull and the Tower of London. Such arms as the King's men had were either 'borrowed' from the trained bands of the counties through which the Royal army had travelled, or they came from private armouries, which meant that they were virtual antiques and as such were often unserviceable. An inventory taken at Tutbury Castle in 1608 had shown that most of the arms and armour stored there was 'cancered, rotten, and not worth anie thing saveinge the heades of bills, pikes, and some few callivers, but all eaten with cancer'.[6] Clarendon described the equipment of the King's army at Edgehill thus:

> ... the foot, (all but three or four hundred who marched without any weapons but a cudgel,) were armed with muskets, and bags for their powder, and pikes; but in the whole body there was not one pikeman who had a corselet, and very few musketeers who had swords. Amongst the horse, the officers had their full desire if they were

able to procure old backs and breasts and pots [helmets], with pistols or carbines for their two or three front ranks, and swords for the rest; themselves (and some soldiers by their examples) having gotten, besides their pistols and swords, a short poleaxe.[7]

The King's army was also deficient in artillery, while this particular arm of the Parliamentary forces was, again, well-equipped, although the balance was redressed a little by the fact that half of Essex's train of artillery was still a full day's march behind his army on the day of the battle.

Both armies were deficient in experienced soldiers; men who had seen service in foreign armies in Europe. Fourteen years earlier, in 1628, Sir Edward Cecil had commented: 'This kingdom hath been too long in peace, our old commanders both by sea and land are worn out, and few men are bred in their places, for the knowledge of war and almost the thought of war is extinguished'.

It is at this point that a popular generalisation, which has no doubt gained credence by appealing to the imagination, should be dispelled. The Royalists did not all wear ringlets, nor did all the Parliamentarians wear their hair cropped at Edgehill, or at any time during the Civil War, as any portrait of the period will show. It is true that for a short time at the start of the Civil War a few Puritan zealots, according to a contemporary account, 'distinguished themselves, both men and women, by several affectations of habit, looks, and words', of which close-cut hair was one. But the writer, who was the wife of Colonel Hutchinson, the Parliamentarian Governor of Nottingham Castle and a prominent Puritan, also records that these affectations were soon foresaken and, 'two or three years after, any stranger that had seen them, would have enquired the reason of that name'. Colonel Hutchinson himself, incidentally, had 'a very fine thickset head of hair' which 'was a great ornament to him'.[8]

The name Roundhead was, of course, used extensively by the Royalists when referring to Parliamentarians. But this must be taken simply as an example of the normal human tendency to affix a name of reproach indiscriminately on those of an opposite party, in order to subject them to hatred and ridicule. Similarly, the appellation Cavalier, often used by Parliamentarians when describing Royalists, was derived from the word *Cavaliero,* a Spanish trooper, which to most Englishmen represented a brutal oppressor of Protestants and the traditional enemy of England. The Royalists, however, proudly adopted this name which later acquired gay and gallant associations which belie the true character of the average cavalier.

It can therefore be accepted that there was very little to distinguish the antagonists. At Edgehill the regiments of both sides were dressed in any colour fancied by their colonels, with the result that practically every colour of the rainbow was represented. The only definite distinction between the two armies was the orange scarf worn by the Parliamentarians and the red scarf worn by the King's forces.

It was 3 o'clock before the two armies finally came to grips on that October Sunday. Battles are commonly perverse products of chance and confusion and this particular battle was no exception, for what followed can, at best, only be described as a confused *mêlée.* The Royal army had advanced down from its superior position on top of Edge Hill exposing itself to the withering fire of the Parliamentarian cannon. Then Rupert, who commanded the right wing of the King's cavalry, led the first charge in which he successfully routed the main body of the Parliamentarian horse. The success of this operation was due in part to the desertion to the Royalist side of the aptly named Sir Faithful Fortescue. Seventeen or eighteen of Fortescue's men were, however, killed by their new allies; 'by the negligence of not throwing away their orange-tawny scarfs'.[9]

The decisive advantage gained by this opening cavalry charge was not followed up. Instead, many of Rupert's men seem to have temporarily forgotten the battle and proceeded to the enemy baggage train for plunder. The remainder pursued the fleeing Parliamentary cavalry until, about a mile beyond Kineton, they met Essex's delayed artillery under the command of John Hampden, who had perceived the situation and had planted a battery across the road. Thus he was able to check, or at least deflect, the pursuers.

The Royalist reserve cavalry on the right wing, contrary to instructions, followed Prince Rupert's charge, leaving the centre of the King's army, with the infantry, the artillery, and the Royal standard, partially exposed. 'To add to our Misfortunes', wrote Sir Richard Bulstrode in his account of Edgehill, 'a careless Soldier in fetching Powder (where a Magazin was), clapt his Hand carelessly into a Barrel of Powder, with his Match lighted betwixt his Fingers, whereby much Powder was blown up and many killed'.[10]

Meanwhile the Parliamentary foot had, unlike the cavalry, stood firm, no doubt because heart had been put into them by 'divers ... eminently pious and learned pastours who ... rode up and downe the Army, through the thickest dangers, and in much personall hazzard, most faithfully and couragiously exhorting and encouraging the Souldiers to fight valiantly, and not to flye, but now, if ever, to stand to it, and fight for their Religion, Laws, and Christian Liberties'.[11] These foot regiments were backed up by two small remaining forces of Parliamentary horse commanded by Sir Philip Stapleton and Sir William Balfour, which had managed to evade the Royalist onslaught. Cavalry and infantry together got to work on the remaining Royalist forces. Balfour succeeded in cutting his way through the enemy to reach their gun battery, putting it out of action, while one of Essex's life guard slew the King's standard bearer, Sir Edmund Verney, and captured the Royal standard, but this was almost immediately retaken for the Royalists by Captain John Smith, a Worcestershire gentleman.

The Parliamentarians managed to surround the King and his retinue, but were temporarily distracted by the return to the field of some of Rupert's horse, which were almost immediately driven off again by Stapleton. But 'by this time it grew so dark, and our Powder and Bullet so spent, that it was not held fit we should Advance upon them',[12] goes the official Parliamentary account of the battle, and so the fighting deteriorated and the two armies gradually disengaged.

The official Royalist account of the battle also gives the poor light as the reason why the battle disintegrated:

> By this time it was grown so dark, that our Chief Commanders durst not charge for fear of mistaking friends for foes (though it was certainly concluded by them all, that if we had light enough, but to have given one charge more, we had totally routed all their army).[13]

It will be noted that the Parliamentarians did not forecast the outcome had the battle continued as the Royalists attempted to do. This was because as the King's forces had, even according to the Royalist Bulstrode, 'retired up the hill, from whence we came down, and left the *champ de battaile* to the enemy',[14] the Parliamentarians felt that technically they were the victors.

Both armies settled down either on or near to the battle-field for the night, 'which proved very cold by reason of a sharp frost'.[15] The Parliamentarian soldiers, however, spent a more comfortable night than their adversaries, victuals being provided by the not unbiased local people. An illustration of the degree to which the inhabitants of this area were disposed to the Parliament's cause is provided by the actions of a local woman named Hester Whyte who, after the battle, took charge of some of the wounded Parliamentarians. These 'continued at her house in great misery by reason of their wounds for three months. She often sat up night and day with them, and, in respect of her tenderness to the Parliaments friends, laid out her own money in supply of their wants'. The Royalists on the other hand were compelled to endure the elements without the comforts enjoyed by their antagonists.

With the arrival of the dawn the battle was not resumed. The Royal army went back to Edgcote and that of the Parliament retired to Warwick. Essex was urged by Hampden to use the fresh troops and artillery he had brought with him to effect a decisive victory against the King. But the earl had been discouraged by the behaviour of the main body of his cavalry and by his heavy losses for, in spite of the short duration and remarkable inefficiency of this first full-scale battle of the Civil War, no less than 1,500 were left dead on the field. And if we are to believe Royalist boasts that 'we have killed five for one', the majority of dead must have been Parliamentarians. Another reason why the battle was not resumed was probably due to the wholesale desertion from both armies during and immediately after the battle. Essex later invited those who had deserted his army to return on the tactful assumption that they had 'gone to visit their friends'.

In the last 300 years there have been numerous tales of
apparitions and the existence of a strange psychic aura at
Edgehill. The first report appeared in a pamphlet[1 6] published
in January 1643 telling of 'Apparitions and Prodigious Noyses
of War and Battels seen on Edge-Hill near Keinton in
Warwickshire', and continues thus:

> At this Edge-Hill, in the very place where the battell was strucken,
> have since and doth appeare, strange and portentuous Apparations
> of two jarring and contrary armies, ... it being certified by men of
> most credit in those parts ... between twelve and one of the clock in
> the morning was heard by some Sheepherds, and other countrymen,
> and travellers, first the sound of drummes afar off, and the noyse of
> souldiers, as it were, giving out their last groanes; ... but then, on the
> sudden ... appeared in the ayre the same incorporeall souldiers that
> made those clamours, and immediately, with Ensignes display'd,
> Drummes beating, Musquets going off, Cannons discharged, Horses
> neyghing ... the alarum ... and so pell mell to it they went ... after
> some three houres fight, that the Army which carryed the King's
> colours withdrew, or rather appeared to flie; the other remaining as
> it were masters of the field ... On Sunday, being Christmas night,
> appeared in the same tumultous warlike manner, the same two
> adverse Armies, fighting with as much spite and spleen as formerly ...
> The rumour whereof coming to his Majestie at Oxford, he
> immediately dispatched thither Colonel Kirke and three other gentle-
> men of Credit, ... who ... heard and saw the fore-mentioned prodigies,
> ... distinctly knowing divers of the apparitions or incorporeall
> substances by their faces, as that of Sir Edmund Varney, and others
> that were slaine.

Although Edgehill was militarily indecisive it was, in
retrospect, a loss politically for Charles. Had the King won
an outright victory against Essex's army he could have
marched on an overawed Parliament and an undefended
capital. As it was, Essex was able to return to London and
organise its defence in the time Charles took to arrive there,
which was three weeks; during which time the King had
satisfied his original desire to take Banbury, the soldiers and
inhabitants of which had, since the Battle of Edgehill,
'surprised many passengers, and soldiers, and others well
affected to his Majesty's service, and detained them prisoners
with great barbarousness and inhumanity'.[1 7] On his arrival
at the outskirts of the capital it became apparent that to take
it by force would be impossible, so Charles retired to Oxford,
'the only city of England that he could say was entirely at

his devotion',[18] for the winter.

CHAPTER THREE

[1] Historical Manuscripts Commission, *Seventh Report* (1879), p.530.

[2] Clarendon, Bk. VI, 83.

[3] *The Memoirs of Edmund Ludlow, 1625-1672* (London, 1894), ed. C.H. Firth, Vol.I, p.41.

[4] *A Letter from a worthy Divine to the Lord Mayor of London* (1643), Thomason Tracts E.124.

[5] Clarendon, Bk. VI, 83.

[6] *Talbot Papers,* Vol.M. p.525; Stebbing Shaw, *The History and Antiquities of Staffordshire* (London, 1798, 1801), Vol. I, p.57 (General History).

[7] Clarendon, Bk.VI, 73.

[8] *Lucy Hutchinson Memoirs of Colonel Hutchinson,* Rev. Julius Hutchinson, ed., (Everyman's Library edition, London, 1908), pp. 95-96.

[9] Clarendon, Bk. VI, 86.

[10] Sir Richard Bulstrode's Account of the Battle of Edgehill, from Peter Young's *Edgehill 1642* (Kineton, 1967),pp. 264-274.

[11] John Vicars, *Magnalia Dei Anglicana, Or, Englands Parliamentary-chronicle* (London, 1644), Parts I and II, p.200.

[12] John Rushworth, *Historical collections of private passages of state* (London, 1680-1701), Pt.III, Vol.II, p.37.

[13] Rushworth, *Historical collections,* Pt.III, Vol.II, p.43.

[14] Bulstrode's Account of Edgehill; Young's *Edgehill 1642*, pp.264-274.

[15] *The Memoirs of Edmund Ludlow, 1625-1672,* Vol.I, p.45.

[16] *A Great Wonder in Heaven, shewing the late Apparitions seen at Edge-Hill,* Thomason Tracts, E.85.

[17] *A Collection of Original Letters and Papers Concerning the Affairs of England, 1641-1660,* T. Carte, ed., (London, 1739) Vol.I, p.13.

[18] Clarendon, Bk. VI, 100.

CHAPTER FOUR

LOYALTIES AFFIRMED

Two and a half years were to elapse before the Midlands witnessed another full-scale battle between the main field armies of Parliament and the King, although these armies did pass through the region on numerous occasions, leaving in their wake a trail of rapine and desolation as evidence of their progress.

The first months of 1643 saw both sides stabilising their positions in the area. Towns were garrisoned and Parliamentarian and Royalist land-owners fortified their residences. More often than not the city corporations and rural patricians would determine the allegiance of the locality over which they exercised jurisdiction and influence. In the counties of Shropshire, Worcester, Hereford, Nottingham and Oxford most of the influential families and corporations espoused the Royalist cause and so, at this particular time, they were universally regarded as Royalist. This was especially so in the case of Shropshire which possessed no Parliamentarian garrison within its borders from the outbreak of the war until August 1643.

In Shrewsbury the appointment of Sir Francis Ottley as Governor and the strong garrison established there under his command, kept in check the element of discontent which existed in the town but not, it seems, without difficulty. All 10 prisoners on the calendar for the Spring (1643) assizes had been 'charged with speacking of ill and malytious speeches against the Kings Majestie', or being 'a Parrson justly suspected to be disaffected in not houlding the Earl of Essex, & those that take his part to be Rebells', and other similar crimes;[1] and a document dated 17 March 1643 among the Ottley papers orders the apprehension of a further 43 disloyal persons for actively displaying 'contempt to his majests person and power'.[2]

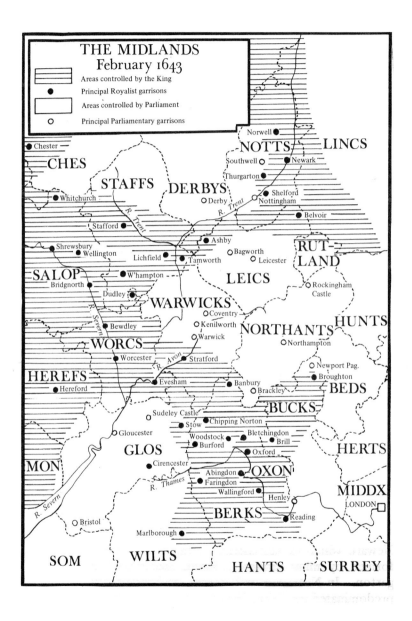

THE MIDLANDS
February 1643

Areas controlled by the King

● Principal Royalist garrisons

Areas controlled by Parliament

○ Principal Parliamentary garrisons

Parliament had lost its toehold in Worcestershire when
Sir William Russell took possession of the city of Worcester
in November 1642, after the commander of the Parliamentary
garrison, left behind by Essex, had decided that local hostility
rendered his position untenable, and had marched his men
out of the city to Gloucester. Supporters of the Parliament
in Worcester had been 'but of the middle rank of people
[artisans and small traders], and none of any great power and
eminence to take their parts'.

The evacuation of Worcester served to isolate the garrison
which Essex had also planted at Hereford, where the
commander, Lord Stamford, experienced the same local
hostility as his colleague had at Worcester. In a letter to
Parliament Stamford writes:

> ... The county, as well as this vile city, are so base and malignant
> that although the roguish army of the Welsh Papists and other
> vagabonds that were beaten in the first battle in Warwickshire do
> plunder, kill, murder, and destroy men and women, take away all
> their goods and cattle, yet such is their hatred to our condition that
> they would rather be so used than be rescued by us.[3]

This disaffection was to some extent caused by the conduct
of Stamford's own men who pillaged 'all that kept faith and
allegeance with the King', and threatened 'that they would
keep them so short that they should eate the very flesh from
their arms'.[4]

It was the attitude of the inhabitants of Hereford towards
Parliament's cause, together with a serious lack of supplies,
that persuaded Stamford to relieve himself of the responsibility
of attempting to hold the city, and so, in December 1642,
he too removed himself and his forces to Gloucester. Thus the
entire counties of Worcester and Hereford fell into the King's
hands.

In the north-eastern extremity of the region, in Nottinghamshire, a large Royalist garrison had been established at
Newark which was surrounded by a ring of outer defences
formed by minor garrisons at Norwell, Shelford and Thur-
garton. In Nottingham itself, however, the Parliamentarians
predominated and Colonel Hutchinson was able to secure the
castle for Parliament and establish a satellite garrison at
nearby Southwell.

The approaches to Oxford, where the King had retired after his abortive attempt to take London, were covered by a ring of garrisons which stretched as far as Marlborough in Wiltshire, Reading in Berkshire, and Broughton in Buckinghamshire. Those in Oxfordshire were at Banbury, Bletchingdon, Burford, Chipping Norton and Woodstock. Thus the Royalists controlled the whole of Oxfordshire except for the extreme south-east, where Parliament held Henley-on-Thames.

The King also had a considerable following in Staffordshire, but then so had Parliament, but it was the Royalists who possessed military supremacy in the county at the beginning of 1643, having established powerful garrisons at Lichfield, Tamworth, Wolverhampton, and at Stafford, where the garrison commander was the High Sheriff of the county, William Cumberford. Of these garrisons Stafford was considered by the Royalists as being of particular importance, 'it being the key of Yorkshire unto Oxford'.[5]

The only effective military force in opposition to the Royalists in the county at this time was furnished by the Moorland Dragoons, a rough troop of soldiers raised in the uplands of north-east Staffordshire around Leek, an area described by one Royalist as 'a woody enclosed country all the way, except the moores on top of the hills; a black earth where they digg and cutt a heathy turfe; a rebellious place'.[6] The Moorlanders appear to have banded together with little outside assistance and were led by one of their own number whom they referred to as 'The Grand Juryman'. Early in February 1643, on their own initiative, and armed, in the main, with only birding guns, clubs, and pieces of scythes,[7] they made a bold but futile attempt to eject the Royalist garrison at Stafford.

The principal magnate and Lord Lieutenant of Derbyshire, the Earl of Devonshire, had, at the commencement of hostilities, decided to absent himself from England and to spend the duration of the war in Europe. Derbyshire, except for the southernmost tip of the county, was thereafter controlled for Parliament by Sir John Gell, who established his headquarters in Derby Town Hall. Gell did not, however, enjoy the confidence of all the Parliamentarians in the county. Many considered him to be a man lacking in principle who had no real heart in the cause. His followers were described by Lucy Hutchinson as 'nimble youths at plunder'. This statement is supported by the observations of other contemporary writers. In a tract entitled *A Case for the City Spectacles* it is related that 'one Hope', an officer in Gell's forces, 'plundered most sacrilegously a Communion cup and was pulled out of his breeches'. But then there were as many who fought more for plunder and personal malice than for the good of the cause in these local armies as in the main field armies.

A similar situation to that in Derbyshire also existed in Warwickshire. Here Parliament held most of the county and, by way of a loan, the inhabitants contributed £1,474 9s. 11d. and 4,385 ounces of plate between August 1642 and June 1643 'towards the maintenance of the garrison in the castle of Warwick'.[8] But the area around Stratford-upon-Avon at the southern end of the county was controlled by the Royalists which, together with Shropshire, Herefordshire and Worcestershire, provided a safe corridor between the King at Oxford and the Marches and North Wales.

Both the county and the town of Gloucester were decisively on the side of the Parliamentary party, which had established garrisons at Sudeley Castle, taken from the Royalists on 29 January 1643, Cirencester and Gloucester, where the corporation had ordered that 'two great gilt bowls ... four old Maces and one old seal of Mayoralty be sold towards the charge for the fortifications of the city'.

Cirencester, 'a stragling and open towne, neither well fortified nor capable of defence',[9] was, however, lost to the King's forces on Thursday 2 February 1643. The Royalists took and carried to Oxford 1,100 prisoners, 'tied to one another with cords and match',[10] 'and fell to plundering that night, all the next day, and on Saturday ... to the utter ruin of many hundred families', so that 'the inhabitants of the miserable distressed Cyrencester' were prompted to dispatch to the King a petition to the effect that they 'having undergone all the heavy effects of your majestie's justly incensed army ... acknowledge us inexcusably faulty, but appeale unto your mercy, and to beg your pardon'.[11] Thus Cirencester found it politic to give its support to the King, which, together with the existence of a Royalist garrison at Stow-on-the-Wold, and the proximity of the county to Oxford, rendered Parliament's control over the county incomplete. But this did not prevent troops from Gloucester and Sudeley from keeping the Welsh occupied in Monmouthshire and South Wales and preventing them from sending reinforcements by the direct route to the King at Oxford.

Northamptonshire, too, supported Parliament. Here Lord Brooke had seized the castle of the county town, which at this time had become the most powerful Parliamentary garrison in the South Midlands, while the ardour of the townsfolk in the cause, or the extent of their desire to benefit from the eight *per cent* interest being offered on all loans made to Parliament, is preserved in the receipt book for the money and plate that they contributed. In one week alone (20 to 25 August 1642) gifts of silver plate, in all some 2,970 ounces, to the value of £1,073 0s. 9d., and £55 4s. 5d. in coin, were made.[1] [2]

The situation in Leicestershire was quite different. Here the southern half of the county, including Leicester itself, was held for Parliament by the Earl of Stamford's heir, Lord Grey of Groby, assisted by the republican Sir Arthur Hesilrige; while the northern part of the county was effectively controlled by the Royalist Henry Hastings, the second son of another local magnate, Lord Huntingdon. From their headquarters at Ashby-de-la-Zouch Hastings and his army, which was mainly recruited from the colliers employed in the Huntingdon family coal mines in Derbyshire, were able to keep up an effective harassing warfare with Lord Grey. They also made incursions into south Derbyshire in an effort to keep open Royalist communications along the Trent Valley.

Leicestershire is of particular interest because it provides a singularly penetrating example of the extent to which political loyalties could, at this time, be closely involved with local issues and power struggles. The rivalry between the Hastingses and Greys went back to personal feuds of far longer standing than the Civil War. In fact, it stemmed from their rivalry for the control of the county since the mid-16th century. Clarendon mentions the 'notable anymosities' of these rival magnates and states that Leicestershire was, in consequence, 'divided passionately enough without any other quarrel',[13] for the lesser gentry of the county were traditionally aligned behind one family or the other. For these two families the Rebellion was, therefore, at one level, simply a further stage in the long-drawn out battle for local domination.

For every Royalist and Parliamentarian partisan within these Midland shires there were many more whose interests were confined to living a life of their own, in which politics played merely an intermittent part, rather than to supporting either 'Roundheads' or 'Cavaliers'. This was especially true of the 'common people', very few of whom, according to the philosopher Hobbes, 'cared much for either of the causes',[14] for they loved 'their pudding at home better than a musket and pike abroad, and if they could have peace, care not what side had the better',[15] and when forced to bear arms they, remarked Sir William Brereton caustically, 'had not much mind to fight, but were glad to take any occasion to make haste home to their cows'.[16] Those like the Earl of Devonshire, whom providence had placed in more fortunate circumstances, and who were 'neither driven by ambition, nor the spirit of blind zeale', and possessed the necessary means, 'deserted the state'.[17]

The desire to maintain a position of neutrality was not confined to the apathetic. Both individuals and corporate bodies desired to preserve their properties and persons from the dangers which threatened them by the collapse of law and order and the outbreak of armed conflict. Thus, when Colonel Hutchinson had first attempted to seize Nottingham Castle, having declared that the town itself was indefensible, the townsfolk, although predominantly Parliamentarian in sympathy, were nevertheless reluctant to aid the Governor in his preparations, for they realised that if the Royalists advanced to besiege the castle they would be exposed to the dangers of war; 'what is the cause to me if my goods be lost' exclaimed one citizen, Doctor Plumtre.[18] The Colonel's offer to receive into the castle, along with their goods, all who cared to go and repair quarters there, did little to assuage the discontent. There were threats to tear the castle stone from stone, and only after the Governor had at length arrested Alderman Dury and 14 others, and sent them as mutineers to be imprisoned by Sir John Gell at Derby, was a sullen acquiescence enforced. The discontent even spread among the soldiery, which was comprised mainly of townsfolk. The soldiers considered that an attempt to hold the castle would provoke the inevitable ruin of their homes beneath its battlements, and for a time their Colonel was forced to contemplate the possibility of having to borrow men from neighbouring garrisons in order to maintain his charge.

Although Leicester, which rivalled Northampton as a stronghold of non-conformity, eventually gravitated to the side of Parliament, at the outbreak of hostilities it nonetheless endeavoured to pursue a policy of neutrality and join neither side in the dispute. The following extract from a letter,[19] written as late as January 1643 by the mayor of Leicester, Richard Ludlam, to Henry Hastings, in the latter's capacity as High Sheriff of the county, not as a Royalist, exemplifies the city's dilemma:

... whereupon havinge in our Towne neither Armes nor power to resist wee resolved to morrow to send to the Right honourable the Lord Grey by our Towne Chamberlaines to desire his Lordshipp to forbeare bringinge any forces into the Towne lest otherwise he should be the meanes to cause our prejudice in this Corporacion. As for admittinge of forces into the Towne I assure you, Sir, I shall be farr from it but if any happen to come I must confess I knowe not how to prevent them of possessinge the Towne.

Another element of neutrality emerged as a result of the inability of many to reconcile the complex and often seemingly anomalous issues with their consciences. The letter[20] reproduced below, from a Shropshire gentleman, addressed jointly to Sir Francis Ottley and the High Sheriff of Shropshire, Henry Bromley, serves to illustrate the unenviable situation in which many honest men found themselves at this time:

From Birmingham
Feb: 22 [1643]

RIGHT WORTHY SIRS,

I take so much boldness on me to write my mind unto you, I have left my Father my Wife and Children, with what Mind there's one above knows, and how much I desire to return you shall see by this.

I never had an Intention, nor yet have, of taking up Arms of neither side, my Reasons this my protestation already taken, binds me both to King and to parliament. I am not so senseless (though it were almost to be wished I were) that there are two Armies each seeking to destroy the other, and by oath bound to preserve both, each Chalenging the Protestant religion for their Standard yet the one takes the Papists the other the sismatikes for their Adherents, and (for my part) my conscience tells me they both intend the Protestant Religion, what reason have I therefore to fall out with either. Now if you'll be pleased to shelter me by your power, to live at Home is my earnest desire, beseeching you that no more protestations be Urged upon me, for I find in my own Conscience I have sufficiently enough of this, nor be compelled to bear Arms, nor clapt up as dissaffected to his Majestie, which very word I abhor from my heart. Thus wishing God to deal with me as I wish to you or either of you I rest yours to be Commanded,

JONATHAN LANGLEY

The attempts by the local armies to consolidate the Midland counties during the remainder of the war made the region an undesirable residence for those who wished to steer a middle course, for it was assumed by both sides that those who did not show positive signs of supporting their party must be opposed to it. 'Delinquents' were punished by being subjected to more frequent plundering and free billeting of troops than was usual, forced to pay more than their share of the additional taxation which the prosecution of the war had rendered necessary, had their property sequestered, or were imprisoned.

But acquiescence in the policies of the party currently in control of an area did not ensure security from the more licensed activities of soldiers from the opposite camp, who would make frequent lightning incursions into enemy held territory in search of booty. And when, in the shifting tide of war, territory changed hands, as so often happened in this area, the victors invariably exacted retribution from those 'malignant' and 'disaffected persons' suspected of collaborating with the ejected party, even if support had been given under duress.

A few of the more fortunate did, however, enjoy a degree of immunity. Parliamentarian soldiers were ordered to forbear to molest goods or chattels of Thomas Littleton, parson of Suckley and vicar of Halesowen, because he was 'a laborious, painfull minister, and well affected to the Parliament'.[21] And a similar order was issued concerning another known Parliamentarian residing in a Royalist controlled area, Robert Willmott, treasurer to the Committee for the county of Stafford. In this instance the soldiers were commanded to forbear to plunder the cloth in Willmott's fulling mills at Kidderminster and Hartlebury.[22] While Prince Rupert ordered the Royalist soldiers 'to doe noe maner of violence, injury, harme, or detriment, by unlawfull plundering, to Sir Henry Herbert, knt. of Ribsford, in the County of Worcester, in his person, family, houses, goods, tenants, woods, cattles, or chattels whatsoever, by yourselves or others, as you will answeare the contrary at your utmost perills'.[23]

But the majority, whether neutral or partisan, experienced no such exemption from the effects of civil war, and like the ass in the fable they were doomed to bear the burden regardless of who might be the master of the hour.

CHAPTER FOUR

[1] 'Ottley Papers', *Salop.Arch.Soc.Trans.*, Vol.VII (1895), pp.269-273.

[2] *Ibid.*, p.279.

[3] J. & T.W. Webb, *Memorials of the Civil War in Herefordshire* (London, 1879), Vol.I, p.204.

[4] Ryves, *Mercurius Rusticus*, Part I, pp.71, 76.

[5] *Hastings Manuscripts*, Hist.MSS.Comm.(1933) Vol.II, p.91.

[6] Richard Symonds, *Diary of the Marches of the Royal Army During the Great Civil War*, ed. C.E. Long (Camden Society, 1859), p.176.

[7] *Hastings MSS.* Hist.MSS.Comm. Vol.II, p.91.

[8] Commonwealth Exchequer Papers - Assessments, loans, and contributions - Accounts and schedules - Warwickshire (S.P. 28/182).

[9] Corbet, *History of the Military Government of Gloucester*, p.20.

[10] Nehemiah Wallington, *Historical Notes of Events Occurring Chiefly in The Reign of Charles I* (London, 1869), Vol.II, p.146.

[11] *A Relation of the Taking of Cicester in the County of Gloucester, on Thursday, Febru.2, 1643;* Bibliotheca Gloucestrensis, ed. John Washbourn (London, 1823/1825), Pt.I, pp.183-4, 189.

[12] Commonwealth Exchequer Papers - Assessments, loans and contributions - Accounts and schedules - Northampton (S.P. 28/172).

[13] Clarendon Bk. VI, 275.

[14] Thomas Hobbes, *Behemoth, or The Long Parliament,* ed. Ferdinand Tönnies (London, 1889), p.2.

[15] Letter from Sir Robert Poyntz to the Marquis of Ormonde, 1 June 1643, *A Collection of Original Letters and Papers 1641-1660,* ed. T. Carte (London, 1739), Vol.I, p.21.

[16] Webb, *Civil War in Herefordshire,* Vol.II, p.208.

[17] Corbet, *History of the Military Government of Gloucester,* p.17.

[18] *Memoirs of Colonel Hutchinson,* p. 126.

[19] H. Stocks, *Leicester Records 1603-1688* p. 320.

[20] 'Ottley Papers', *Salop. Arch. Soc. Trans.,* Vol.VII (1895), p.263.

[21] Hist. MSS.Comm.*(Fourth Report, 1874),* p.265

[22] *Ibid.,* p.267.

[23] Letter from Prince Rupert to all Commanders, Officers, Souldiers in the King's army, 2 Jan. 1644, *Epistolary Curiosities,* ed. Rebecca Warner (London, 1818), pp.32-34.

CHAPTER FIVE

EARLY ATTEMPTS TO CONSOLIDATE THE MIDLANDS

The first serious attempts by the Royalists and Parliamentarians in the Midlands to increase the territory under their individual control began in the spring of 1643. To this end Parliament issued Ordinances of Association by which the local Parliamentary armies in specified counties

> should associate themselves to protect the counties, raise horse and foot, money and plate, give battle, fight, and levy war, put to execution of death, and destroy all who should levy war against the Parliament. [1]

In accordance with these decrees the Parliamentary forces of Warwickshire, Staffordshire, Lichfield and Coventry were 'associated' under Lord Brooke; those of Northamptonshire, Rutland, Leicestershire, Derbyshire and Nottinghamshire were united with the Parliamentary forces of Buckinghamshire, Bedfordshire and Huntingdonshire under Lord Grey of Groby; while responsibility for Parliament's interests in Gloucestershire, Shropshire and Worcestershire rested with Sir William Waller, Commander of the Western Association.

The Royalists, too, attempted to amalgamate their local forces in the region. In February 1643, the counties of Leicester, Derby, Nottingham, Lincoln and Rutland were associated by the King's order, and Colonel Henry Hastings was made Colonel-General of all the Royalist forces in them.[2] And in February 1644 it was proposed that all the Royalist forces in Worcestershire, Shropshire, Herefordshire and Staffordshire should be amalgamated, with 'Prince Charles his Highness to be General of these Associated Counties'.[3]

The full potential of these novel instruments of military power was, however, never fully realised in the Midlands, for people's attitudes and ways of thinking were still local rather than national. Thus the first allegiance of the local armies was to their immediate neighbourhood and they were often reluctant to leave their homes to the mercy of the opposition while they were fighting with other armies elsewhere. In this respect they were little better than the trained bands.

The primary phase in Parliament's plan to consolidate Staffordshire was the successful occupation, albeit temporary, of Lichfield Close. The Cathedral Close had been fortified at the beginning of March 1643 by two prominent local Royalists, Lord Chesterfield and Sir Richard Dyott, assisted by the burgesses of the city.

Lord Brooke, 'having taken Stratford upon Avon, and settled that town and county of Warwicke in peace', marched with his forces against Lichfield. On 2 March (which, ironically, is St. Chad's day, the saint to whom the Cathedral is dedicated) the Parliamentarians commenced a bombardment of the garrison. On that same day, while directing operations, Brooke was shot through the eye and killed by Sir Richard Dyott's son who was perched upon one of the Cathedral towers. The result of young Dyott's compensatory sure-sightedness (the youth was both deaf and dumb) put considerable heart into the defenders of the Close. But by the same token it also strengthened the determination of the besiegers. From Derby came Sir John Gell with further forces to help in the siege; and from the Royalist garrisons of Tamworth and Rushall came help for the besieged. By 5 March, however, the strength and morale of the Royalists had flagged and the garrison surrendered on honourable terms. The Royalists were allowed to leave Lichfield to seek temporary refuge in Stafford, unmolested.

But 'though', according to John Vicars, 'the souldiers were mercifull to the men, yet were they void of all pitty toward the organ-pipes, copes, surpluces, and such like popish trumperies found in the Minster, affoording these no quarter, except quartering and mangling them in peeces'.[4] The Royalist Sir William Dugdale, also recorded the activities of the Parliamentary soldiers in Lichfield Cathedral: 'They stabled their horses in the body of it, kept courts of guard in the cross isles; broke up the pavements, poluted the qire with their excrement; every day hunted a cat with hounds throughout the church, delighting themselves in the eccho from the goodly vaulted roof: and to add to their wickedness, brought a calf into it, wrapt in linnen; carried it to the font; sprinkled it with water; and gave it a name in scorn and derision of that holy sacrament of baptism'.[5]

In the city itself, the besiegers destroyed the ornate eight-arched market cross, which had been erected by Dean Denton in the earlier part of the 16th century.

After Lichfield the county town itself was to be the next objective. On 19 March Sir John Gell moved out of Lichfield with 750 men to rendezvous at Hopton Heath with another Parliamentary force of similar strength from Cheshire, under Sir William Brereton. From the heath their forces were to carry out a combined attack on Stafford, two miles away. The garrison was, however, well prepared for this assault. Apart from the Royalist troops which had been allowed to seek refuge there after the siege at Lichfield, there was, in the town, another force under the command of the Earl of Northampton. The earl had been sent from Banbury to relieve Lichfield, but finding that he was too late decided to billet his troops in Stafford.

Northampton, cognisant of the enemy's plan, seized the initiative and assumed the offensive before the two Parliamentarian armies could unite. With 900 men, all mounted, he attacked Gell's small force as it waited on the heath for Brereton. Gell's cavalry was soon overwhelmed by the superior Royalist horse and his infantry was treated to a murderous bombardment by a 29-pound or demi-cannon, named appropriately *Roaring Meg,* which, according to an eye witness account, 'made such a lane through them that they had little minde to close agayne'.[6]

Brereton, when he arrived, could do little to save the day and eventually both commanders were forced to quit the field, having failed in their objective. Parliament lost in all 500 men, or a third of their forces; the Royalists lost about 50, including their commander, Northampton, whose skull had been cleft by a halbert from behind. Gell and Brereton refused to return the earl's body unless the Royalists would in exchange, return their captured artillery. This the Royalists refused to contemplate. It could be said that such a bargain was contrary to the rules of war as they then stood, but with the price of cannon being what it was it is difficult not to condone this action.

After the battle Gell, of whom a Royalist eye witness caustically remarked, 'is certainly hurt [it is thought by Northampton himself], but not killed. He is not too forward to come into danger',[7] retired to Uttoxeter with his 'prize', the body of Northampton, while Brereton made for Stone where he rested before returning to his base in Cheshire.

The failure to take Stafford was redeemed a little by the successes in Gloucestershire and Herefordshire of Sir William Waller. In February 1643 a force of about 1,600 'well and sufficiently armed' but as yet untrained Welsh infantry, some horse and artillery, raised by Lord Herbert, arrived on the west bank of the Severn at Highnam, opposite the Parliamentary city of Gloucester. They entrenched themselves there awaiting reinforcements from Oxford which would enable them to take Gloucester and also provide them with an escort through Waller's domain to the safety of the King's capital. But they waited too long. While the Deputy Governor of Gloucester, Colonel Massey, kept the Royalists engaged in repeated skirmishes, Waller was able to cross the river by an improvised bridge of boats at Frampton Passage, about 10 miles below Gloucester, march up the west bank, through the Forest of Dean, to Huntley, and attack the enemy from behind.

Most of the Welsh, seeing the hopelessness of their position, surrendered, while a few attempted to flee with the cavalry. They were, alas, caught by Waller's troops as they attempted to ford the River Leadon, a tributary of the Severn, at a spot now crossed by Barber's Bridge, and nearly 100 were slain. A grisly reminder of this action is provided by a monument at Barber's Bridge which marks the spot where the skeletons of 86 men were found in 1868.

At the battle, which took place on 24 March 1643, nearly 1,600 potential Royalist troops, among them some of the most powerful magnates in Herefordshire and Monmouthshire, were taken, together with a considerable supply of arms and ammunition. The Royalists regarded the battle of Highnam, as it came to be called, as a major disaster. Clarendon blamed both Lord Herbert and his brother Lord John Somerset. Lord Herbert was not with the army he had raised, at an estimated cost of £60,000, and which he was supposed to be commanding when the fateful attack took place, but was instead dabbling in court intrigue at Oxford. His brother, who commanded the cavalry, is reported to have kept at a safe distance from the conflict and was therefore conspicuous by his absence among the prisoners taken into Gloucester. Clarendon, in referring to this 'mushroom army', observes that 'if the money which was laid out in the raising, arming, and paying that body of men, which never advanced the King's service in the least degree, had been brought into the King's receipt at Oxford, I am persuaded the war might have ended the next summer'.[8]

CHAPTER FIVE

[1] Rushworth, *Historical collections abridged and improved*, Vol.V, p.103.

[2] *Hastings MSS.*, Hist.MSS.Comm, Vol.II, pp. 89-90.

[3] *Diary of Henry Townshend of Elmley Lovett, 1640-1663*, ed. J.W. Willis Bund (Worcestershire Historial Society, 1916), Vol.III,p.190.

[4] Vicars, *Magnalia Dei Anglicana*, Parts I and II, p.273.

[5] Sir William Dugdale, *A Short View of the Late Troubles in England* (Oxford, 1681), pp.559-60.

[6] 'Dunrobin MSS' transcribed by D.E.A. Horne, *Collections for a History of Staffordshire* (The Staffordshire Record Society, 1936), pp.181-184.

[7] *The Battaile of Hopton Heath between His Majestie's Forces under the Earle of Northampton and those of the Rebels, March 19, 1643.* Thomason Tracts, E.99.

[8] Clarendon, Bk.VI, 293.

CHAPTER SIX

PRINCE RUPERT'S CAMPAIGN IN THE MIDLANDS
SPRING 1643

At Oxford the blow of the battle of Highnam was softened by news of the arrival in England of the King's wife, Henrietta Maria. The Queen had gone to Holland 13 months earlier in order to procure munitions with the proceeds from the sale of the crown jewels. Now she had returned with an impressive range of war-wares, some of which may have been furnished by Anton Krupp of Essen, who was at that time making a profitable living out of the war then raging in Germany. Some of these supplies were to go to the King's northern army, commanded by the Earl of Newcastle and based on York, and the remainder to the King himself at Oxford. These two armies, when fully equipped and ready, were, together with a third army from Devon and Cornwall, under Sir Ralph Hopton, to take part in a three-pronged attack on London.

This was the King's new strategy, but before it could be implemented the valuable supplies allocated to the King's own army had to be conveyed from Bridlington, where the Queen had landed, to Oxford. This meant that they would have to pass through the web of Parliamentarian garrisons which were scattered throughout the Midlands. Rupert was, therefore, sent north 'to clear these obstructions'[1] and provide for the Queen's convoy a safe route through the Midland counties.

From Oxford the Prince and his small army travelled first to Chipping Norton, then on to Shipston-on-Stour, Stratford-on-Avon, to Henley-in-Arden, where they hovered about for four days 'pillaging the countrie extremely as their manner is', arriving at Birmingham on Easter Monday, 3 April.

Although Birmingham was not in fact a garrison, 'being built in such a form as was indeed hardly capable of being fortified',² it did present a possible threat to the safety of the convoy. Rupert had not forgotten how the townsfolk of this 'incurably Parliamentarian town' had attacked the King's baggage train as it passed through in the autumn of 1642 and had since then, with great industry and vigilance, apprehended any messenger whom they thought might be in the King's service. This in itself was sufficient to engender that bitter feeling against the town of 'Bromigham' which the Royalists felt. It was also, in their eyes, sufficient excuse for a punitive expedition against its inhabitants, which might discourage them from such activities in the future.

But the inhabitants of Birmingham had done a great deal more in their desire to distinguish themselves from the King's 'good subjects', for they kept the Parliamentarian armies well supplied with war-wares while assiduously refusing to ply their skills, for which they were renowned, in the manufacture of weapons for the King, whom they were soon to curse as the 'man of blood'.

These same men, whom Thomas Hutton in his *History of Birmingham* called 'the sturdy sons of freedom', had, on hearing of Rupert's approach, thrown up earthworks around the town and barricaded the streets. With the aid of 140 musketeers from the nearby garrison of Lichfield, thought to have been commanded by Colonel Richard Graves, Squire of King's Norton, the townsfolk were boldly but characteristically determined to resist the Prince's attack.

In the ensuing struggle the defenders, who with opprobrious speeches reviled the enemy 'calling them Cursed dogs, develish Cavaliers, Popish traytors'³ fought 'with mettle equal to their malice'.⁴ Even after the Royalists, 'like so many furyes or bedlams',⁵ had finally entered the town they still met with considerable resistance. They were fired upon from the upper windows of houses and in the 'long pretty street called Dirtey', now called Deritend, a group of smiths, nailors and cutlers made a last brave attempt to push the 'Cavaliers' back, before being trampled under foot by Rupert's cavalry. A Parliamentary tract⁶ continues the story:

> Having thus possessed themselves of the Town, they ran into every house cursing and damning, threatening and terrifying the poore Women most terribly, setting naked Swords and Pistols to

their breasts, they fell to plundering all the Town before them, as well Malignants [Royalists] as others, picking purses, and pockets, searching in holes and corners, Tiles of houses, Wells, Pooles, Vaults, Gardens and every other place they could suspect for money or goods, forcing people to deliver all the money they had ... They beastly assaulted many Womens chastity, and impudently made their brags of it afterwards, how many they had ravished; glorying in their shame especially the French among them, were outragiously lascivious and letcherous ... That night few or none went to Bed, but sate up revelling, robbing, and Tyranising over the poore affrighted Women and Prisoners, drinking drunke, healthing upon their knees, yea, drinking drunk Healths to Prince Rupert's Dog.

Nor did their Rage here cease, but when on next day they were to march forth of the Towne, they used all possible diligence in every Streete to kindle fire in the Towne with Gunpowder, Match, Wispes of Straw, and Besomes, burning coales of fire, etc., flung into Straw, Hay, Kid piles, Coffers, Thatch and any other places, where it was likely to catch hold ... .

The account of the 'Birmingham Butcheries', as this incident came to be called, given in this recriminatory pamphlet, and in the one reproduced as Plate 1 (p. 84), both published by Parliament, tally closely with the Royalist versions, one of which is recorded in a letter written by a Walsall Royalist to a friend at Oxford and published as a pamphlet on 14 April 1643. In this the writer refers to 'the miserable destruction of Burningham by fire which I must confesse tooke the deepest apprehension with me of any one accident since the beginning of these unhappy distractions'.[7]

The only inaccuracies in the Parliamentary reports concern Lord Digby and the Earl of Denbigh. Digby was not among the 'divers chiefe Commanders and men of great quality' slain at Birmingham and, in fact, survived the Civil War. The death of the Earl of Denbigh actually occurred at Cannock five days after the attack on Birmingham, although this was as a direct result of injuries sustained there. His demise was, perhaps, the most serious direct consequence of this action for the earl's heir was of the opposite faction, thus transferring the influence of the head of this powerful Warwickshire family from the King's side to that of the Parliament.

The raid on Birmingham also had a considerable psychological effect. The fact that a mere handful of largely untrained men were able to hold off two attacks by an enemy who had infantry, cavalry, and artillery at their disposal did much to cast doubt on the popular conception of Rupert as a brilliant commander. John Vicars saw in this the hand of God who 'fought for those poore unarmed inhabitants, who were for the most part, Smiths, whose profession or trade was to make nailes, sythes and such like iron-commodities'.[8] The Prince also had to endure a rating from his uncle, the King, who, on hearing of the slaughter and burning at Birmingham, wrote to the Prince advising him on the future treatment of the King's 'misled subjects'. In future he was to 'take their affections rather than their towns'.

The upbraiding of Rupert did little to remove the animosity that the townspeople of Birmingham felt towards the Prince and the King's party, which, by all accounts, they were able to communicate to their descendants. This is borne out by the following song, entitled *The Armourer's Widow,* featured in Thomas A. Vaughton's collection of *Tales of Sutton Town and Chase* which, he claims, was still being sung in the middle of the last century:

> When Rupert came to Byrmingeham
> We were in sorry plyght,
> Our blood God's earth ystained by daye,
> Our homes in blazing ruins laye
> And stained the skye at night.
>
> With matchlock and with culverin,
> With caliver and drake,
> He battered down our ancient town,
> He shot our sons and fathers down,
> And Hell on earth did make.
>
> Our children's cries, our widows' prayers
> Ascended with the flame,
> And called down the wrath divine
> Upon the Royal Murderer's line,
> And brought his kin to shame.

The day after the assault on Birmingham Rupert moved northwards again to Walsall, from where he attacked Rushall Hall, the home of a prominent Puritan and scholar, Colonel Edward Leigh. The hall had been fortified and held for

Parliament by the Colonel and was of considerable importance owing to its strategic position. When Rupert arrived there Colonel Leigh 'was absent, but his wife, together with her household, put up a spirited but short defence. In the end they were forced to surrender and because of their gallant action were treated kindly. Thereafter, under its Royalist commander, Colonel John Lane, this garrison was to prove a constant threat to the Parliamentarian convoys travelling from Manchester to Coventry and London.

From Rushall the Prince, who had been joined by three or four hundred 'proper fellowes from Walsal, who came with bills and hooks to serve the King', continued in a northerly direction to Cannock and then, turning due west, made for Lichfield, arriving there on Saturday 8 April.

Rupert immediately called upon Colonel Russell, Governor of the newly acquired Parliamentarian garrison in the Cathedral Close, to surrender. But Russell refused to surrender to a man capable of such atrocities as had been carried out at Birmingham; '... an act', according to the Colonel, 'not becoming a gentleman, a Christian, or Englishman, much less a Prince'.[9] (Whatever else Prince Rupert of the Rhine might be he was not, at this time, an Englishman, although he was made a free denizen of England in January 1644, when he received the additional title of Duke of Cumberland, which the Parliamentarians soon transmuted to 'Prince Robber, Duke of Plunderland'.) An intensive bombardment achieved little result and so Rupert obtained some 50 miners from the neighbouring collieries, and using techniques learnt in his European campaigns, he tunnelled his way to the walls of the Close. Finally, on 20 April, the miners made a breach in the wall with the aid of gunpowder; the first time in England that gunpowder had been thus employed. Through the gap poured Rupert's men and after fierce fighting the Parliamentarians surrendered. The Royalists had regained Lichfield, which they held until July 1646.

CHAPTER SIX

[1] *Ibid.*, Bk. VII, 31.

[2] *Ibid.*

[3] *A letter written from Walshall, by a Worthy Gentleman to his Friend in Oxford, concerning Burmingham (1643)*, Thomas on Tracts E. 96.

[4] Clarendon, Bk. VII, 32.

[5] *A True Relation of Prince Ruperts Barbarous Cruelty against the Towne of Brumingham* (1643), Birmingham Reference Library.

[6] *Prince Rupert's Burning Love to England, discovered in Birmingham's Flames* (1643), Birmingham Reference Library.

[7] *A letter written from Walshall concerning Burmingham*, Thomason Tracts E. 96

[8] Vicars, *Magnalia Dei Anglicana*, Parts I and II, p.296.

[9] Webb, *Civil War in Herefordshire*, Vol.I, p.305.

CHAPTER SEVEN
FURTHER ATTEMPTS AT CONSOLIDATION

Again, the successes of Waller, or 'William the Conqueror' as he came to be called, went some way towards redressing Parliament's failure in Staffordshire. In spite of a serious setback at Ripple Field on 13 April, Waller was able to thwart an attempt by Rupert's brother, Prince Maurice, to destroy his forces in the field and take Gloucester for the King.

'The Conqueror' followed this with a successful attempt to secure positive control over Herefordshire. Leaving Gloucester on Sunday 25 April, he marched on Hereford, which was held by Sir William Coningsby. After a bombardment and several sallies, Coningsby requested a parley and agreed to deliver up 'the government of the town' if Waller would promise 'that gentlemen should have quarter and civil usage, ladies be treated honourable, the citizens, bishop, dean and chapter, preserved from plunder [a lot to ask of Parliamentarian soldiers] and not imprisoned for anything past'.[1] But Waller offered quarter and no more. After much argument his terms were reluctantly accepted and on Tuesday 27 April, Waller occupied the town; an event which was said to be 'as great a deliverance as the Israelites passing the Red Sea'.

According to *Mercurius Aulicus* the victorious Parliamentarians took only 60 arms, 'the rest being all conveyed away' by the Royalist soldiers who had 'shifted out of towne ... while the parley lasted'.[2] Nevertheless considerable quantities of powder and ammunition were taken and also a number of 'persons of quality', including the Governor, who were despatched as prisoners to Gloucester. 'All this (through mercy) with the loss of one man and the hurt of three or four soldiers',[3] proclaimed a Parliamentary report.

From Hereford Waller called in the county to take the following oath:[4]

I, A.B., do swear in the presence of Almighty God that I will defend with my life and estate the King's Majesty's person and both

Houses of Parliament now sitting at Westminster, and to the utmost of my power maintain and assist the army raised by the authority of both houses, under the Command of the Earl of Essex, and will to the hazard of my life and fortunes oppose all forces raised or to be raised without the consent of both houses of parliament. So help me God.

The Parliamentarians did not stay long in Hereford for, like Stamford before him, Waller soon began to doubt the wisdom of attempting to hold it. On 18 May the Parliamentary soldiers were returned to Gloucester, and two days later the Royalists reoccupied the city.

After Hereford Waller decided to devote his energies to taking a far more valuable prize, Worcester. The city, he was informed, was ripe for capitulation, since it was seething with unrest, and there existed a Parliamentary fifth column within ready to assist in the downfall of the Royalist garrison there. The fifth columnists distributed post-dated propaganda leaflets[5] addressed:

To all gentlemen, and other inhabitants of the City of Worcester.

As many of you as are sensible of the danger of your religion, your persons and goods, and the privileges of your Corporation, are desired to declare yourselves sensible of them at this opportunity. It being my errand (by the help of God) to secure them from the oppression of your present governors. And I promise that all such as shall appear willing to welcome my endeavour shall not only be received to free quarter, but protected to the utmost of my power.

May 29th, 1643   William Waller.

This prior warning of the intended attack on Worcester gave the Governor sufficient time to make the necessary preparations for the defence of the city as the following order,[6] signed by the Governor's deputy, testifies:

To all Constables, Petty Constables and all other his Majesty's loving subjects within the County of Worcester.

Forasmuch as there are a multitude of armed men come within this County of Worcester and against the City of Worcester this 29th day to the great disturbance of this County and the hazard of the loss of the said City from their loyalty and obedience, these are to command you suddenly upon receipt hereof and with all haste to summon all persons within 16 and 60 years of age to repair with all such arms and weapons as they have to the City of Worcester to help, assist and defend the said City and County from all opposition whatsoever. And that every person bring with him three days' provision at the least. And hereof fail not at your perils. Dated this 28th day of May 1643.

Sam Sandys

Waller arrived before Worcester with an army of 3,000 men, including his crack Gloucester Blue Regiment, and eight pieces of artillery, at daybreak on 29 May, after a night march from Gloucester. The customary punctilio of calling upon the city to surrender was observed, in answer to which Sandys advised Waller 'that he was not now at Hereford, and bad him be gone'.[7] Then followed two days of artillery bombardment during which the Parliamentarians succeeded only in gaining the outer suburbs of the city. Waller requested reinforcements from Sir William Brereton but he, as will be revealed later, was consolidating his position in Staffordshire and was unable to assist, although it is debatable whether Brereton would, in fact, have assisted anyhow as events in Worcestershire would, unlike those in Staffordshire, have had little effect on the situation in his native county, Cheshire.   In view of this, and the knowledge that Prince Maurice was on his way from Oxford with a large force, Waller decided to abandon the siege. In the early hours of Monday 31 May, Sir William, leaving behind 160 dead, retreated towards Tewkesbury, from whence he extracted the 1,000-odd soldiers which comprised the Parliamentary garrison there, before proceeding to Gloucester. The purpose behind this was to give his army sufficient strength to resist if it was attacked on the march.

The Parliamentarian fifth column was of little help at Worcester and the pamphlets they distributed, one feels, were ignored. The citizens did not desire to be rescued from the 'oppression' of their 'present governors'.

Waller's attack on Worcester, which had lost the city '2 men only and 3 women',[8] revealed certain weaknesses in its defences. It was therefore decreed that

> all the trees, hedges, mounds and fences which might any manner prejudice the City and help and succour the Assailants or enemies and likewise all Houses or buildings be immediately plucked down and levelled. To effect which the ordinary sort of women out of every ward within the City joined in companies ... slighting all such fortifications as were left by Essex at his being here, and throwing down ditches ... which was done rather by the reason some of them were killed in the siege, though casually; also to ease the soldiers, who, being weary of their late hot service, desired some rest, and to

prevent Sir William Waller's approach near if he should return against them .[9]

Parliament's reply to the capture of Lichfield came on 16 May when Brereton finally succeeded in taking Stafford with his own forces from Cheshire and aided by reinforcements from Newcastle-under-Lyme and Leek. The reinforcements from Leek were the Moorlanders referred to earlier. Since their lone attempt at taking Stafford, Parliament had despatched some officers to Leek to train them. But in spite of the rigid training they received these 'stout fighting men' remained 'the most ungovernable wretches that belonged to the Parliament'. Brereton surreptitiously entered the town at 3 o'clock in the morning and the citizens 'all being asleep in their beds', he took possession without loss of life. Only the aged Lady Stafford and her retinue ensconced in the castle offered resistance, firing upon any soldier who attempted to approach. When the castle was finally gained it was found to be empty, the occupants having fled by a secret route. Stafford now became the administrative centre for the county wherein would now reside the County Committee with wide powers of control including the gathering of the 'weekly pay'. There will be a full description of the County Committees and their functions in a later chapter.

Brereton followed up his success with the capture of Wolverhampton in which he used the same strategy as in the capture of Stafford. Sir William himself records, we 'went towards Wolverhampton, which towne wee entered about three o'clock in the morninge, without any opposition or resistance, the greatest malignants were fled, those that remained were summoned and appeared, and theire armes, whereof wee brought two or three cart-loades, and some cannon-bulletts, from Mr. Folies forges; and the moulds which made these bullets, which were intended for Lichfield, all which were brought into Stafford; reservinge the ransome and compositione of that towne for some more seasonable opportunity, when the greate and rich men were returned'.[10]

The church of St. Peter's again received the now standard treatment afforded to religious buildings by the soldiers of both sides. The church chest was broken into and many records and papers disappeared and tombs were destroyed.

Although the Royalists had regained Lichfield, the loss of

Wolverhampton and particularly Stafford was a severe blow
to them and prompted the King at Oxford to observe 'to our
great displeasure that few places in that our county of
Stafford, of any consideration (besides the castle of Dudley),
but are possessed and held by those now in actual rebellion
against us'.

In spite of this Queen Henrietta Maria's convoy, which left
York on 4 June with an escort of 5,000 men, passed through
the Midlands unmolested on its way to Oxford - a singularly
striking commentary on the real effectiveness of the local
armies, the result, no doubt, of the inability of local
commanders to agree on what action should be taken. A close
watch was, however, kept on the convoy by Essex's Scoutmaster General, Sir Samuel Luke, whose diary contains the
following entry for Sunday 9 July 1643:[11]

> William Sherwood [a Parliamentary spy] returned this day and
> saith that the King's forces quartered the last night at Weeden and
> Daventry, and marched this day towards Ashby de la Zouch in
> Leicestershire, where (hee heares) the Queen is .

The King's forces referred to had been despatched from
Oxford to strengthen the Queen's escort lest Essex should
attempt an attack with the main Parliamentary field army
based on London.

After Ashby the Queen next halted at Burton-on-Trent,
a town which even at this early stage in the war had already
withstood a number of sieges. Originally it had been
garrisoned for the King, as had nearby Tutbury Castle, and the
Earl of Chesterfield's house at Bretby. In the late autumn
of 1642, Bretby was sacked by the Parliamentarians who
afterwards took Burton, 'for their better security'.[12] Towards
the end of January 1643 the town was recaptured by the
Royalists under Henry Hastings who lost it again to the
combined forces of Sir John Gell and Lord Grey in April.
When the Queen and her convoy arrived at Burton it was still
in the hands of the Parliamentarians, although the number of
soldiers garrisoned there was quite small. Even so, according
to *Mercurius Aulicus* the town 'had faire warning given it by
two severall summons, and yet had that rebellious impudence
to stand it out the third time, so as they [the Queen's
soldiers] were forced to take it by assault; wherein they took
Master Haughton the Governour of the towne, and his

seditious lady who (to the disgrace of her sex) shewed her-
selfe as active against the Queen's majesty as her husband and
his fellow rebels had been against the King. And yet her
majesties goodnesse and clemency was so exemplary, and like
her royall selfe, that she forbad any violence to be offered to
the town'.[13]

The Parliamentarian version, which, as one would expect,
is rather different, took the form of a report sent to Sir
Samuel Luke by one of his spies.

> Some of her [the Queen's] forces lately came to Burton upon Trent
> and fell upon the townesmen and drove 30 of them into the church
> whoe defended themselves bravely and kild many of the Cavallyers
> but at last were glad to demand quarter. But they refused to grant
> it but came in the night and cutt all their throats, doing great spoile
> in the towne, ravashing the woomen, forcing many of them to take
> the river, where they drowned insomuch that above 20 were found
> and taken upp dead this weeke, and they dayly find more. [14]

It is left to the inclinations of the individual reader to
select the account that seems the most plausible. It should be
said, however, that in a letter to her husband the Queen wrote
that the soldiers 'got so much plunder they could not well
march with their bundles' and the convoy was delayed at
Walsall while the soldiers rested.

The Queen left Walsall on Monday 10 July, wisely by-
passing Birmingham, and on the following day arrived at
Stratford-upon-Avon where she was joined by Prince Rupert.
According to local tradition the Queen and Rupert were the
guests of Shakespeare's elder daughter, Mrs. Susanna Hall
of New Place, during their three days' stay. The occasion of
what was the town's first known royal visit was appropriately
celebrated by bell-ringing and feasting, as is shown by the
following details of expenditure which appear in the
accounts[15] of Thomas Horne, Chamberlain at the time:

Moneyes disbursed and payd when the Queene maiestye laye in
the Towne

	£	s.	d.
Payd to 6 foote men for their fee	1	10	—
pd to ten Cochmen and porters for their fee	1	10	—
pd for 4 Quayles		4	—
pd for 3 heens 1 Coke 8 chikins		5	4
pd for Cakes presented to the Queene	5	-	-
pd for 6 maltshires for them		6	-
payd to the Buchers for meate	3	18	6

pd to Wm. Hopkins for Beare   15   8
pd for 1 quarter of Oates and 6 strike of Beanes   1   2   -
pd for Mr. Bayliffe of Warwicke for their fortifications   3   -   -
pd to John Copland for Bread cheese and Beare   12   6
pd to the Bellringers   2   -

Summe totalis (including Mr. Bayliffe's bill on
previous page) 28Li 2s. 11d.

The Queen, who was met by Charles himself at Kineton, eventually reached the safety of Oxford on 14 July. She was received by the mayor and city council who had resolved to 'repaire to Penniles bench in their best aray and there stande readie against her Majesties comeinge'.[16] According to the city accounts the council also expended the sum of 6s. 6d. 'for strewing flowers when the Queen came to Oxford'.[17]

CHAPTER SEVEN
[1] *Mercurius Bellicus* .... *Wherein is the relation of the taking of Hereford by Sir William Waller* (30 April, 1643), Thomason Tracts E.100.

[2] *Mercurius Aulicus* 1 May, 1643.

[3] *Mercurius Bellicus,* 30 April, 1643, Thomason Tracts E.100.

[4] *Diary of Henry Townshend of Elmley Lovett,* Vol.II, pp.120, 121.

[5] *Mercurius Aulicus,* 30 May, 1643.

[6] *Diary of Henry Townshend of Elmley Lovett,* Vol.II, p.122.

[7] *Mercurius Aulicus,* 30 May, 1643.

[8] *Diary of Henry Townshend of Elmley Lovett,* Vol.II, p.123.

[9] *Ibid.,* pp.123-4.

[10] Shaw, *The History and Antiquities of Staffordshire,* Vol.I, p.53. (General History).

[11] *Journal of Sir Samuel Luke,* ed. I.G. Philip (Oxfordshire Record Society, 1947), p.114.

[12] Shaw, *Op;cit.,* Vol.I, p.17.

[13] *Mercurius Aulicus,* 18 July, 1643.

[14] *Journal of Sir Samuel Luke,* p.117.

[15] Levi Fox, *The Borough Town of Stratford-upon-Avon* (Stratford-upon-Avon, 1953), p.24.

[16] *Oxford Council Acts, 1626-1665,* ed. M.G. Hobson and H.E. Salter (Oxford Historical Society, 1933), p. 113.

[17] *Ibid.,* p.425.

CHAPTER EIGHT

THE KING'S CAPITAL

Oxford had changed much between Charles's state entry into the city after Edgehill and the arrival of the Queen. In that time it had become the Royalist capital and military headquarters. Not for the first time in its long history Oxford was to be 'the frontier fortress of middle England'.[1] Here the King, claiming to be the only just and authentic government, set up an administrative machine to rival Parliament's at London. He appointed a Lord Chief Justice of his own and decreed that he and the Royalist peers and members of the House of Commons with him at Oxford were the legal government of England.

'The scholars (were) put (out) of their colleges: and those that remained bore arms for the King in the garrison',[2] and the university buildings assumed functions commensurate with the city's new role. Arms and powder were put in New College cloister and tower, 'whereupon', we are informed, 'the master of the school there, with his scholars were removed to the coristers' chamber at the east end of the common hall of the said Coll. It was then a dark nasty room and very unfit for such a purpose, which made the scholars often complaine, but in vaine'.[3] The law and logic schools became a granary while in Magdalen Grove twenty pieces of artillery and their carriages were parked. The King and his Court occupied Christ Church, into the great quadrangle of which 'a drove of fatt oxen and about 300 sheepe' were driven to provide sustenance for the army, while accommodation was found for the Queen and her Court in Merton. Of the Parliament assembled at Oxford, the Lords met in the Upper Schools and the Commons in the Great Convocation House. In the music and astronomy schools tailors worked busily on uniforms, the material for which had been plundered from the great cloth manufacturing area of nearby Gloucestershire.

In the town itself a powder mill was set up in the ruins of Osney Abbey and a sword factory was established at Wolvercote. Part of the castle was used to house Parliamentary prisoners. But alas, the Royalists were not very particular in their treatment of prisoners of war and those unfortunate enough to be incarcerated in Oxford were, according to Parliamentary reports, 'used like dogs rather than Christians'. It is not surprising, therefore, that most of the 1,100 prisoners taken at Circencester accepted the option to join the King's army.

The mint, brought down from Shrewsbury by Bushell in December 1642, was established in New Inn Hall, whence came the celebrated 'Oxford crown piece', beautifully executed by Rawlins in 1644. A printing press was also set up on which was produced the news-sheet *Mercurius Aulicus*. This, the Royalist answer to the Parliamentarian pamphlets, was published at regular intervals from 1643 to 1645 and can thus claim to be England's first regular newspaper, although production often suffered through lack of materials; a deficiency exemplified by the publication shortly after the battle of Edgehill of Sir John Denham's poem *Cowper's Hill* which 'was printed at Oxford, in a sort of browne paper, for then they could gett no better'.[4]

The statement made by Clarendon that Oxford was the only city in England that Charles could say was entirely at his disposal, was, in fact, largely true of the university only, and the extent to which this was so is illustrated by Parliament's reaction to it:

> ... our schollars have turned the University to an Accadamy of Cavaliers, Master Sherwood some times curate of Saint Pulchers for the good service he hath done is made a doctor, being a man greatly in favour here, whose wit and ingennuity is of great use amongst the great ones, he wants nothing but good sack which is somewhat scarce at Oxford. [5]

The city itself was, in common with most commercial centres throughout the country, Puritan in inclination and Parliamentarian in its sympathies. Thus, whilst protesting loyalty to the King, the citizens employed every means of obstruction and non-co-operation open to them.

When they were asked to pay a contribution towards fortifying the city (an operation that was to cost £30,000) they refused, but offered to do the work themselves. This they did for a while but what little enthusiasm there was soon flagged and the King was forced to insist on one day's work a week from every able bodied citizen, or the payment of a fine. An appeal to the citizens to 'bring in their brasse to furnish his Majesty with freelie this 4th of April 1643', was responded to by only 40 people who between them contributed a mere 7 cwt.[6]

On considering the inconvenience of 'entertaining' the King within their walls, the attitude of the citizens is hardly surprising. For, apart from making incessant financial demands, the Royalists also demolished many private residences in order to facilitate fortification. Anthony à Wood, the celebrated Oxford antiquarian, then a schoolboy attending New College School, recalled further privations: 'the plate which had been given to [him] at his christening by his godfathers and godmother - which was considerable - was (with all other plate in Oxon) carried by his majesties command to the mint at Newe Inne, and there turned into money to pay his majesties armies'.[7] Also, 'his father's house opposite Merton Coll. was taken up for the quarters of John Lord Colepeper, Master of the Rolls, and of the privie councill to his majestie; whereupon Mr. Wood's father with his familie removed to a little house in his backside, which he about two or three yeares before had new built'.[8]

The citizens also had to endure continuous abuse from the soldiery who, due to long periods of inactivity were, it appears, seldom sober. In fact, intemperance became so rife that Charles was prompted to issue an order to the effect 'that neither vintner nor any other victualer in Oxford should afford any wyne or drinke to be sold in his house to any body after nine of the clocke at night &c. uppon payne of forefeyting 10s.'

When the soldiers were not abusing the townsfolk they quarrelled among themselves. An entry in Dugdale's Diary recorded: 'Sir Arthur Aston wounded in the side in the darke, by a scuffle in the streete'.[9] And a Parliamentary spy, sent into Oxford by Essex's Scoutmaster General, reported 'that at Court twoe gentlemen fell out and fought for a horse that was given betweene them, and one of them runne the horse through, and that Prince Rupert came forth with a poleaxe and parted them'.

A Gloucestershire man in the King's service, Captain Richard Atkyns, relates in his memoirs that 'in Oxford a knight provoked me with so ill language that I could not forbear striking of him; and being very angry, I took his periwig off his head and trampled it under my feet: the next morning he sent me a challenge by his second'.[10] The intended duel 'with sword and pistols' on Bullingdon Green did not, however, take place.

The occupation of the city by the King's army also resulted in frequent outbreaks of 'the epidemicall disease',[11] which contemporaries called *morbus campestris,* or camp fever, caused undoubtedly by overcrowding in filthy conditions. Edward Greaves, an Oxford surgeon, favoured the residence of the army as the principal cause 'it being seldom or never known that an Army where there is so much filth and nastiness of diet, worse lodging, unshifted apparell, &c., should continue long without contagious diseases'.[12] Another of Luke's spies, Robert Cox, reported on 10 July 1643, 'that there dyes about 40 a weeke of plague in Oxford, besides many of other diseases'.[13]

The churchwardens' accounts[14] for one Oxford parish alone, St. Martin (Carfax), show how deadly were the combined effects of war and plague on the city during the first year of its military occupation:

		£	s.	d.
1643 Rec^d for graves in the church this yeare		12	4	2
" for the goeing of the bell this yeare		4	9	2
" for the use of the paule this yeare		6	6	8
p^d for a shrudd for a souldier			3	0
" for 8 graves making in the churchyard for poore souldiers			4	0
" for 2 shrudds for poore souldiers			6	0
" for making of 10 graves in the churchyard for souldiers			3	4
" for a shrudd for a souldier that died at the Crosse Inne			3	0
" for another shrudd for a souldier that died				

under Penylesse Bench	3	0
" for another shrudd for a souldier that died at the Crosse Inne	3	0
" to four souldiers for conveying a sick souldier to St. Thomas parish	1	0
" for carrying a sick souldier to Bridewell		4

The total receipts for graves in the church, the going of the bell, and the use of the pall, amounted to £23. This implies a great mortality, as the receipts from the same sources in ordinary years averaged under £3. The burials, too, registered from 26 March 1643 to 17 March 1644, were 90 in number, while the yearly average of the four preceding years was only 15. Items in the accounts for 1644 and 1645 'for frankincense and other fumes for the church', for which a total of 3s. 8d. was paid, were not only a safeguard from infection, but also to kill the bad smells arising from superficial overburying.

CHAPTER EIGHT

[1] Charles W. Boase, *Oxford* (London, 1887), p.151.

[2] *The Life and Times of Anthony Wood, antiquary of Oxford, 1632-1695, described by Himself*, ed. Andrew Clark (The Oxford Historical Society 1891 – 1900), Vol.I,p.69.

[3] *Ibid.* p.69.

[4] John Aubrey, *Brief Lives and other Selected Writings*, ed. A. Powell (London, 1949), p.81.

[5] *A Perfect Diurnall*, No. 38 (1643).

[6] *Oxford Council Acts, 1626-1665*, p.372.

[7] *The Life and Times of Anthony Wood*, Vol.I, pp.94, 95.

[8] *Ibid.* p.67.

[9] *The Life, Diary and Correspondence of Sir William Dugdale*, ed. William Hamper (London, 1827), p.57.

[10] *Military Memoirs of the Civil War - The Vindication of Richard Atkyns, Esquire,* ed. Peter Young & Norman Tucker (London, 1967), p.31.

[11] *The Life and Times of Anthony Wood,* Vol.I, p.104.

[12] F.J. Varley, *The Siege of Oxford* (Oxford, 1932), p.96.

[13] *Journal of Sir Samuel Luke,* p.114.

[14] The Rev. Carteret J.H. Fletcher, A *History of the Church of St. Martin (Carfax), Oxford* (Oxford, 1896), pp.46-48.

CHAPTER NINE

THE SIEGE OF GLOUCESTER

As Gloster stood against the numerous Powers
Of the Besiegers, who with Thunder-showers
Charg'd her old ribs, but vanisht like a storm
With their own losse, and did no more perform
Then Squibs cast in the air, which throw about
The Siege of Gloucester
Some furious sparks, and so in smoke go out.[1]

His army now fully equipped Charles was ready to put his plan to take the capital into effect. But the northern and western armies were not yet ready to take part in a concerted attack on London. There was, however, little doubt both in the Royalist and Parliamentarian camps that with a swift thrust from Oxford Charles could take the capital alone. For in that sultry August of 1643 pacifist elements had momentarily gained the upper hand, and, as is the wont of those addicted to a policy of appeasement, they had successfully permeated a mood of defeatism throughout the metropolis which was tending to sap potential resistance.

'That storm of fortune', wrote a chronicler of the war, Thomas May, 'was strong enough to shake divers of the loose leaves that seemed to grow on the Parliament side, and unsettle the resolutions of such as were not enough rooted in that cause which they had chosen. For divers men of great quality, and members of both Houses, some lords, and many of the Commons, did at that time desert the Parliament, and fly to Oxford.'[2]

Matters were exacerbated by Rupert seizing Bristol on 26 July, which dealt Parliament its severest single blow of the war so far, and by the condition of the main Parliamentary field army, the strength of which had been reduced to 6,000 foot, of whom 3,000 were sick, and 2,500 cavalry.

Thus the way seemed open for the successful occupation

of London by the King. But Charles was advised to consolidate his position in the Severn Valley by taking Gloucester,
'the most considerable Garrison in all that part of the
Realm',[3] before marching on the capital. Such an action
would give the Royalists complete control of the River
Severn from its source to the Bristol estuary, thus enabling the
levies still being recruited in South Wales to join the Royal
army, as well as opening up a direct route to the iron
foundries of the Forest of Dean.

This campaign, in the opinion of Richard Atkyns, would
finish the war. He writes, 'When we were possessed of Bristoll,
and the lesser garrisons came tumbling in to the obedience of
the King, I took the King's crown to be settled upon his head
again; and my place of Major to the Prince, being supplied by
a more knowing officer [Major Robert Legge], I desired leave
to return to my private condition as before, and to march
with the army that was to besiege Gloucester, hoping to
possess my estate there; offering my lieutenant, cornet, and
several other gentlemen the command of my troops'.[4]
Atkyns, no doubt, reflects the mood of most Royalists at
this time.

The decision to take Gloucester before marching on London
proved to be a cardinal error of judgment. Not only did the
'godly city', as the Royalists opprobriously, but with great
truth, called it, prove a difficult nut to crack, but its plight
also rekindled the resolution of the Parliamentary party in
London against the King. The peace party was soon silenced
and Londoners listened instead to the exhortations of the
Puritan divines who, from their pulpits, urged the citizens
'to go forth and fight for the Lord against the mighty'.

The King, comforted, albeit unintentionally, by the words
of the late Parliamentary Governor of Bristol, who had said
of Gloucester that 'he would be hanged if it could hold out
two days', arrived before the walls of the city on 10 August
1643. He called upon the citizens of Gloucester to surrender
themselves and the city, 'with great promises ... of prefer-
ment',[5] assuring them 'that they nor any of them shall receive
the least dammage or prejudice by Our Army in their persons,
or estates'.[6]

The King also attempted to strike a respectful fear into the hearts of the defenders of Gloucester with boasts of the greatness of the army sent against them, which comprised 'all Prince Rupert's forces from Bristoll, with addition of fifteen hundred armed Welch, and two thousand club-men out of Wales, and armes sufficient to arme them at Bristoll, eight hundred foote with a regiment of horse from Worcester, and five thousand foote with a brigado of Horse from Worcester, and five thousand foote with a brigado of horse of the queene's forces from Oxford'.[7]

The reply to the King's demand that Gloucester should be surrendered to him, signed by the mayor, Dennis Wyse, the Governor, Edward Massey, the aldermen and some prominent citizens, declared that

> We the Inhabitants, Magistrates, Officers, and Souldiers, within this Garrison of Gloucester, onto his Majesties gratious Message return this humble Answer. That we doe keep this City according to our Oath and Allegiance, to and for the use of his Majesty, and his royall Posterity, and doe accordingly conceive ourselves wholly bound to obey the Commands of his Majesty signified by both Houses of Parliament; and are resolved by God's help to keep this city accordingly.[8]

This apparently contradictory' reply is not as it first appears. When the citizens refer to the commands of his Majesty signified by both Houses of Parliament, they imply that any order issued by the King without the approval of Parliament at Westminster is unlawful and cannot command their obedience.

Charles was incredulous at the audacity of the inhabitants of Gloucester, the garrison of which numbered a mere 1,500 men, and possessed less than 10 pieces of ordnance. John Corbet, chaplain to the Governor, recorded the King's reaction: 'His Majesty with all mildnesse seemed to receive this answer, onely to wonder at our confidence, and whence wee expected succour, adding these words, Waller is extinct, and Essex connot come'.[9]

But Charles was wrong. The 'Conqueror', now also known as 'the Knight Owle' on account of his rapid marches between sunset and sunrise, had, it must be admitted, lost his army in a collision with the King's western army at the battle of Roundway Down on 13 July. This is why Rupert was able to take Bristol so easily on 26th and, of course, the reason

why the King felt so sure of taking Gloucester. Waller was, in
fact, now in London assisting Essex to raise a new army for
the relief of Gloucester.

Meanwhile the King, who had taken up quarters at Matson
House, had ruled out the possibility of taking Gloucester by
storm and decided instead upon a siege. As a preliminary to
this the pipes which supplied the city with water from
Robin's Wood Hill were cut, and the stream which flows from
Upton St. Leonards was diverted from its course. But as
Massey was able to pump water into the city from the Severn
these tactics proved to be ineffectual.

Royalist engineers then commenced digging trenches on
Gawdy Green (now Brunswick Square) while the defenders
destroyed £29,000 worth of real estate, including some
'very fair dwelling houses', which nestled against the Barton
Street side of the city wall, 'for the necessary safety of
the ... City'.[10]

Defects in the fortifications were repaired by the willing
hands of the citizens, men, women and children, who toiled
with apparent indefatigability in spite of the almost constant
bombardments from batteries on Gawdy Green and at
Lanthony, from which the Royalists shot 'melting hot iron
bullets, some eighteen pound, others twenty-two pound
waight'.[11]

According to the Royalist news-sheet *Mercurius Aulicus*
these cannonades 'made foule work upon that citie ... battering
the walls in sundry places, beating down divers of the houses,
and killing very many men, both in the works, and about the
streets ... which lasting almost all the day did so tire the
soldiers in the towne they were hardly able to hold it out.
Insomuch that one of their best canoneers ... at the breake of
day leaped over the walls into the Severne, and did swimme
the river, and came safely to his Majesties camp, informing
them of the astonishment and affright which the town was in,
that the soldiers were so tired with the continuall dueties
that they were not able to stand out long'.[12]

It seems, however, that at this stage in the siege the soldiers
of the beleaguered garrison were, in fact, far from being
unable to hold out, and were, to a limited extent, indulging
in offensive tactics. On Wednesday 16 August, for instance,

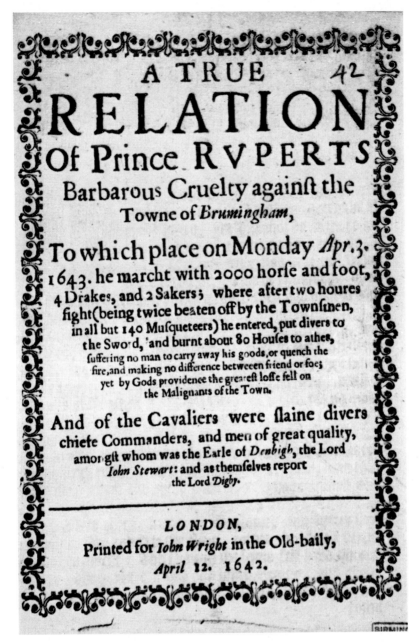

A TRUE 42

RELATION

Of Prince RVPERTS
Barbarous Cruelty againſt the
Towne of *Brumingham*,

To which place on Monday *Apr.*3. 1643. he marcht with 2000 horſe and foot, 4 Drakes, and 2 Sakers; where after two houres fight(being twice beaten off by the Townſmen, in all but 140 Muſqueteers) he entered, put divers to the Sword, and burnt about 80 Houſes to aſhes, ſuffering no man to carry away his goods,or quench the fire,and making no difference betweeen friend or foe; yet by Gods providence the greateſt loſſe fell on the Malignants of the Town.

And of the Cavaliers were ſlaine divers chiefe Commanders, and men of great quality, amongſt whom was the Earle of *Denbigh*, the Lord *Iohn Stewart*: and as themſelves report the Lord *Digby.*

LONDON,
Printed for *Iohn Wright* in the Old-baily, *April* 12. 1642.

Plate 1.   Title-page of the Parliamentarian pamphlet referred to on page 60. (The date of publication given as 1642 is a printer's error and should have read 1643.)

Birmingham Reference Library.

Plate 2. Deritend, Birmingham, today showing the point at which the 'sturdy sons of freedom' made their stand against Rupert's cavalry.

The 14th-century half-timbered building, a medieval oasis in an industrial wilderness, is the only extant witness of this incident.

Photograph: R. E. Sherwood.

Plate 3. A dramatic representation of Charles I receiving Gloucester's reply to his call that the city should surrender to him.

Gloucester City Library.

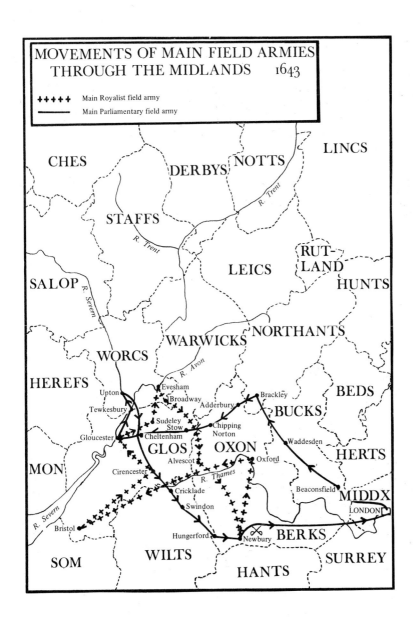

MOVEMENTS OF MAIN FIELD ARMIES
THROUGH THE MIDLANDS   1643

+++++   Main Royalist field army

———   Main Parliamentary field army

'about one hundred and fifty musketeers commanded by Captain Crispe, sallied forth at the north port, and fell upon the enemies trenches upon the east side of the Friar's orchard, killed above one hundred men (as is confessed by some of the enemies themselves) wounded many, beat them out of their trenches, took some spades, shovels, and arms, and retreated without the loss of any, only two wounded after an exceeding hot skirmish for the space of halfe an hour or more, the cannon and muskets on both sides playing most furiously'.[13]

The Royalists also reported on these attempts to harass their besieging army. The instances which *Mercurius Aulicus* chose to publish, however, were apparently not as successful as the one quoted above (which emanated from a Parliamentary source) and were given as examples of the garrison's growing desperation:

> It was advertised that on Tuesday night [22 August] the distressed rebells in Gloucester had made two sallies, the one upon the Lord General's quarters, the other on Sir Jacob Astley's, but were soon beaten back againe (as who could expect otherwise) with the losse of many of their men. And (which is worth your notice) those rebels, which were taken prisoners at both these sallies, were most purely drunke, the faction in the city having (for the cause as they call it) filled the poor soldiers full of strong drinke, as the onely meanes to make them stand, that is, to poure out their owne bloud in the act of rebellion. [14]

By the 15th day of the siege the King's sappers had mined up to the walls of the city and were preparing to blast an entrance. But fortune continued to favour the beleaguered citizens of Gloucester, for at the 11th hour the tunnels were rendered inaccessible, and the powder useless, by an unexpected downpour.

The Royalists now resorted to psychological warfare by means of a paper fixed to an arrow and fired into the city, on which was written:

> These are to let you understand your God, Waller, hath forsaken you and hath returned himself to the Tower of London, Essex is beaten like a dog, yeelde to the kings mercie in time, otherwise and if we enter perforce, no quarter for such obstinate traterly rogues.
>
> From a well wisher. [15]

To which the recipients of these comforting words replied, by a similar means of delivery, with the following piece of defiant doggerel:

> Waller's no God of ours, base rogues ye lie,
> Our God survives from all eternity;
> Though Essex is beaten be, as you doe say,
> Rome's yoke we are resolv'd nere to obey:
> But for our cabages which ye have eaten,
> Be sure ere long ye shall be soundly beaten.
> Quarter we aske you none if we fall downe,
> King Charles will lose true subjects with the towne.
> So saith your best friend, if you make timely use of him,
> > Nicholas Cudgel you well. [16]

By the end of August, however, it seemed apparent that Gloucester would indeed fall. Provisions were running dangerously low and only three barrels of powder remained. Added to this Charles had received considerable reinforcements during the siege, including two regiments from Ireland, bringing the total strength of the Royal army to 30,000 men, at that time the largest army ever assembled on English soil.

An atmosphere of justifiable confidence, therefore, permeated the ranks of the King's forces, prompting Prince Rupert to wager £5,000 with his uncle that the city would fall before 6 September.[17]   And Lord Spencer, in a letter to his wife written on 25 August from the trenches 'before Gloucester', after a brief reference to a small boil, 'in such a place, that as I cannot ride without paine, so I cannot with modesty, make a more perticular description', remarked that 'many of the souldiers are confident, that we shall have the town, within this four days'.[18]

But help was near, although this was unbeknown to the defenders of Gloucester. On 26 August, following a proclamation by Parliament 'that the city of London and parts adjacent cannot be long in safety if that city [Gloucester] is lost', Essex marched out of London intent on relieving Gloucester. By 1 September the Parliamentary army, comprising 15,000 men and 40 pieces of artillery, had covered about 50 miles, having skirted Oxford to the north, and crossed the Cherwell at Clifton, near Aynho.   A Royalist source claims that as the army passed through Chipping Norton 'a woman of that towne (whose zeal for the King and the justice of his cause could not containe itselfe though in the mid'st of mortal enemies) said in the hearing of some of the rebells, "God blesse the

Cavaliers" ... This expression of the poore womans affection
to the King and his loyal subjects in so innocent a prayer,
so highly incensed the rebells, that to punish so hainous a
crime, ... they tyed her to the taile of one of their carts, and
stripping her to the middle, for two miles marched whipped
her ... They left her a lamentable spectacle of their cruelty ...
and [has] since died of those wounds which she received
from them'.[19]

The army entered Gloucestershire at Adlestrop, and at
Stow-on-the-Wold it was met by a detachment of cavalry
under Prince Rupert who had been sent to head Essex off.
But the Parliamentarians easily routed Rupert's forces and
'drave them seven miles'.[20] The Prince refers to this encounter
in his journal thus:[21]

> *September 4.   Munday, faced Essex by Stowe in the Wold.*
> *Wee retreated and that night lay in the field*
> *by Compton.*

When he received intelligence of Rupert's failure to check
Essex's advance, Charles abandoned the siege of Gloucester
and proceeded to Sudeley Castle, which is about 12 miles
north east of Gloucester, positioned his men on a line between
Worcester and Evesham, and awaited developments.

On 5 September Essex, 'like a blazing-starr', appeared on
the hill above Prestbury to the immense relief of the lately
beleaguered citizens of Gloucester. The inhabitants of the
surrounding countryside were, no doubt, less enthusiastic in
their welcome of Gloucester's deliverers. During the siege
homes and sheep herds for miles around had been plundered
mercilessly by the commissaries of the Royal army and, as the
needs of the Parliamentary army were no less than those of
the King's, it was expected that the misery inflicted on the
countryfolk of Gloucestershire by the King would be repeated
by Essex.

Because of this the attitude of the people living about
Gloucester towards those in the city and their cause had
tended to be hostile rather than sympathetic. A contemporary, Thomas May, in a reference to the citizens of Gloucester
and their stand makes mention of the fact that:

> The whole country round about them, instead of incouraging this
> resolution of theirs, did rather indeavour to shake and weaken it,

by intimations of the danger, and persuasions to make peace with such an enemy. For they had revolted from the Parliament, or resolved so to do, and wished, for their own interests, that the King were quietly possessed of that city. For they conceived (not without reason) that the standing out of Gloucester would be unhappy for that country, because, by the falling downe of a great army, they could not but expect a destruction of their corne, cattle, and all other provisions. And at the last, if it should so fall out that the King should faile of taking that towne, they must be inforced to stoop perpetually under two burdens, and be cast into a sadd condition of poverty and misery. Whereas if that army did prevaile they were sure to rest in the heart of the King's country, farre from spoile and plunder, and for an easie contribution, injoy free and ample trade. [22]

Essex, realising that the King had already retreated, made first for the then insignificant market town of Cheltenham, where, after driving out a detachment of Royalist cavalry, he rested his troops. On 8 September Essex entered Gloucester to the acclamation of its citizens. But he remained there only long enough to furnish the city with ammunition, money and other necessities, which took three days, for the King's powerful army was still intact and the road to London lay open. It was essential, therefore, that Essex should reach the metropolis before the King, also, moved in that direction.

But there was a danger that Charles would attempt to destroy the Parliamentary army somewhere on its march home, and so he employed various ruses to put the enemy off the scent, the first of these being a feint towards Worcester by a forced march to Tewkesbury.

It seems that this move meant that Mr. Bartlett of Castle Morton was once again visited by Parliamentary troops. It will be remembered that Bartlett was twice reported as being plundered during the autumn of 1642 'and', relates *Mercurius Rusticus,* 'though these two plunders, one upon the neck of the other, left Master Bartlet a desolate, naked house, yet when the Earle of Essex came lately downe towards Gloucester and hid himself, and his army in hedges, ditches, and the inclosures about Teuxbury, on three severall dayes, three severall companies came to visit Master Bartlets house, presuming that in almost a twelve months time, the house might be new furnished, nor were they altogether deceived in their expectation; without they plunder him of eight horses, and within, what ever they found, they made clean work'.[2][3]

Essex stayed at Tewkesbury until 15 September and then pushed south to Cirencester where the Royalists had 'laid in a great store of provisions for their army'.[2][4] But in spite of Essex's stratagem Charles eventually caught up with the Parliamentarian army at Newbury on 20 September, and a bloody battle followed. But this, like Edgehill, proved indecisive and Essex was able to continue his march on London, while the King, despondent and disillusioned, returned to Oxford.

The summer that had begun with so much promise had ended in disaster for Charles. Never again would conditions be so favourably disposed to the Royalist cause, and never again would the King command an army of such strength.

In that summer of 1643 Gloucester became, in the words of Thomas May, 'the chiefe scene on which this civill tragedy was acted, and place of great concernment in the kingdom, where the first turne of fortune grew'.[2][5] And another contemporary, Bulstrode Whitelocke, recorded that 'most men were of opinion that when the King went to Gloucester, if he had marched up to London, he had done his work'.[2][6]

The siege of Gloucester is probably the most glorious incident in that city's history. Even the Royalists who, in cynical tones had earlier described Gloucester as the 'godly city', admitted that 'they in the town behaved themselves with great courage and resolution, and made many sharp and bold sallies on the kings forces, and did more hurt commonly than they received'. The last statement is borne out by the casualty figures. While the Royalists lost 1,500 men in the siege the city lost only 50, of whom two were 'a boy and a girle through their indiscretion gazing over the walles' during a bombardment.

When news of the relief of Gloucester reached London Parliament ordered 'that Public Thanksgiving be given on the next Lord's Day in all the churches of London and Westminster ... in acknowledgement of God's great mercy and goodness shown in the relief of Gloucester'. Parliament also voted £1,000 as a reward to Massey. In Gloucester itself 5 September was, until the Restoration in 1660, called 'Gloucester holiday' and celebrated by much feasting and ceremony; while upon the south gate, demolished in the late 18th century, two mottos were inscribed: 'A City assaulted by Man but saved by God', and 'Ever remember the 5th September, 1643. Give God the Glory.' But as the main focus of attention shifted elsewhere and the exigence passed, Gloucester's heroic stand was soon forgotten by all except the citizens themselves. Essex had been unable to leave behind either sufficient men or money for the necessities of the city, and so, although the siege had been raised, the hardships of the citizens increased rather than diminished. Massey had, however, petitioned Parliament for £10,000 and 1,000 men for the immediate relief and future defence of Gloucester. But the request for money was ignored and only 50 soldiers actually arrived.

Naturally the citizens of Gloucester felt betrayed by the Parliamentary party for whose cause they had endured so much misery. A mood of despondency prevailed in the city, exacerbated by the knowledge that the enemy were again making a renewed effort to consolidate their position in the Severn Valley. In furtherance of this policy the Royalists strengthened their garrisons at Berkeley, Beverstone, Sudeley, Lydney, Hereford, Worcester and Monmouth. Besides these, garrisons were also placed at Newnham, Dymock, Newent, Highleadon, Taynton, Salperton and Tewkesbury. This meant that Gloucester was hemmed in on every side and was to be squeezed out of existence by blockade. Trade naturally came to an end and the fear of famine was always present. The soldiers had not been paid for months and were soon on the verge of mutiny. Corbet relates how 'in most of the officers there was a general lack of duty, and for the least check would throw up their commissions'.

Life was, however, eventually made a little tolerable by the energetic ingenuity of Massey. Realising that he could expect no further aid from Parliament the Governor resolved to utilise the resources at hand for the preservation of the city. By plundering Royal barges on the Severn and supply ships in the Bristol estuary, he was able to provide the citizens of Gloucester with the necessities of life, if not some of its luxuries. By levying taxes on those areas in the immediate vicinity not under Royalist control he was also able to provide sufficient money to pay his garrison troops, which he kept occupied by waging guerrilla warfare against the Royalist garrisons ringing the city. Thus, by his cheerfulness and personal magnetism, the irrepressible Massey kept the spirit of the siege of Gloucester alive during its virtual blockade.

CHAPTER NINE

[1] From an anonymous poem prefixed to Corbet's *History of the Military Government of Gloucester.*

[2] Thomas May, *The History of the Parliament of England* (London, 1647), Part III, pp.91, 92.

[3] Dugdale, *A Short View of the Late Troubles in England,* p.187.

[4] *Military Memoirs of the Civil War - The Vindication of Richard Atkyns, Esquire,* p.29.

[5] *A Brief and Exact Relation of the Most Materiall and Remarkable Passages that Hapned in the Late Well-Formed (and as valiently defended) Seige laid before the City of Gloucester (1643);* Bibliotheca Gloucestrensis, Pt.I, p.207.

[6] *Mercurius Aulicus,* 11 August 1643.

[7] *A Brief and Exact Relation;* Bibliotheca Gloucestrensis, Pt.I, p.207.

[8] Corbet, *History of the Military Government of Gloucester,* p.43.

[9] *Ibid.*

[10] Bibliotheca Gloucestrensis, Pt.II, Appendix V, p.380.

[11] *A Brief and Exact Relation;* Bibliotheca Gloucestrensis, Pt.I, p.220.

[12] *Mercurius Aulicus,* 20 August 1643.

[13] *A Brief and Exact Relation;* Bibliotheca Gloucestrensis, Pt.I, p.215.

[14] *Mercurius Aulicus,* 24 August 1643.

[15] *A Brief and Exact Relation;* Bibliotheca Gloucestrensis, Pt.I, p.224.

[16] *Ibid.,* pp.224-225.

[17] *Journal of Sir Samuel Luke*, p.145.

[18] *Letters and Memorials of State (Sidney Papers)*, ed. Arthur Collins (London, 1746), Vol. II, p.669.

[19] Ryves, *Mercurius Rusticus*, pt. I, p.145.

[20] *A True Relation of the Late Expedition of His Excellency, Robert Earle of Essex, for the Relief of Gloucester* (1643), Bibliotheca Gloucestrensis, Pt.I, p.239.

[21] 'The Journal of Prince Rupert's Marches, 5 Sept. 1642 to 4 July 1646', ed. C.H. Firth, *English Historical Review*, Vol.XIII (1898).

[22] May, *The History of the Parliament of England*, Part III, p.94.

[23] Ryves, *Mercurius Rusticus*, Part I, pp. 164, 165.

[24] *A True Relation;* Bibliotheca Gloucestrensis, Pt.I, p.240.

[25] May, *The History of the Parliament of England*, Part III, p.92.

[26] Whitelocke, *Memorials of the English Affairs*, p.69.

CHAPTER TEN

OTHER MILITARY ACTIVITY IN THE MIDLANDS -
SUMMER AND AUTUMN 1643

While the chief focus of attention during the summer of 1643
had rested upon Gloucester, local struggles between Royalist
and Parliamentarian continued unabated throughout the rest
of the Midlands. In Rutland, Burley was taken for the King,
while in Staffordshire Tamworth was taken by local Parliamentary forces, and 'upon Wednesday, August 30 1643,
being the Fast-day of that moneth, and therefore as in many
more of our former victories so much the more memorable,
the brave and strong Castle, called Eccleshall Castle, was
taken by Stafford soldiers',[1] assisted by 'that valiant and ever-
renowned active gentleman, Sir William Brereton, with some
forces from Cheshire'.[2] Thus, according to contemporary
accounts, the home of the Bishop of Coventry and Lichfield,
which had been garrisoned for the King by Lord Capel,
General of His Majesty's forces in the counties of Worcester,
Salop, Chester and North Wales, fell to Parliament. This was
after a siege lasting over two months, and a determined
attempt by Lord Capel's 'fellow rob-carriers, Colonel Hastings',[3] and Colonel Bagot, 'the son of a good and powerful
family in the county', to raise it.

When the besiegers finally entered the castle most of its
defenders had fled, leaving behind 'a trunck of plate, which
they had brought out to have carried away with them',[4] one
third of which was sent to the Stafford Committee to be
'disposed of for the use of the Publique', 40 barrels of beer
and the body of the recently expired Bishop. His Lordship
had died about a week before of natural causes but preparations for his burial were incomplete when the garrison fell.

The Shropshire Parliamentarians were just as active as their
Staffordshire brethren in that August of 1643, and with good
reason for, in a newspaper report dated 29 October 1642, it

was stated that 'taxes, billeting of soldiers, and plundering of men's houses, hath quite undone the whole county of Shropshire. The Cavaliers take men's horses away violently, and if they refuse to let them go, they have pistols and swords presently at their breasts. The whole county of Shropshire is so impoverished with the robbings and ransacking of these Rebels, that the length of an age will scarce recover their losses, and make them reparations'.[5]

In April 1643 Parliament appointed a Committee 'for the Association of the Counties of Warwick, Stafford and Salop'. Its members were the chief local opponents of the King and included Sir John Corbet, Richard More, and Thomas Hunt, who were, respectively, Members of Parliament for Shropshire, Bishops Castle and Shrewsbury, together with Mr. Thomas Mytton of Halston, Robert Corbet and Humphrey Mackworth.

One of the Committee's first tasks was to discover where the most effective garrison could be established for the annoyance of their adversaries, who for so long had enjoyed military supremacy in the area. The choice fell upon Wem, the only unoccupied town near to the centre of the county. And so, at the end of August, Mytton, Mackworth and Hunt, having raised a small body of troops, and being spiritually fortified by the attendance of Mr. Richard Baxter, the famous dissenting minister, settled a garrison at Wem, Parliament's first in the county.

It was not long before this newly established garrison received the attention of Lord Capel, who was no doubt anxious to redress his failure to raise the siege at Eccleshall. Commanding a force of 5,000 men, Capel set out from Shrewsbury on 17 October and laid siege to the garrison, which contained about 500 soldiers, protected only by hastily thrown up earthworks, as the town had no wall. These makeshift fortifications were mainly the work of the townspeople of Wem, who to a man gave the Governor, Thomas Mytton, their enthusiastic support.

If the Parliamentary version of the siege is correct the defenders of Wem certainly gave a very good account of themselves, for they successfully resisted the repeated sallies of the Royalists and 'one of Colonel Mytton's case of drakes

[3 lb. cannon] killed sixty of the King's party at one shot'.[6] The women of the town particularly distinguished themselves during the siege, for which service they are immortalised in the rhyme:

> The women of Wem, and a few musketteers,
> Beat the Lord Capel, and all his cavaliers.

With the approach of Sir William Brereton out of Chester the Royalists broke off the engagement and, after a minor battle at Lee Bridge, they dispersed to Shrewsbury and Whitchurch.

Parliament's success at Wem encouraged the Parliamentarian sympathisers in Shrewsbury to hatch a plot for the betrayal of the town. But the conspiracy was discovered by the ever vigilant Ottley, who had the ringleaders executed. The following extract from the mayor's accounts, dated 29 December 1643, probably alludes to the intended demise of Ottley's victims:

Item, for timber to make a gibett	0	9	0
It. for three men, theyer work at the same	0	3	6
It. for John Davies his time to carry the same	0	1	6

Also in October Sir William Vavasour, who had lately been appointed Colonel-General of the Royal forces in Gloucestershire, furthered his scheme to tighten the blockade on Gloucester by taking Tewkesbury, which he entered with little resistance, promising the townsfolk that 'as their governor, he would behave with moderation'.

Massey was, however, reluctant to part with Tewkesbury without a struggle. He sent up on the tide a boatload of soldiers at the sight of which Vavasour's men promptly deserted leaving the Colonel and a few officers to defend the town. Resistance was obviously impossible and so Vavasour made a tactical withdrawal to Hereford.

When Massey had occupied the town he wrote a despatch to Essex containing the usual request for assistance: 'Your Excellency well knowest how impossible it will be to maintain the garrison without supply of strength, many of the townsmen here being weary of the service, and the country already desire not or will not look upon us, being also likely to lose our markets, since we are not able to defend them from the enemy's seizure.' It is easy to appreciate the attitude of the inhabitants of the town and the countryside immediately surrounding it, for Massey's occupation of Tewkesbury in October 1643 was the sixth time that the town had changed hands since the war began.

In November the first tangible result of Charles's treaty with the Irish landed at Bristol in the form of 1,000 foot, 100 horse and eight pieces of assorted artillery. These were initially seconded to Vavasour and were to be billeted on the unfortunate inhabitants of Newent in Gloucestershire. While they were marching thence through Wootton-under-Edge these Irish troops were attacked by a detachment of Massey's army under the command of Captain Robert Backhouse. The Parliamentarians were, however, repulsed in the attack and the reinforcements proceeded on their way through Cheltenham to their destination.

By now the struggle between Massey and Vavasour had assumed the character of a duel between the two men, and both had by now lost sight of the real issues involved. In his almost fanatical desire to reduce Massey, Vavasour resorted to the most insidious tactics. The Captain Backhouse mentioned above was, in a letter addressed to him dated 19 November 1643, informed indirectly by Vavasour that 'you may not only have your pardon, but raise yourself a greater fortune, than the condition of those you serve are able to afford you. This you may gaine by the delivery, you may guesse my meaning of what place, which is not hard for you to do'.[7] The person who delivered the letter told Backhouse that if he undertook the business referred to he would receive the sum of £5,000. But the Captain, out of fear or honesty, informed his Colonel who ordered him to proceed with the affair but to temporize by entering into a detailed correspondence with the enemy. This lasted for most of the winter, during which time Vavasour released his vigilance, enabling Massey to obtain supplies with less difficulty, thus relieving the pressure which was telling so heavily upon the garrison.

Also in November the home of the Catholic Throckmortons, Coughton Court, was taken over by troops from the Parliamentary garrison at Warwick. From Coughton, which is on the Warwickshire/Worcestershire border, the Parliamentarians could keep an eye on Royalist activity in nearby Worcester.

As soon as the Royalists at Worcester received intelligence of
the occupation of Coughton Court, a force was sent against
this newly established Parliamentarian garrison but the
soldiers 'could not agree about their commands, and soe
returned without doing anything'.[8]

On the 28th of the month some 2,000 Moorlanders were
attacked by a smaller force of Royalist cavalry commanded
by Colonel Dud Dudley and although 'at first the rebels came
on hansomely',[9] being in the main foot soldiers, they were
after two hours of fighting, eventually worn down and
defeated, after which Leek was finally taken for the King.
This defeat was, however, soon avenged. Early in December
Colonel Hastings, fearing for the safety of Tutbury, moved
into Staffordshire in order to rid the area around the castle
of Parliamentary troops. This was, like the capture of Leek,
part of a desperate attempt to keep open the corridor, formed
by North Staffordshire, which connected the main Royalist
areas of the west and the north. But if the Parliamentary
news-sheet *A Perfect Diurnal* for Saturday 2 December 1643
can be believed it would seem that the Moorlanders saw to it
that Hastings's contribution to the scheme was not a success:

> Colonel Hasting's, that eminent rob-carrier, we heare for certaine
> by letters to the House of Commons, upon a designe to releave
> Tutbury Castle in Staffordshire, which is kept against the Parliament,
> marching from Ashby de la Zooch into Staffordshire, was set upon
> by valient Morelanders, who made a miserable route of his troopes,
> killed above an 100, tooke about 150 horse, an 100 armes, all their
> baggage, many prisoners, whereof most of his captaines and officers
> (all but one) some say himselfe very narrowly escaping, and is gone
> backe to Ashby to bemone his bad success.[10]

The triumph of the Moorlanders was, however, offset by
Parliament's loss to the Royalists of one of Stafford's satellite
garrisons, Lapley House. This was effected at midnight on
21 December by a party of men belonging to 'Colonel
Leveson, the vigilent Governor of Dudley Castle', and
commanded by Captain Heaveningham:

> Being come to Lapley they began to reare ladders to the court wall,
> which gave the Rebels an alarme; notwithstanding which the Captaine
> and six more got up the ladder, and leaped down into the yard,
> where there passed some blowes against 15 Rebels, for so many were
> then on the guard in the gate-house, but two or three of the Rebels
> being slaine, and as many hurt, gave the Captaine time to open the

gate and let the rest of his musketteirs into the yard, who received some shot from the Rebels, out of the windowes, but without losse, except one onely hurt. This done, the Captaine reared ladders to the windowes, and most valiantly entred in despight of the Rebels (above 70 in number) whom he tooke prisoners, with all their armes, ammunition, and baggage. Twelve musketteirs kept garrison in the church adjoyning, who hearing the house already taken, yeilded themselves prisoners, and were with their fellowes sent all prisoners to Chillington, which also was lately a garrison of Rebels, till Colonell Leveson tooke it by assault, and all the Rebels in it prisoners. Lieutenant Staley with 24 musquetiers was left to keepe Lapley house, and a Coronet with 10 others to keepe the church, till more might be sent from Dudley Castle.[11]

An attempt by some troops from Stafford to retake the garrison resulted in their rout by Colonel Leveson in which they were forced to leave behind them one of their pieces of cannon 'which', taunted *Mercurius Aulicus,* 'be brought backe to Lapley, where 'tis ready for them when ever they please to fetch it'.[12]

The year ended with the capture of Tong Castle in Shropshire by Parliamentary forces from Eccleshall, on 28 December, and with the siege of Aston Hall. The Hall, it will be remembered, was the home of Sir Thomas Holte, who had entertained the King on his march to Edgehill in the autumn of 1642. Since then the baronet's son and heir, Edward, had died in the King's service at Oxford of the plague; an event which the celebrated Royalist antiquarian, Sir William Dugdale, of Shustock, Warwickshire, considered of sufficient importance to record in his diary:

August 28 [1643] Mr. Edward Holte (sonne and heire of Sir Thomas Holte of Aston juxta Bermingham) dyed in Oxford: buried in Christ Church, under that window in the chappell on the south side of the Quire, wherein the picture of a Bishop is sett.[13]

On 18 December Colonel Leveson of Dudley Castle, acting on a request from Sir Thomas, placed 40 musketeers in the Hall, which was assaulted on the 26th by a Parliamentary force numbering some 1,200 men, drawn mainly from Birmingham and the surrounding garrisons. After being subjected to a considerable bombardment, to which a shattered balustrade and newel post in the Hall's principal staircase remain as mute reminders, the defenders finally surrendered on 28 December. In this two-day siege the Royalists lost 12 of their own men and killed 60 of the enemy, some of whom were interred in the graveyard of Aston Church, as the following extract from the parish register testifies:

1643   Five soldiers were buried on the eight twentieth day of Dece'ber.

In terms of military success it would appear that, on balance, Parliament had fared rather better than the King during this, the first full year of war. But nothing palls so quickly as military successes that do not bring the conclusion of hostilities any nearer, and the supporters of Parliament were by now as heartily sick of the war as were the King's supporters. John Pym, the one man capable of holding together the disunited and factious Parliamentary party, and instilling it with renewed vitality and sense of common purpose, died on 8 December 1643. Thus the Parliamentarians were, in addition to experiencing that debilitating sense of despondency which they shared with their adversaries, rendered acephalous.

CHAPTER TEN

[1] Vicars, *Magnalia Dei Anglicana*, Parts I and II, p.411.

[2] *A Perfect Diurnal*, No.8 (1643).

[3] *Ibid.*

[4] Vicars, *Magnalia Dei Anglicana*, Parts I and II, p.412.

[5] *England's Memorable Accidents*, No. 57 (1642).

[6] *A True relation of a Great Victory obtained by the Parliaments Forces against the Cavaliers neere Chester, 17 and 18 Oct. 1643* Thomason Tracts E.77.

[7] *A True Relation of A Wicked Plot intended ... against the City of Gloucester* (1644); Bibliotheca Gloucestrensis, Pt.I, p.287.

[8] Dugdale, *Life, Diary, and Correspondence*, p.56.

[9] *Mercurius Aulicus*, 2 December 1643.

[10] *A Perfect Diurnal* No. 20.

Plate 4. The oak staircase at Aston Hall showing the shattered balustrade and newel post.

'Country Life' magazine.

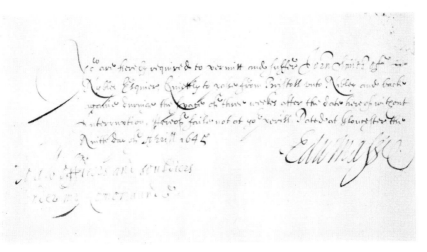

Plate 5. Pass issued by Edward Massey.

Gloucester City Library.

12

By virtue of severall orders of the Com[itt]ee (the first of them bearing date the 12 of Aprill 1645) I had the Contribution of these townes underwritten (at the rates expressed) assigned unto me for the last 19 monethes beginning January 1644 and ending July 1646 / the first 3 monethes whereof were paid to the Committee or their Officers

The townships	monthly assessment	months	the totall summe	receipts	arreares
Bredon cum membris	36 13 4 / 50 00 0 im	17	783 6 8	752 02 10	51 03 10
Kilmington and Woollershall	15 00 0 / 18 02 7 im	19	322 11 0	237 05 00	85 06 00
Pensham	05 14 7 / 07 16 3 im	19	133 17 1	133 17 01	00 00 00
Wicke	11 09 0 / 15 00 0 im	16	225 16 0	225 16 00	00 00 00
Quttenhill	04 18 0 / 06 13 4 im	19	114 06 0	094 00 00	20 06 00
Comberton Magna	07 06 8 / 10 00 0 im	12	101 06 8	084 17 9	16 08 11
Comberton Parva	07 06 8 / 10 00 0 im	12	101 06 8	100 03 10	01 02 10
Strensham	12 10 0 im	12	150 00 0	078 12 00	71 08 00
Ripple	28 00 0 im	07	196 00 0	136 00 00	60 00 00
			2128 10 01	1822 14 6	305 15 01

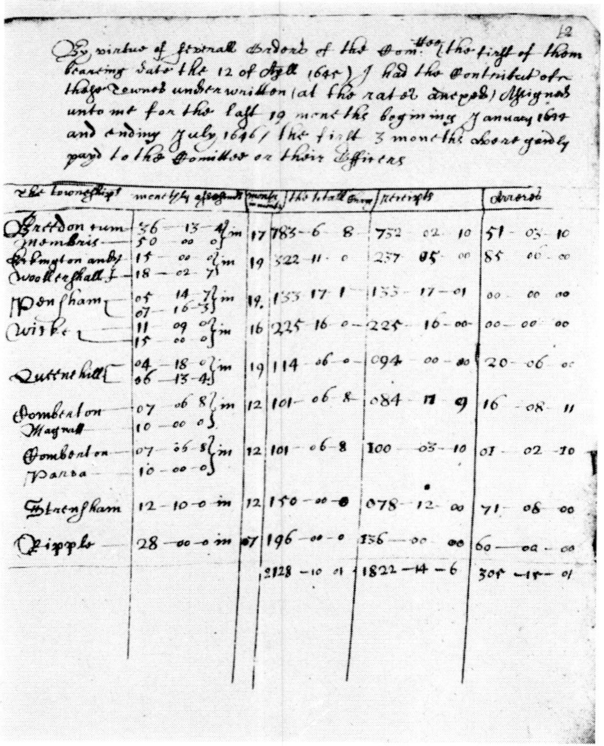

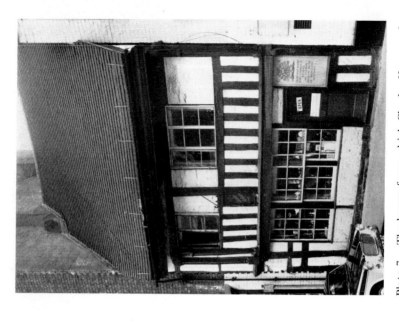

Plate 6. Extract from the account book of Captain Euseby Dormer.

Public Record Office, London. Crown Copyright Reserved.

Plate 7. The house from which Charles II escaped after the Battle of Worcester.

Photograph: Michael Dowty, Worcester.

[11] *Mercurius Aulicus,* 26 December 1643.

[12] *Ibid.*

[13] Dugdale, *Life, Diary, and Correspondence,* p.54.

CHAPTER ELEVEN

THE COST TO THE COMMUNITY -
SOME EXTRA-MILITARY CONSEQUENCES OF THE WAR

(i) The Towns

Fighting was not the only evil that the war had brought about. Civil strife also led to the complete dislocation of the region's economy. There was an almost total cessation of traffic upon the roads bringing considerable distress, especially to the towns, many of which were already objects of siege and plunder. Goods transported from one commercial centre to another were often confiscated *en route* by the army in consequence of which markets and whole industries were ruined. At Shrewsbury the fear that 'a want of all commodities, not native with us, will follow the intercourse betweene us and London being interdicted' soon became manifest; the town 'being exhausted of wine, vinegar, hops, paper; and pepper at four shillings the pound'.[1] And of Burton upon Trent the Staffordshire antiquarian, Sir Simon Degge, said that 'it was before the last wars a town given much to cloathing, their kersies being in great esteem in this country; but since the war it hath declined in trade having suffered much by the plunder'.[2] While as early in the war as April 1643 Birmingham was described as 'having for a long time been without trade'.[3]

It was not altogether the persistant confiscation of merchandise by the soldiery that brought about this state of affairs. The fact that both parties had issued orders forbidding trade with those parts of the country at emnity with themselves assisted considerably in the debilitation of the region's commerce. In November 1643 Charles prohibited the free passage of cloth to London, because, in the words of the Royal edict, 'most of the merchants residing therein are in actual rebellion against his Majestie'.[4] And, on 10 December 1645, the Committee of Both Kingdoms wrote to the County Committees and their military commanders in the Midlands warning them that 'owing to the connivance at trade between London, and Worcester, Hereford, and other of the King's garrisons in those parts, both the people are enabled to pay the contributions laid on them by the enemy for their maintenance, and the garrisons are supplied with what information and other necessaries they require'. The letter goes on: 'If this trade were stopped it would soon reduce those garrisons to such want as they could not long hold out, and besides, it would put the people under so great necessity that they would compel the surrender of those places, so as to enjoy their trade again. We therefore recommend to your especial care strictly to inhibit and prevent all manner of trade from the City and other places under the power of the Parliament to Worcester, Hereford, and other Royalist garrison towns, as likewise from those places to London'.[5]

The economic importance of this policy is further exemplified by the petitioning of Charles by the manufacturers and traders of Worcester who pointed out that as they were forbidden to trade with London they could find no sale for their goods and were thus unable to pay the taxes imposed upon them for the maintenance of the King's army.

It was ironic that the war should have brought such distress to the towns because they, or rather the merchants therein, had been one of the elements that instigated the conflict with the King, for they considered that Charles's economic policies prevented England from gaining the necessary strength to enable her to compete with Europe and further modify English trade. To the commercial classes of England 'a small country and few people, by its situation, trade and policy, may be equivalent in wealth and strength, to a greater people and territory'.[6] As their exemplar they took the Spanish Netherlands: 'the city of London and other great towns of trade', wrote Hobbes, 'having in admiration the great prosperity of the Low Countries after they had revolted from their monarch, the King of Spain, were inclined to think that the like change of government here would to them produce the like prosperity'.[7]

But for the English merchants the struggle against Charles
was not progressing towards what these Calvinists of Commerce
regarded as its predestined end. Instead it had produced
nothing but adversity and even those merchants of good
estate and credit 'were', complained a contemporary, 'hardly
able to go on with trade or to pay their debts and maintain
their charge' and many were forced to emigrate.

(ii) Passes

Traders who did attempt to pursue their business activities,
and anyone else for that matter, required an official pass for
even the shortest of journeys. The following letter[8] addressed
to Sir Francis Ottley at Shrewsbury is a request for such a
permit:

> Sir,
>   I have sent my Servants with some Carts to fetch away my Goods
> which I left in my House in Shrewsbury, I shall desire they may have
> your Ticket to pass the Gate without interuption, I am by the Kings
> command to stay some time in Chester, where I shall be ready to
> serve you as
>
>   Your Friend & Servant
>   T. HANMER.

Hanmer was, of course, a Royalist requesting safe conduct
through what was, on the date of the letter, Royalist controlled territory. It was, however, not uncommon for passes to be
issued by Parliament to Royalists or to those living or visiting
Royalist held areas allowing the latter to travel through
Parliamentary country. The warrant (see Plate 5 at page
96) issued by Edward Massey, for instance, gave John
Smith of Nibley in Parliamentarian controlled Gloucestershire permission to travel from the Royalist garrison town of
Bristol to his native village and back.

Such acts were usually instigated by enlightened self-
interest for the recipients of these passes were usually
performing some service of benefit to Parliament, like
Margary Davies, a Dudley haberdasher, who received a warrant
issued by Parliament at Tipton Green, Staffordshire, giving
her 'full power and authority to carry sell and vent all such
hatts as she shall make, to Coventry to Mr. Binks (as formerly
she hath done); provided she carrys nothinge with her pre-
judiciall to the state, or doth not convey any of her hatts to

the enemyes garrisons'.[9]

The case of another inhabitant of the Royalist town of Dudley, Henry Finch, an ironmonger, further exemplifies the selfishness behind Parliament's apparent magnanimity. Finch attempted to return home from the East of England laiden with bags of hops and a barrel of soap, but without a travel warrant, and in consequence found himself 'stayed at Birmingham by Colonel Foxe', who refused to allow him to proceed without a pass from Lord Denbigh. Only after Finch had petitioned Denbigh to the effect that he was a man well affected to Parliament and constantly employed 100 men at work, and that 'if he may not pass with his commodities it will be a general loss to the whole country',[10] was he allowed to pass into the Associated Counties.

There were, however, some instances of passes being issued for purely conciliatory purposes. Two of the King's physicians, Sir Theodore Mayerne and Doctor Frayzer, together with a Royal apothecary, were permitted by Parliament to travel from London to their master at Oxford. Safe passage between London and Oxford was also granted to what Charles and his Court would no doubt have considered to be the necessities of life. The King's favourite wine was sent regularly to him from London and the House of Lords ordered 'Jemmey Jacke to have a pass quietly to go to Oxford with a Birding piece, and a case of Pistols for the use of the Prince'. The Lords also instructed that passes should be granted to permit 'three boys to carry to Oxford some Beagles, for the Prince his Highness' and 'that John Damntry and Joseph Atkinson, Servants to His Majesty, shall have a pass, quietly to go to Oxford with Gloves and other Necessaries for His Majesty'.[11]

Such deeds were not confined to Parliament at Westminster nor to intercourse between London and Oxford. When the Royalist garrison at Lichfield Close was being besieged by Sir William Brereton during April and May 1646, one of the Royalist officers in the Close, Lord Walter Aston, requested safe conduct for one of his servants from the beleaguered garrison to Bridgnorth, which had recently been 'delivered up' to Parliament. The purpose of the journey was expounded in a letter written to Brereton in which Aston asked that 'a

Servant of mine passe ... to Bridgnorth to enquire if he can find what is become of some Writeings of mine that were left in the Castle in Sir Lewis Kerks tyme [Sir Lewis had been the Royalist governor of Bridgnorth]. Sir they are writings only that concerne my barony which cannot any way advantage any body but my selfe and posterity'.[12]   Brereton, in his reply, agreed to this request.

Unfortunately Royalists and Parliamentarians alike rarely honoured passes issued by the opposite faction and the bearers of such documents were not infrequently treated as enemy collaborators and hanged as spies.

It would also appear that passes were not always fully honoured even by members of the issuing party.   On 2 November 1643, Colonel Mainwaring provided Mr. Thomas Green with a permit which was supposed to give the bearer and his horse safe conduct through Parliamentarian held territory between London and Coventry. 'This passe (one would thinke)'. declares a Royalist report dated 5 November 1643, 'is particular enough to secure one of their own faction, but truly it was not; for (as Mr. Green himself confesses) when he came to passe through Northamptonshire, the rebels souldiers stayed him, and told him, that though Colonell Mainwaring had given license for him and his horse to passe their guards, yet there was no saddle mentioned in his passe, which therefore they tooke from him. Master Green being met by some of his majesties scouts, riding (very meloncholy) without a saddle, was conceived to have stolen the horse, and was thereupon brought into his majesties quarters yesterday, to give accompt how a man of his coat came to want a saddle.'[13]

(iii) Taxation

To the dislocation of the region's economy and the restricted mobility of its inhabitants was added the burden of taxation.   In the first few months of the war the King and his adversary, Parliament, had relied on gifts and loans from their respective supporters to prosecute the war. But when it became evident that the struggle was to be long and serious both sides began to turn their attentions to more systematic means for securing the necessary funds. With this end in view novel forms of taxation were introduced and these became the chief bone of contention between the warring parties and the population at large.

Every parish in the land was rated at so much in the pound by one side or the other, or by both. A small proportion of the levy realised went towards the maintenance of the main field armies but the majority was allocated to local troop commanders who had the contributions of specified districts assigned to them.

The collection of this tax was made by the parish constables and paid by them to the high-constables, who handed over the money to specially appointed receivers. They in turn would pass each district's contribution unto its assigned officer. Sir Thomas Pope, for instance, was appointed receiver for the Hundreds of Banbury and Bloxham, and moneys raised therein were apportioned to Sir Thomas Byron, towards the maintenance of the six troops of Prince Rupert's regiment.[14]

The allocation of districts to local commanders was left by Parliament in the hands of County Committees. These Committees, on which sat local dignitaries sympathetic to the Parliamentary cause, soon developed into comprehensive units of local government, but their chief function continued to be to keep the machinery of taxation running smoothly for the maintenance of the Parliamentary local and main field armies.

The Royalists exacted their tribute by authority of a warrant signed by the King, and Parliament under the aegis of an Act of Parliament, dated 24 February 1643, and described in its preamble as 'An Ordinance for the speedy raising and levying of Money for the maintenance of the Army Raised by the Parliament, And other great Affairs of the Commonwealth, by a Weekly Assessment upon the Cities of London and Westminster, and every County and City of the Kingdome of England, and the Dominion of Wales'.[15]

In this 'pretended ordinance' as Charles called it, for it was 'contrived ... without Our Royall assent', and therefore 'clearly unlawfull, and unwarrantable',[16] the weekly tax payable to Parliament by the Midland Counties and Cities was initially assessed thus: Coventry, £37 10s.; Derby, £175;

Gloucesterhsire, £750; Gloucester, £62 10s.; Hereford,£437 10s.; Leicester, £187 10s.; Lichfield, £5; Northampton,£425; Nottingham, £187 10s.; Oxford, £650; Rutland, £62 10s.; Shropshire,£375; Stafford, £212 10s.; Warwick, £562 10s.; Worcester £16 13s.; Worcestershire, £550.

Parliament could perhaps be accused of displaying unwarranted optimism in rating such places as Hereford, Oxfordshire, Shropshire, Staffordshire and Worcestershire where, on the date that the ordinance was passed, it had no power; and this was soon taken up by the Royalist wits at Oxford, 'if the worthey Members will come to these places, the money lyes ready for them',[17] they jibed. There is no doubt, however, that Parliament did succeed in realising at least a part of the levies that it had imposed on territory held by the enemy, just as the Royalists were successful in wringing taxes from Parliamentarian held territory.

This occurred frequently in the Midlands, where Royalist garrisons and Parliamentary Committees existed side by side and where the boundaries of Royalist and Parliamentarian controlled areas were conterminous or overlapped, and resulted in the unfortunate inhabitants of such places having to render tribute to both parties.

In the case of Royalist Worcestershire, for instance, a County Committee 'appoynted by Parliament' was set up first at Coventry in Warwickshire and later at Evesham, 'for raysinge and maynteneing of horse and foote for restoring and continuing the County and City of Worcester into and under the obediance of King and Parliament'.[18] The Worcester Committee exacted tribute from those Worcestershire villages such as Inkberrow, Bromsgrove, Alvechurch, Redditch, Boeley, Hanbury and Kings Norton and Yardley (both now suburbs of Birmingham) that were situated close to the border of Parliamentarian controlled Warwickshire. This was in addition to the impositions demanded of these townships by the Royalist garrison at Worcester which had levied an initial tax of £3,000 on the county 'to be paid monthly towards the payment of His Majesty's forces sent and raised for the defence of the County of Worcester'.

As Parliament increased its control over Gloucestershire during 1644 those Worcestershire villages that were close to the Gloucestershire border also began to experience the iniquity of double taxation. A number of these South Worcestershire townships, including Bredon, Eckington, Wick, Little Comberton, Great Comberton and Strensham were assigned by the Worcester Committee at Coventry to Captain Euseby Dormer and his troop of horse 'for 100 weeks and foure days, beginning October the 7th 1644 and ending September the 11th 1646 at £5. 5s. per weeke', the contributions for the first three months of each year being forwarded 'to the Committee or their Officers'.[19] During the same period these villages were also rendering tribute to the Royalist garrison at Worcester, Bredon being assessed at £52 per month, Eckington at £12, Wick at £15 2s. 2d., Comberton 'magna and parva' at £20, and Strensham at £12 10s. 0d. per month.[20] The considerable arrears listed in Captain Dormer's account book (see Plate 6) illustrate the reluctance, or inability, of the inhabitants of these villages to be the milch cow of both warring parties.

Another instance of double taxation in South Worcestershire is provided by the estate of Blackmoor Park situated close to the Malvern Hills. Although the owner of the Park, John Hornyold, had died on 1 May 1643, the Royalist garrisons at Worcester and Madresfield, and the Parliamentary Committee at Gloucester, were still able to realise during one period the sum of £12 per month each from the estate.

There is evidence that similar circumstances existed in Staffordshire. On 15 March 1644 the Staffordshire Committee ordered that the weekly pay of Uttoxeter 'shall be assigned to Capt. Walter Snowe for the payment of his Officers and Souldiers'.[21] But the Royalist garrison at Tutbury Castle, barely eight miles away, had so far withstood all attempts to dislodge it and was inflicting considerable distress on the surrounding countryside; so much so that Uttoxeter was forced to pay 'to Tutbury castle money and returns' to the value of £50 on 11 March 1644, a further payment of £47 18s. 0d. on 8 July 1644, and yet another payment of £50 on 8 August 1644, added to which was the cost of provisioning the castle with oats, cheese, butter and sheep skins.[22]

The constable's accounts of Mavesyn Ridware, also in

Staffordshire, show that between 24 November 1643, and 25 October 1644, the inhabitants of this hamlet, which is situated between Lichfield and Stafford, at about the same distance from each, rendered a total of £109 18s. 0d. in weekly paid contributions to the Royalists 'for the garrison at Lichfield', and from 17 February to 20 July 1644 they paid £41 3s. 10d. to the Staffordshire Committee 'towards the mentenance of the garrison at Stafford'. These payments were continued during 1645, a total of £131 13s. 3d. being paid to Lichfield and £85 7s. 9d. to Stafford.[2 3]

In December 1644 the Staffordshire Committee assessed the weekly pay of Seisdon Hundred, which included such townships as Wolverhampton, Bilston, Pen, Amblecote, Sedgeley, Kinver, Codsall, Clent (now in Worcestershire) and Wrottesley at £102 10s. 0d. The tribute was 'assigned to the Captaines and Officers of horse belonginge to the garrison of Stafford for the payment of themselves and their Troops'.[2 4]

Seventeen months earlier, in July 1643, the King had issued a warrant permitting Colonel Thomas Leveson, governor of Dudley Castle, to levy taxes on Seisden Hundred. Leveson, in turn, ordered the constable of that same Hundred 'in his majestie's name' to levy and gather his rateable part of £300 in this Hundred 'for and towards the paying of a greater number of souldiers than formerly; now lately raysed, for the defence of the castle of Dudley, and country adjacent'.

Wrottesley, for instance, of which 'the rateable part' to be paid to the Parliamentary Commissioners at Stafford on 16 December 1644 was £2 0s. 5d. per week, received, on 4 July 1644, a demand for the villages rateable portion of £300 ... for the moneth of July ... together with the arrearages due for all former monethes ... for contribution, at the said castle of Dudley, upon the 13th of the said moneth of July'.[2 5] This followed similar demands for monthly contributions in money and provisions, including rates and 'seaven schore bedds' and other furnishings dated 21 November 1643, 13 December 1643, 25 June 1644, and a warrant[2 6] signed by Leveson himself, dated Dudley Castle, 19 December 1643, and addressed to the constable of Wrottesley, or his deputy, to the effect that

Whereas, at severall times, you have contemptiously disobeyed my warrants, in not sending so many teames as hath been required (and sometimes none at all) to his majesties garrison at Dudley castle, there to be employed in his service.

These are, therefore, once more to give you notice, to presse, charg, and bring out of your constableweeke, four sufficient able teams; and the same to be ready to-morrow at Pepperhill parke, by seaven of the clocke in the morning, then and there to load tymber, to be imployed for his majesties use at Dudley castle. If you fayle in performance you will enforce me to send to you in such a way, so unpleasing to you, that you will ever wish hereafter you had yealded more obedience to my warrants, issued forth for the advancement of his majesties' proceedings, therefore fayle you not.

It is almost certain that Leveson was still exacting his levies, or at least some part of them, at the same time that Seisdon Hundred was paying tribute to the County Committee at Stafford.

Leveson also held a warrant from the King, dated 10 September 1643, 'to levy money in the nearest parts and hundreds of Warwickshire for the payment of the garrison of Dudley Castle'.[27] As the parts of Warwickshire that bordered on South Staffordshire, in which Dudley is a Worcestershire enclave, were controlled at that time by Parliament, then this warrant must be accepted as further evidence of double taxation.

The iniquity of double taxation was not only endured by those unfortunate enough to live in areas where Royalist and Parliamentarian control conjoined, or where the influence of both parties could be easily effected, but it was also experienced by those living well inside the territories controlled by the two parties.

In a 'humble petition' to Parliament at Westminster, dated October 1643, the inhabitants of the city and county of Coventry, which was situated in an area that was solidly Parliamentarian, complained:

That great is the pressure under which at this time our country doth groane and mourne, it being brought into a disconsolate and heartlesse condition through our daily oppressions for want of due protection, not onely from the often robberies and spoylings, but the unjust taxes and rates imposed upon the severall inhabitants by the adverse party, even almost to the walls of our garrison, to the great disadvantage and dishearting of many, and daily falling off of others, who have largely contributed to the Parliament for their future safety.[28]

Some of those who had been subjected to 'the unjust taxes and rates' of 'the adverse party' in all probability lived in such villages as Ryton-on-Dunsmore and Bedworth, both of which are within a five mile radius of Coventry, and Meriden and Cubbington, which are about six miles from Coventry. All four villages were at the time of the petition paying regular contributions to the Warwickshire County Committee at Coventry through Thomas Basnet, Esquire.[29]

Henry Townshend of Elmley Lovett, a village situated in the heart of Royalist Worcestershire, and at least 10 miles from the county boundary, also paid contributions to both sides throughout the war.

Such deep penetrations into enemy held territory as those cited tended, however, to be sporadic and were more in the nature of plundering expeditions than a serious attempt at exacting regular tribute.

Elmley Lovett, like many other Worcestershire villages was, however, taxed retrospectively by Parliament after Massey had seized Evesham on 26 May 1645. On 14 October 1645, from its new headquarters at Evesham, the Parliamentary Committee for Worcestershire demanded contributions of £10 per month from Elmley Lovett, back-dated 12 months, which the Committee considered to be arrears. The inhabitants were given three days, until the 17th, to raise the money and submit it to a commissioner 'at Evesham at Mr. Heralite's house'. The order ended 'hereof fail you not as you will answer the contrary at your perils of pillaging, and plundering, and your houses fired, and your persons imprisoned'.[30] During the same twelvemonth period the parish had already paid a monthly levy of £10 18s. 0d. to the Royalists as their part of the £4,000 assessment levied on the county in February 1644.

The authorities were not always insensible to the effects of double taxation and there were instances of relief being granted to those thus afflicted. Captain William Acocke entreated Lord Denbigh to consider the state of Alcester, oppressed by taxes and plundered by the adverse party. Acocke pointed out that he had received only £10 in money in lieu of the five horses demanded on the earl's warrant and conveyed to Denbigh the prayer of the inhabitants of Alcester that they may be excused the remainder. 'And though I doe not absolutely desire so', pleaded Acocke, 'yet my humble suite unto your honor is that att most you will not impose above £5 more upon them, less if you please'.[31]

An entry in the Staffordshire Committee Order Book records a similar act of charity: 'Whereas the weekely pay of Horninglow and Branson assigned to Col. Edward Ashenhurst for the pay of his officers and souldiers are in areare the summe of £12 a peice, it is ordered that in regard of theyr greate sufferings by the Enemy and that they are still under theyr power that they shall pay but £6 areare apeice and likewise whereas they are to pay 30s. a weeke a peice since the assignment to their said Colonell it is ordered that they shall pay but 15s. a weeke a peice.'[32]

(iv) Forced Loans and Excise

The imposition of forced loans was another means employed by both sides in an attempt to meet their liabilities. As already stated, reliance on voluntary contributions as a means of financing the war proved unsatisfactory. Parliament's first general appeal for a loan made in June 1642 had, by December of that same year, realised only £76,000, even though the Public Faith was pledged for its repayment with interest at 8 *per cent*. It was decided therefore that contributions made under this scheme, known as 'the Public Faith' or 'Propositions', were to be compulsory, for which an ordinance was passed in May 1643. The provisions of this statute were based on those for the levying of Weekly Pay, and stipulated that all persons worth more than £10 a year in land, or £100 in personal estate, must loan an amount not exceeding one-fifth of their revenue from land, or one twentieth of their goods. This was, of course, in addition to their Weekly Pay contribution. These loans were still subject to the original terms under the voluntary scheme, except when force or distraint had to be used in obtaining payment and then no guarantee of repayment was given.

According to an entry in the Order Book of the Staffordshire Committee it would appear that an inhabitant of Uttoxeter was one of those who declined to render this further tribute. The entry, dated 19 March 1644, concerns

William Eyton 'sent to for £30 and refusing to pay is to be imprisoned untill hee make performance'.[33]

But Eyton's reluctance to make his Public Faith loan was probably less from recalcitrance than from his impecuniosity resulting from the inordinately heavy double taxation to which Uttoxeter was subjected. This is reflected in another entry in the Staffordshire Committee's Order Book, dated 6 February 1644, at which time Uttoxeter was already £50 in arrears in its contributions, which it was ordered 'shall be paid in one thursday seaventhnight being the 15th day of this instant month'.[34]

Charles imitated the Parliamentary Compositions by raising forced loans of his own under the Privy Seal. The Privy Seals were issued 'By the Advice of the Members of Both Houses Assembled at Oxford', on printed forms, with blank spaces into which could be inserted the name of the lender and the sum required from him. The entry of Scotland into the Civil War on the side of Parliament was the occasion and the excuse for the raising of money by this means as the wording on the loan forms suggests. The recipients of these forms were reminded by Charles that with the 'invasion' of England by 'our subjects of Scotland ... by lawe your personall service, attended in a warlike manner for the resistance of this invasion, may be required by us, which we desire to spare, chusing rather to invite your assistance for the maintenance of our army in a free and voluntary expression of your affections to our service, and the safety of this Kingdome'.[35] Naturally, possession of London gave Parliament a decided advantage over Charles in raising money by this means.

The King and *his* Parliament at Oxford also attempted to imitate another Parliamentarian form of taxation introduced by a statute dated 22 July 1643 by which excise was levied on all alcoholic beverages manufactured in England, such as wine, ale and beer, and also cider and perry, for which the Midland counties of Gloucester, Hereford and Worcester were already renowned. The excise also covered importations into England of tobacco, groceries, cloth, silks, furs, hats, leather goods, lace, linen, thread and wire. This wartime measure which, incidentally, has yet to be repealed, was initiated to ensure a degree of equity in 'the future maintenance of the

Parliament Forces and other great affairs of the Commonwealth', as some 'Malignants and Neutrals' had thus far
contrived to evade payment of their weekly assessment.
Through this Act it was felt that defaulters would be compelled to give some support to the cause, albeit involuntarily.

(v) Sequestration

Yet another means of taxation involved the sequestration
of the estates of 'notorious delinquents', whom Parliament
defined in an ordinance passed on 1 April 1643, as 'all
persons, ecclesiastical or temporal, as have raised or shall
raise arms against the Parliament, or have been, are, or shall
be in actual war against the same, or have voluntarily
contributed or shall voluntarily contribute, not being under
any power of any part of the King's army at the time of such
Contributing, any money, horses, plate, arms, munitions, or
other aid or assistance for or towards the maintenance of any
forces raised against the Parliament, or for opposing any force
or power raised by authority of both Houses of Parliament'.[36]
By this act, and by the King's authority, known Royalist
or Parliamentarian sympathisers residing within the territories
controlled by the party at enmity with that which they were
in sympathy, forfeited their lands and possessions. The
sequestered property was either rented out, or sold, to
provide a further means of realising revenue for the continuance of the war.
Both sides appointed special commissioners of sequestrations who were the sole judges of whether or not a person
came within the definition of delinquent. The iniquity with
which these commissioners often effected their business is
illustrated by the case of Sir Edward Powell of Pengethly
Hall, Sellack, in Herefordshire who, because of his advancing
years, had taken up residence in London. To the Royalist
Commissioners for Sequestrations Powell's decision to live in
a Parliamentarian stronghold was cogent and compelling
evidence that he was a disaffected person, even though his
motives were non-political. And so, on 10 February 1644,
Powell's servants and tenants received a summons to 'appeare
before us his Majesty's Commissioners at Mr. Normans house
in Hereford upon munday next the 12th day of this inst-

ant february by 9 of the clocke in the morninge to give us
an accompt of the rents of the said Sir Edward Powell, and
what rent shall appeare to be due from any the said tenants
they are then to pay us accordingly'.[37]

Sequestration served Parliament rather better than the
Royalists whose territory decreased consistently as the war
progressed, giving Parliament fresh crops of 'delinquents'
estates to sequester. As Parliament consolidated its position
in Staffordshire the power given to Colonel Leveson of Dudley,
by a warrant dated 2 July 1643, to seize the estates and pro-
fits of those inhabitants of Cuttleston and Seisdon Hundreds
in rebellion against the King, was transferred to the local
Parliamentary Commissioners. They inflicted like punishment
on those guilty of assisting the enemy, usually notwithstand-
ing the fact that assistance may have been rendered to the
Royalist cause involuntarily.

Although the Committees of Sequestration were considered
by contemporaries as harbingers of 'the dismemberment of
estates and ruin of families',[38] there were instances of Parliamentary Committees making provision for the maintenance
of the wives and dependents of delinquents, and even instances
of delinquents renting their own property back off the
Committees.

The administration of sequestered estates soon became
irksome, however, and a system of compounding, which had
been developed during 1644, was officially introduced by
Parliament in the spring of 1645, whereby delinquents could
pay a fine in lieu of forfeiting their estates. A composition
tariff was laid down, ranging from one half to one tenth of
the pre-war value of the estate according to the degree of the
owner's delinquency. In Nottinghamshire the sums paid for
the compounding of estates ranged from £8,698 7s. 6d.
imposed on the Earl of Chesterfield, to a few shillings paid
by small freeholders to redeem their fields. And in Shropshire
they ranged from the heavy fine of £5,284 plus a payment of
£170 per annum paid by Francis Newport of Eyton to the
sum of £1 paid by Thomas Jones of Ludlow.

In certain circumstances those who paid regular fines could
apply to the Commissioners of Sequestration for their payments to be adjusted. John Milton, the Puritan poet,

petitioned the Commissioners concerning an estate at Wheatley in Oxfordshire that had belonged to his late father-in-law, Mr. Richard Powell, who like his daughter, Milton's wife, had been a zealous Royalist. Milton requested that 'the Order of sequestring may be recalled, and that the composition may be modified' on the grounds that Mrs. Powell 'hath her thirds [widow's portion] out of that land, which was not considered when her husband followed his Composition, and ... the taxes, freequartering, and finding of armes were not then considered, which have bin since very great, and are likely to be greater'.[39]

(vi) Irregular Impositions

In addition to the regular impositions there were other incidental requisitions of money, goods, men and materials occasioned by such exigencies as the arrival, and subsequent activities in the district, of either local troops or those belonging to the main field armies.

An order from the high constable of Staffordshire, one Cartwright, to the constable of Wrottesley, and dated Nether Penn, 24 April 1644, obviously relates to Prince Rupert's Midland campaign of that year, during which he several times traversed Staffordshire. 'According to a warrant from Colonel Leveson, to me directed', wrote Cartwright, 'shewing that he hath received two severall orders from his highness prince Rupert, for the sending in for provision for his army, to be in readiness against the time he shall send for the same: These are, therefore, to charg and command you to bring into his majesties garrison, at Dudley Castle, upon Friday next, your rateable part of twenty quarter of wheate ... forty quarter of malt ... twenty hundred weight of salt butter ... twenty hundred weight of bacon ... and also your ratable parte of forty hundred weight of good and sound cheese ... All.which provision the said colonell saith is to be safely kept at Dudley castle until his highness send for the same; which, if he doe not, he saith it shall be restored unto the countrey againe, or satisfaction in money for the same'. To these instructions was appended the warning to 'faile not, lest the prince's forces be enforced to fetch it'.[40]

An intelligence report from Colonel Fox to Lord Denbigh

dated Edgbaston, 18 March 1644, also refers to this campaign. Fox tells of the arrival at Lichfield of Prince Rupert's forces on the evening of 17 March and that Colonel Richard Bagot, the governor of Lichfield, 'sent forth warrants to his neighboringe parishoners to bringe in provisions for 4,000 of his [the Prince's] soldiers. Its credably thought they are bound for Newarke'.[41]

Another order from Cartwright at Nether Penn to the constable of Wrottesley, and dated 13 May 1644, is possibly in anticipation of Lord Denbigh's investment of Dudley Castle which took place in the following month. The warrant ordered that Wrottesley supply 37 men, 'furnished with materials; viz. spades, mattocks, crowes of iron, baskets, and such like tooles, for fortification, to bee employed uppon his majesties' important service'. The men were to be brought 'to his majesties garrison at Dudley Castle' at 6 a.m. the day following the date of the order.

Yet another order[42] addressed to the constable of Wrottesley, this time from a Parliamentarian commissary, was dated two days after Lord Denbigh had been forced to abandon the siege of Dudley Castle following a brush with a Royalist force under Lord Wilmot.

> These are to will and require you, to bring unto the house of Dudley, these severall proportions of victalls and other provisions, here under written, for the reliefe of the king and Parliament's army, now under the command of the right honorable the earle of Denbigh. And, if you faile in the dew performance hereof, you are then to be reputed and taken as enemies to the king, Parliament, and kingdome, and forthwith to be proceeded against accordingly.
>
> Given under my hand, this 14th day of June, 1644.
>
> GEORGE LIDDIATT, Commissary.

400 pound of bread	3 flitches of bacon
300 pound of cheese	2 quarter of oates
2 pots of butter	2 quarter of maulte
3 muttons, 3 veales	

It would appear from this warrant that Denbigh's troops remained in and around the town of Dudley for several days after the siege of the castle had been raised.

On 22 June 1644, Cartwright again ordered the constable of Wrottesley to bring workmen 'unto his majesties garrison at Dudley castle ... with spades, mattocks, picks, and baskets, to continue there during the space of a month, and you are to provide provision to maintain them during the said time; and in case you bring noe men, you are to hire men for the said time, after the rate of XIId. a day for a man'. An additional instruction, dated 23 June, ordered the constable to furnish teams of horses 'to carry lime, coales, wood, timber, stone, and hay'.[4 3] These last orders no doubt refer to the damage inflicted on Dudley Castle during Denbigh's abortive siege.

A later siege of Dudley Castle, that carried out by Sir William Brereton in 1646, also placed a considerable burden on the local population. In a letter to the Speaker of the House of Commons Brereton reported that 'when we first entred the towne wee rescued out of the markett place manie hundreds of cattell which the enemy had taken from the neighbourhood upon the approach of our fforces'. If Brereton can be believed, the cattle were, in this instance, 'restored to the severall owners'.[4 4]

Entries in the churchwardens' and constables' accounts of Marchington cum membris and Uttoxeter tell of the protracted siege of the Royalist garrison at Tutbury and its eventual capitulation to Sir William Brereton. There is a demand from the besieged garrison commander, Sir Gilbert Gerard, to the constable of Marchington 'immediately upon sight hereof, to bringe to Tedbury castle to me foure sufficient able horses, or twenty pounds in money; to provide the same towards the recruiting of my troope'. This was followed by an instruction dated seven days later from one of the castle's besiegers, Colonel John Bowyer, ordering the constable 'to provide and bring in to our quarters at Tutburie, upon sight hereof, provision for 100 foote ... to continue the same dayly, untill further order'.[4 5] Both warrants were appended with the customary threat to 'fayle not at your perills'.

The sum of £18 7s. 3d. was expended on behalf of the inhabitants of Uttoxeter 'for provisions to the leaguer at Tutbury' on 30 March, and 8 April 1646. This was followed by a further seven shillings 'for bread, beer, cheese, and drink, for Leek souldiers Marching to Tutbury', on 21 April, and £16 'paid to Sir William Brereton, for gaining Tudbury, and marching against Dudley', on 4 May 1646.[4 6]

At the same time Tutbury Castle also attempted to raise provisions from Hanbury and its neighbouring parishes and also from Coton, a hamlet some eight miles west of Uttoxeter.

On 18 December 1645, Colonels Morgan and John Birch attacked and took Hereford for Parliament, but not before the governor of the Royalist garrison, Barnabas Scudamore, had attempted to take preemptive action, indicated by the following warrant[47] addressed to the constable of a neighbouring parish:

> These are straightly to Charge and Command you to send to my Garrison,at Hereford out of your hundred, a hundred able men, with spades, shovells, pickaxes, and other necessaries fit for Pioneers, for his Majesties Service, whereof you are not to faile, as you will answer the contrary, at your utmost perill.

> Given under my hand this   BARNABAS SCUDAMORE
> 14 of Decemb. 1645

Other more general impositions of a similar nature included a tax, often called 'British Moneys', for the relief of Parliament's army fighting in Ireland, which was levied from October 1644 and later doubled. This was followed in February 1645 by a £21,000 per month levy for the maintenance of the Scottish Army fighting on the side of Parliament.

(vii) Conclusion

Such were the encumbrances of Midland folk. The fact that the area was the scene of continual warfare and bloodshed was in itself sufficient to bring about a serious dislocation in industry and trade and to impoverish and distress the population; but in addition there were these crippling exactions which were hardly calculated to stimulate trade or to nurture voluntary support for either cause.

The insatiable appetite of war was such that the impositions increased, not only in variety but in volume. The £3,000 per month tax levied by the King on Worcestershire in April 1643 was increased to £4,000 in February 1644.[48] Parliament also increased its Weekly Pay contributions as well as other taxes including the rate for compounding sequestered estates which, during 1644, increased from one tenth the pre-war value of the estate to one-third the pre-war value. These increases coincided with a universal realisation that there was little likelihood of either King or Parliament ever repaying their forced loans in full let alone the interest. Not for the first time in history Public Faith meant in reality *Punic* faith.

One of the principal reasons for the dramatic rise in taxation was undoubtedly the persistance of both sides in establishing so many garrisons, the maintenance of which was always disproportionate to their actual needs. The total moneys for pay alone expended by Colonel Thomas Waite, Governor of Rutland's miniscule garrison at Burley House, was never less than £100 per week and was often nearer £200.[49] While the 'money paid out of the publique treasurie' for the maintenance of the garrison at Edgbaston in an 18-month period from October 1643 to April 1645 was £2,544 18s.[50] It is hardly surprising, therefore, that Symonds, when referring to the five garrisons of Leicestershire, complained that 'the yearly contribution amounted to fourscore and seaventeene thousand pounds, within this county of Leicester onely ... And the whole number of men were not above 1,500 in all these garrisons'.[51]

In addition to their disproportionately high maintenance costs many garrisons tended to overawe the surrounding countryside rather than protect it and were, in fact, little more than dens of thieves. In theory those who paid the prescribed levies were free from all extraordinary payments and allowed to enjoy their horses, cattle and goods quietly. Also, no troops were to be quartered on them, except at times of extreme necessity; in which case they were to receive payment. In practice, however, these relatively equitable conditions were rarely adhered to by the more rapacious garrison commanders. In March 1644 Colonel Fox petitioned his commander in chief, Lord Denbigh, on behalf of the inhabitants of Warwickshire regarding the earl's recently established garrisons in that county which were exacting provisions, pillaging, and issuing warrants for money in Denbigh's name in places obedient to Fox's impositions and under his protection.[52] But it would appear from a report in *Mercurius Aulicus* that Fox had himself grown 'so stout a plunderer that many of his contributers petitioned against him, whereupon he was brought before the Committee at Coventry' to whom he 'offered a sound summe to be restored to his place and liberty'.[53]

Denbigh received similar intelligence to that contained in Fox's petition from Colonel Waldyne Wyllington, governor of Tamworth. 'One Lieut. Col. Moore came yesterday to Tamworth with a party of horse', wrote Wyllington, 'and after them came several complaints by poor country men (who pay weekly tax to me) that he had taken their horses from them by force, without leaving others in their stead. I sent to Lieut. Col. Moore requesting him to come to speak with me, he answered the officer that I might come to him, for he was governor as well as I; and said further to the officer that if he spake another word he would cut off his head. Upon this affront, I sent a party of musketeers, who brought him to me. He justified taking the horses, but I restored them to their owners. I hear that since they left Tamworth, however, he has taken others out of my assignations, and I much doubt that in their return towards Stafford they will continue the practice'.[54]

Denbigh also received a petition from the inhabitants of Cubbington near Leamington who prayed that no more troops might be quartered upon them, as those already sent had consumed all their provisions.

The perpetrators of these misdeeds were, in fact, all acting under Denbigh's orders and the earl was later charged by Parliament with 'raising monies by his own warrant',[55] his defence being that his share of the revenue of Warwickshire by Weekly Pay, Sequestrations, and on the Public Faith, was being withheld by the County Committee.[56]

But Denbigh's malfeasance did not prevent him from complaining to the Committee of Both Kingdoms about the activities of a brother officer, Commissary-General Hans Behr, obviously a foreigner, whom the earl regarded as a personal enemy. In a letter dated Coventry, 6 April 1644, Denbigh wrote of the insolent behaviour of Behr's soldiers, of their unjust levy of horses, money and provisions, and how as many as 20 or 30 at a time supplied themselves with diet and provender at the cost of one poor family. 'Theire injuries', Denbigh continued, 'had been more unsufferable had not an officer of mine fritened them away with the report of Prince Rupert's drawinge neare; and giving the same alarum to the

Commissary, then at my cozen Sir William Boughton's house, he held it then fitt to remove with his forces at a further distance into Northamptonshire'.[5,7]

The rapacity of some civilian officials often added to the miserable condition of those thus ill used. Lucy Hutchinson tells us that in Nottinghamshire 'Salisbury and one Silvester had, for their own profit, gotten a commission to set on foot the excise in the county, and joined with them one Sherwin. These two were such pragmatical knaves, that they justly became odious to all men ... For when plundering troops killed all the poor country men's sheep and swine, and other provisions, whereby many honest families were ruined and beggared, these unmerciful people would force excise out of them for those very goods which the others had robbed them of'.[5,8]

Despite the persistent malfeasance of Parliamentarian army officers and civilian officials a document among the papers of a Worcestershire Royalist, Henry Townshend of Elmley Lovett tells us that 'the people ... do not stick to say that they can find more justice, and more money, in the enemy's quarters than in the King's'.[5,9]

CHAPTER ELEVEN
[1] Letter from Edward Lord Herbert to Sir Henry Herbert, 25 Aug. 1643, *Epistolary Curiosities*, pp. 31, 32.

[2] Shaw, *History and Antiquities of Staffordshire*, Vol.I, p.18, (General History).

[3] *Special Passages*, No. 35 (1643).

[4] *Mercurius Aulicus*, 22 November 1643.

[5] *Cal. S.P. Dom.* 1645-1647, p.258.

[6] *The Economic Writings of Sir William Petty*, ed. Charles Henry Hall (Cambridge, 1899), Vol.I, p.249.

[7] Hobbes, *Behemouth*, p.4.

[8] 'Ottley Papers', *Salop.Arch.Soc.Trans.*, Vol.VII (1895), p.274.

[9] *Denbigh MSS.* (Hist. MSS. Comm. *4th Rep.*), p.267.

[10] *Ibid.* Part V, p.79.

[11] *Journals of the House of Lords,* Vol.V, p.643.

[12] Letter from Lord Walter Aston to Sir William Brereton, 1 May 1646, Letter Book of Sir William Brereton Referring to The Time of the Leaguers at Dudley and Tutbury Castles, and Lichfield Close, 4 April to 29 May, 1646, pp. 142, 143, Birmingham Reference Library.

[13] *Mercurius Aulicus,* 5 November 1643.

[14] *Agreement betwixt His Majesty and the inhabitants of the County of Oxon* (1642).

[15] *Acts and Ordinances of the Interregnum, 1642-1660,* ed. C.H. Firth and R.S. Rait (London, 1911), pp.85-100.

[16] 'A Proclamation prohibiting the assessing collecting or paying any Weekly Taxes, etc.', *A Collection of all the publicke Orders and Ordinances and Declarations of both Houses of Parliament, from the Ninth of March 1642 untill December 1646* (London, 1646), p.27.

[17] *Mercurius Aulicus,* 12 August 1643.

[18] Commonwealth Exchequer Papers - Assessments, loans and contributions - Accounts and schedules - Worcester (S.P. 28/188).

[19] S.P. 28/188.

[20] *Diary of Henry Townshend of Elmley Lovett,* Vol.III, p.220.

[21] *The Committee at Stafford, 1643-1645,* ed. D.H. Pennington and I.A. Rootes (Manchester, 1957) p.73.

[22] Shaw, *History and Antiquities of Staffordshire,* Vol. I, p.48 (Tutbury).

[23] *Ibid.,* p.198 (Mavesyn Ridware).

[24] *Ibid.,* p.66 (General History).

[25] *Ibid.,* p.62.

[26] *Ibid.,* p.61.

[27] *Hastings' MSS,* Vol.II (Hist.MSS.Comm.), p.104.

[28] *Mercurius Aulicus,* 23 October 1643.

[29] Commonwealth Exchequer Papers - Assessments, loans and contributions - Accounts and schedules - Warwickshire (S.P. 28/184).

[30] *Diary of Henry Townshend of Elmley Lovett,* Vol.III, p.239.

[31] *Denbigh MSS.* (Hist.MSS.Comm. *4th Rep.*), p.266.

[32] *The Committee at Stafford,* p.260.

[33] *Ibid.,* p.76.

[34] *Ibid.,* p.50.

[35] 'Ottley Papers', *Salop.Arch.Soc.Trans.,* Vol.VIII, (1896), pp.219-221.

[36] *Acts and Ordinances of the Interregnum, 1642-1660,* Vol.I, pp.106-117.

[37] Webb, *Civil War in Herefordshire,* Vol.I, p.354.

[38] *Ibid.,* Vol.II, Appendix XXXI.

[39] *Committee for Compounding with delinquents* (S.P. 23/101, p.925).

[40] Shaw, *History and Antiquities of Staffordshire,* Vol.I, p.61, (General History).

[41] *Denbigh MSS.* (Hist.MSS.Comm. *4th Rep.*), pp. 264,265.

[42] Shaw, *Op.cit.,* p.62.

[43] *Ibid.*

[44] Letter to the Speaker of the House of Commons from Sr. Wm. Brereton touching the surrender of Dudley Castle, Letter Book of Sir William Brereton, p.172.

[45] Shaw, *Op.cit.,* p.48 (Tutbury).

[46] *Ibid.*

[47] Vicars, *Magnalia Dei Anglicana* (1646) Part IV, p.331.

[48] *Diary of Henry Townshend of Elmley Lovett,* Vol.II, p.160.

[49] Commonwealth Exchequer Papers - Army-Accounts (Military officers, etc.) - Rutland (S.P. 28/133).

[50] *Ibid.* - Assessments, loans, and contributions - Accounts and schedules - Warwickshire (S.P. 28/182).

[51] Symonds, *Diary of the Marches of the Royal Army,* p.178.

[52] *Denbigh* MSS. (Hist.MSS.Comm. *4th Rep.*), p.264.

[53] *Mercurius Aulicus,* 23 February 1644.

[54] *Denbigh MSS.,* Pt.V (Hist.MSS.Comm.) p.76.

[55] *Journals of the House of Commons,* Vol.III, p.700.

[56] *Journals of the House of Lords,* Vol.VI, p.652.

[57] *Denbigh MSS.* (Hist.MSS.Comm. *4th Rep.*), p.265.

[58] *Memoirs of Colonel Hutchinson,* p.216.

[59] *Diary of Henry Townshend of Elmley Lovett,* Vol.III, p.240.

CHAPTER TWELVE

1644 - THE WAR CONTINUES THROUGH THE WINTER

Military activity of a desultory nature, which had become so much a part of everyday life for many in the region, did not diminish with the advent of winter. Towards the end of January 1644 Massey carried out a daring raid on Chepstow, in which he took the Royalist regiment of horse garrisoned there completely by surprise, and seized a Bristol ship lying close by laden with sack, tobacco and ammunition destined for the Worcester garrison. The suddenness of this attack, which Massey effected by dropping down the Severn to the mouth of the Wye in a boat built by his own men, is recorded in Chepstow parish register:

> Captain Carvine who was killed in his Chambers in the George Inn by certain Souldiers which came from Gloucester was buried 20th January.

Two more instances of bellicose activity, diarised by Dugdale,[1] concern Northamptonshire and Staffordshire:

> February 21 [1644] The Rebells of Northamptonshire having about a weeke since put 60 muskettiers and a troope of Horse into the Earle of Northampton's house at Castle Ashby, did this day begin to fortifye that house.

> February 22 [1644] Biddulph House neare Leeke ... taken by the rebells under the command of Colonell Ashanhurst (who had besieged the same from the tyme that the siege of Nantwich was raysed [25 January 1644] wherein was taken prisoners the Lord Brereton, and 140 souldiers.

Mr. Thomas Smith, a lawyer, was present at the fall of Biddulph House, and later, in 1651, he recalled the event in a deposition,[2] now preserved in the Public Record Office:

> ... He, being in the service of the Parliament, was in Biddulph House in Staffordshire (being the house of Mr. Francis Biddulph, as this deponent verily beleiveth) within about an houre after the same was taken by Parliament's forces, and sawe severall writeings of concernement in some of the souldiers' custody, some of them torne

and many throwne about and spoiled; and this deponent diswaded them from soe doing but they would not cease, to this deponent's best remembrance, and he beleives most of them were carryed away by the souldierye.

But the first major action of 1644 took place in the north eastern corner of the region, in Nottinghamshire. Soon after the King had left Nottingham for Shrewsbury in the autumn of 1642 the Castle had been garrisoned for Parliament by Colonel Hutchinson. In the months that followed the garrison sustained numerous attacks by the strong Royalist garrison from nearby Newark. The effect of this belligerency between these two garrisons on the county is poignantly illustrated by a solitary entry in the Sessions Book of Nottinghamshire county records dated October 1642:

> Here the warres between the King and Parliament began and interrupted all legall proceedings.

The next entry is dated 4 October 1652.

In January 1644 Nottingham received yet another attack from the Newark garrison; and this time the Royalists succeeded in overrunning the outer suburbs of the city. By a miracle Hutchinson was just able to hold the castle, from where he was able to counter attack and, after a day of street fighting, clear the town of enemy soldiers who 'for two miles ... left a great track of blood, which froze as it fell upon the snow'.[3]

By now Parliament was becoming concerned at the vulnerability of Nottingham, which was far too important strategically to lose. It was, therefore, decided that Newark must be reduced. To this end a locally raised Parliamentary force, variously computed at between 5,000 and 8,000 men, and a powerful train of artillery, were assembled before Newark, under the command of Sir John Meldrum. But the besieged garrison proved as difficult to take as Gloucester had been, for after ten days of repeated bombardment and sallies it still held fast.

While Meldrum had been collecting his forces together for the siege of Newark Prince Rupert was preparing to leave Oxford for Shrewsbury. The reason for this expedition was the recently-signed treaty between Parliament and the Scots, upon the invocation of which a Scottish army, commanded by Lord Leven, had crossed the border and was threatening the King's northern army. Rupert's orders were to prevent the Parliamentary troops operating in the Midlands from isolating the north by providing for the security of Shrewsbury, Chester and North Wales.

On Tuesday 5 February, Rupert's men left Oxford for Chipping Norton where they were joined the following day by the Prince himself. Thursday 7 February, saw them at Pershore and on Friday they entered Worcester. Rupert went thence to Bewdley where he attended a meeting of local Royalist grandees, which included Colonel Sandys, Sir Gilbert Gerard, and Colonel Washington, respectively governors of Hartlebury, Worcester and Evesham, together with Sir William Russell and Lord Herbert.

The following extract from the borough accounts[4] shows the cost to the town of entertaining these dignatories:

	£	s.	d.
for a hoggeshead of Claret wine for Prince Rupert	4	10	0
for a pottle of sack and pottle of Claret for the Lord Herbert	0	3	4
for a quart of sack and quart of Claret for Coll. Sandes	0	2	8
for a pottle of sack for Sir Wm. Russell	0	2	0
for a pottle of sack for Sir Gilbt. Gerard	0	2	0
for a pottle of sack for Major Savage	0	2	0
for wine for Coll. Washington	0	2	4
for wine for Mr. Towneshend	0	7	4

After the deliberations at Bewdley, Rupert proceeded to Bridgnorth and on 18 February he arrived at Shrewsbury, taking up his quarters at the house of 'Master Jones, the lawyer' at the west end of St. Mary's church.

During the next fortnight Rupert, aided by the local Royalist commander, Lord Capel, carried out a systematic, and characteristically brutal, campaign to clear the area of Parliamentary troops, which met with only limited success. At Market Drayton the Prince routed a force under Colonel Thomas Mytton and Sir Thomas Fairfax, while 'some of Lord Capel's men went against Hopton Castle ... where there were not above thirty men in it, but they made good the Castle, till their ammunition was all spent, then yielded upon fair and honourable quarter, which the enemy so dishonourable broke, and as soon as they entered, laid hold of them, and caused a great pit to be made, into which they cast them, and buried them alive'.[5] A further expedition to dislodge the Parliamentary garrison at Wem proved abortive, however, possibly because the fate of Hopton stiffened the garrison's resistance.

Being informed of the siege at Newark Rupert left Shrewsbury for the beleaguered garrison on 14 March, travelling thence by way of Bridgnorth, Wolverhampton, Lichfield, Ashby de la Zouch and Remstone. He drew up his men at Coddington, and before Meldrum had time to assess the size and nature of the force opposed to him, the Prince, with his accustomed, and in this instance singularly fruitful, impetuosity, charged down Beacon Hill and, with a shout of 'For God and the King', carried all before him. Meldrum was compelled to sue for peace and leaving behind 4,000 muskets, as many pistols, and 30 pieces of cannon, was allowed to retreat to Hull. After three weeks the siege of Newark had been relieved.

There is little doubt that Meldrum had sufficient forces to beat off Rupert's attack and continue with the siege, but, as Lucy Hutchinson reports, 'the forces that Sir John Meldrum Commanded before this town, were gathered out of several associated counties [Lincolnshire, Leicestershire, Nottinghamshire and Derbyshire], and the commanders were emulous of one another, and so refractory to commands, and so piquing to all punctilios of superiority, that it galled the poor gentleman to the heart', for they 'disputed all his commands, and lost their time and honour in a fruitless expedition, through their own vain contentions'.[6]

The effect of the relief of Newark on the morale of local Parliamentary supporters was so great that according to Mrs. Hutchinson 'such a blow was given to the parliament interest, in these parts, that ... even the most zealous were cast down, and gave up all for lost'.[7]

Rupert afterward contemplated taking Nottingham but at the last moment decided against it, returning instead to his headquarters at Shrewsbury, where he remained for some 18 days. From Shrewsbury he travelled to Oxford, where there was great rejoicing at his triumph at Newark, and on the strength of the somewhat optimistic prediction that he would save the north,· discomfort the Scots, and carry his uncle's cause to a final and brilliant victory.

Events in Worcestershire and Staffordshire during the early summer of 1644 went some way to redress the humiliation sustained by Parliament at Newark. In Worcestershire the Royalist garrison at Bewdley received the attention of Colonel John Fox. To his antagonists Fox was known as the 'Jovial Tinker', an appellation which was both a cynical reference to his singularly dour countenance and to the trade which he is supposed to have followed in his native town, thought to have been either Tamworth or Walsall.

This swashbuckling adventurer of Puritan persuasions had gathered together a band of like-minded men from Birmingham and the surrounding districts, and formed them into a regiment in which he commissioned himself colonel. For his headquarters Fox seized Edgbaston Hall, at that time the home of the Middlemores, and also Hawkesley House on Clent Ridge. From these two bases of operation the 'Jovial Tinker' would take out raiding parties to terrorise and plunder local Royalists. He also kept Lord Denbigh informed of enemy activity in the area. On 18 March 1644, for instance, Fox reported the presence and condition of Prince Rupert's army at Lichfield on their way to relieve Newark.[8]

The 'Tinker's' most noteworthy action to date had been the capture of Stourton Castle from the Royalists, who had garrisoned it in March 1643. But he was unable to hold the Castle in the face of a massive attack by troops from Worcester garrison under Colonel Gilbert Gerard. A request to Lord Denbigh for aid was not forthcoming as the earl was at that time inundated with similar pleas from other garrisons in the region. One of these was contained in a letter from the Committee at Nottingham, and dated 26 March 1644, informing Denbigh that following the rout of Meldrum at Newark by Rupert it was likely that Nottingham would be assaulted the next day: 'wee cannot long hould out; yett if itt please God to move your Lordship and other of our friends to joyne in our assistance it will be an extreame incoragment unto us'.[9] Another letter, dated Coventry, 27 March 1644, from Humphrey Mackworth refers to the 'bleedinge condition' of Shropshire which requires the earl's

help. The writer speaks of recent increases in the Royalist
forces in that county and of the wasted condition of those
of the Parliament, and if Lord Denbigh cannot come to their
aid the writer will advise them to retreat to Nantwich or
Stafford.[10]

The upshot of the matter was that in an attempt to drive
off the besiegers without the assistance of Denbigh, Fox and
his men were themselves driven off and, in the words of a
Royalist account of the incident, were 'pitiously bang'd',
after which they were pursued across Stourbridge Heath,
'the first running rebel' being 'the jovial Tinker himselfe,
whose example was well followed by all his worthy trayne'.[11]

Fox, undaunted by the Stourton *débâcle*, resolved on a
plan to enter the Royalist stronghold of Bewdley and capture
the Governor, Sir Thomas Lyttelton. And so, that 'active
and resolute commander',[12] as Vicars described Fox, left
Edgbaston Hall one afternoon in early April 1644, accompanied by 60 picked men, for Bewdley.

It was evening before Fox and his men reached the town,
into which they gained admittance by claiming to be a detachment of Prince Rupert's horse that had lost its way. Once
inside the town Fox's men were able to silence the guards
and secure an entry into Lyttelton's residence, Ticknell
House, described by the antiquarian John Leland a century
earlier as 'a faire manner place ... standing in a goodly parke
well wooddyd, on the very knappe of an hill that the towne
standithe in'.[13] The sleeping governor and his officers were
taken completely by surprise, and seeing that resistance was
useless they surrendered themselves to Fox.

As dawn broke the intrepid 'Tinker' left Bewdley accompanied by his illustrious prisoner, Sir Thomas Lyttelton,
together with '4 brave Flanders mares, and great store of
provisions, all which with 40 most gallant horses of the
king's cormorants, and as many prisoners'.[14] Lyttelton and
his retinue were first taken to Coventry, thence to London,
where the luckless knight was imprisoned in the Tower.

An interesting picture of Bewdley at this time is drawn by
Captain Richard Symonds in his journal of the King's marches.
'The onely manufacture of this towne', wrote Symonds,
'is making of capps called Monmouth capps. Knitted by

poore people for 2d. a piece, ordinary ones sold for 2s., 3s., 4s. First they are knitt, then they mill them, then block them, then they worke them withe tasells, then they sheere them.'[15]

Less successful than 'Tinker' Fox's escapade was an attempt by Parliamentarian troops to establish a garrison midway between Northampton and Banbury at Canons Ashby by commandeering the church and the hall of Dreydon. 'They began', *Mercurius Aulicus* tells us, 'to rayse taxes by order and appointment of the Committee of Northampton. But a party of the Earle of Northampton's horse, with 80 foot from Banbury, went thither, tooke a petard, and hung it upon the doore before the young Rebels knew of their comming; which presently gave them entrance into the church, where they took them all. Such as fled into the steeple were instantly smoaked downe. Hereupon those in Sir John Dreydon's house yeelded themselves prisoners, who, with good booty, and store of provision, were brought all to Banbury Castle.'[16]

But in Staffordshire Lord Denbigh took Rushall Hall, 'a place very considerable for trade from Cheshire, Staffordshire, and other parts',[17] from the Royalists. In the preliminary bombardment the Royalists found themselves on the receiving end of the big gun, *Roaring Meg,* which had been used against the Parliamentarians at Hopton Heath and had been captured at the fall of Stafford. While Sir John Gell, after capturing a Royalist regiment which was commanded by Colonel Eyre, encamped at Boylston Church, maiched on Burton-on-Trent where he defeated Colonel Harvey Bagot, the governor of Lichfield garrison, and drove him from the town. Thus, after almost a year, Parliament had regained Burton; the obvious delight at this time of this predominantly anti-Royalist town being dampened only a little 'by the occasion of two barrells of gunpowder, casually fired in the church, which blew up the roof and burst all the windows'.[18]

Events in Gloucestershire at this time also augured well for Parliament, especially for the Gloucester garrison. Vavasour's failure to destroy Massey, and his obvious gullibility in the Backhouse letter incident, had reached the ears of the military pundits at Oxford and on 2 June an order was issued from Oxford relieving the Royalist commander of his post. Some time elapsed before a new appointment was made and this gave Massey an excellent opportunity to obtain supplies from London. The convoy crossed the Cotswolds safely, successfully evading the web of Royalist garrisons covering the area, and a detachment of Rupert's horse sent to intercept it. Thus the straitened circumstances of Gloucester were finally relieved and Massey could now make a serious attempt at reducing the effectiveness of the Royalists in his vicinity, instead of devoting his energies to mere foraging expeditions.

CHAPTER TWELVE

[1] Dugdale, *Life, Diary and Correspondence*, p.61.

[2] *Staffordshire and the Great Rebellion*, ed. D.A. Johnson and D.G. Vaisey (Staffordshire County Council, 1964), p.35.

[3] *Memoirs of Colonel Hutchinson*, p.164.

[4] John R. Burton, *A History of Bewdley; with concise accounts of some neighbouring parishes* (London, 1883), Appendix, p.XXXII.

[5] Wallington, *Historical Notes of Events*, Vol.II, p.216.

[6] *Memoirs of Colonel Hutchinson*, p.173.

[7] *Ibid.*, p.177.

[8] *Denbigh MSS*. (Hist.MSS.Comm. *4th Rep.*), pp.264,265.

[9] *Ibid.*, p.265.

[10] *Ibid.*

[11] *Mercurius Aulicus*, 28 March 1644.

[12] Vicars, *Magnalia Dei Anglicana*, Part IV, p.217.

[13] *The Itinerary of John Leland in or about the years 1535-1543*, ed. Lucy Toulmin Smith (London, 1907-10), Pt.V, p.88.

[14] Vicars, *Op.cit.*, p.177.

[15] Symonds, *Diary of the Marches of the Royal Army*, p.14.

[16] *Mercurius Aulicus*, 20 April 1644, Thomason Tracts, E.45.

[17] *Cal.S.P.Dom.* 1644, p.177.

[18] Shaw, *History and Antiquities of Staffordshire,* Vol.I, p.18 (General History).

CHAPTER THIRTEEN

SPRING OFFENSIVE,
THE KING ON THE MOVE AGAIN

With the approach of summer the Committee of Both Kingdoms, which was the instrument through which Parliament prosecuted the war, began making plans for a final victory against the King. The Scots, whom Parliament had secured as allies in September 1643, and who had kept the King's northern army occupied since January 1644, were joined in April by an English army under Lord Fairfax; while two more Parliamentary field armies under Essex and Waller were ordered to advance against the King at Oxford.

Essex left London on 14 May and Waller on 15th, and by the end of the month the two commanders had successfully penetrated the ring of protective garrisons around Oxford. On 2 June Waller forced his way across the Thames at Newbridge and on the same day Essex took Bletchingdon, while an advance party of Parliamentary horse occupied Woodstock. It was natural, therefore, that, in the words of Sir Edward Walker, Secretary for War to the King, 'the Rebels thought their game sure'.[1]

It had become obvious that 'it was now high time for the King to provide for his own security, and to escape the danger he was in of being shut up in Oxford',[2] and so at 9 o'clock on the evening of 3 June Charles and his army quitted the city and, slipping passed Essex under cover of darkness, headed for Bourton on the Water.

On receiving intelligence that the King had escaped from Oxford, Essex and Waller immediately combined forces and were in full cry after him. But Charles's plan was to avoid contact with the Parliamentary army until such time as the two commanders should separate. He would then be strong enough to attack each army in turn with a good chance of victory, after which, with Rupert aiding Newcastle in the

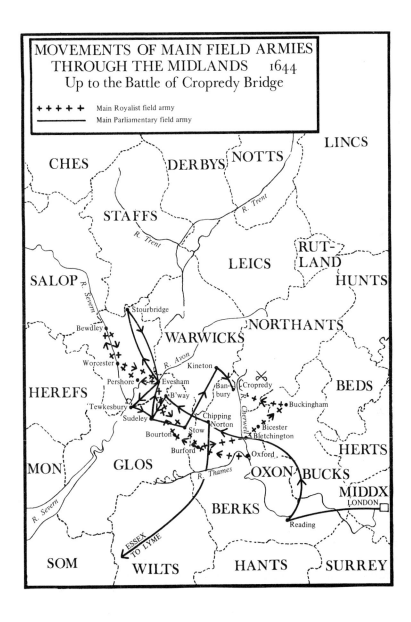

MOVEMENTS OF MAIN FIELD ARMIES
THROUGH THE MIDLANDS   1644
Up to the Battle of Cropredy Bridge

+ + + + +   Main Royalist field army
─────────   Main Parliamentary field army

north, the road to London would then be open.

With Essex and Waller dogging his every step Charles moved on to Evesham ·and thence to Pershore via Charlton and Cropthorne. At Pershore the King ordered the demolition of the bridge spanning the Avon in an effort to protect his rear. The operation was carried out with characteristic 'Cavalier' efficiency, 30 soldiers and some eight civilians being drowned owing to the bridge disappearing prematurely from under them.

On 6 June the King entered the comparative safety of Worcester where, owing to 'the loyalty of that good town and the affection of the gentry of that county ... he procured both shoes and stockings and money for his soldiers'.[3] No doubt 'the loyalty of that good town' became somewhat strained by the King's order for the reparation of the fortifications there, which required the destruction of all the houses in North Street.

The situation at Worcester, however, very soon became as bleak as it had been at Oxford. The King's plight was confessed to Rupert in a letter from George Digby who, it will be remembered, was reputedly 'slain' at Birmingham in April 1643, and was now one of Charles's principal advisers and court favourites. He wrote, 'Essex comes upon us one way, Waller likely to go about us on the Welsh side by Gloucester ... Massey and the Lord Denbigh towards Kidderminster, both with considerable forces'.

Then providence, or rather crass stupidity, took a hand. Essex and Waller, after a council of war at Stow-on-the-Wold, decided to implement a plan formulated by Parliament in London whereby only one army was to pursue Charles and the other was to relieve the Parliamentarian held port of Lyme in Dorset which was being besieged by Royalist forces. And so Essex marched his army to the West Country while Waller kept doggedly on after the King and, after compelling Sudeley Castle to surrender, which provided him with useful plunder - three cannon, ammunition, horses, and 100 quarters of grain, he stationed himself at Evesham 'where', to Clarendon's chagrin, 'the evil inhabitants received him willingly'.[4]

Here Waller hoped that he would be joined by the forces of Lord Denbigh and Massey, but both of these Midland commanders had other fish to fry. Denbigh was engaged on what was to be an abortive siege of Dudley Castle and was reluctant to break off the engagement, while Massey, who had just retaken Tewkesbury, was unwilling to risk the possibility of losing his recently won gains in Gloucestershire by leaving the county.

The hostile armies facing Charles were now reduced to one but even this, although equal in number to the King's, possessed advantages in superior arms, equipment and discipline. For sometime now the Royal army had been cut off from its main source of supply, Oxford, and had been unable to sustain itself completely on the provisions and money supplied by the local Royalists and by plunder. Hungry and unpaid many of the King's men deserted. Waller himself reported on the condition of the enemy in a number of despatches to the Committee of Both Kingdoms. 'His [the King's] army is mouldered away and to a very small proportion, and I think it lessens every day', wrote the Parliamentarian commander. This appraisal was followed almost immediately by two more. In one Waller informed the Committee that 'I cannot find that his Majesty has above seven or eight hundred foot left, and about two thousand horse',[5] and in another he opined that 'the King's army is in a most discouraged broken condition and if it be well plied will be utterly broken'.

On 12 June Charles left Worcester and marched in a northerly direction to Bewdley, which prompted Waller to think that the King was intent on gaining Shrewsbury, thence to join Rupert and the northern army, and then march back with this very considerable force to crush first his own army and then that of Essex. Waller, therefore, left Evesham on the 13th for Stourbridge, sending his cavalry to Kidderminster, with instructions to watch the Bridgnorth road and intercept Charles if he tried to march northwards.

At Stourbridge, his centre of operations, Waller convened a meeting of all the local military commanders who, rather surprisingly, assured him of their co-operation. Present at the meeting were Lord Denbigh, who had been forced to abandon the siege of Dudley Castle when Charles sent a detachment of troops to assist the beleaguered garrison, Sir William Brereton,

Colonel Henry Brooke, Colonels Rugeley and Mytton, Sir
Edward Leigh of Rushall, and Colonel Roper. All agreed
that the King would very likely attempt to join with his
nephew, Rupert, and the northern army and that the only
way of preventing this was to consolidate their forces.

But the King had no intention of marching north. He had,
in fact, decided to return to Oxford and collect reinforcements
so that he could give battle to Waller, who, with the departure
of Essex from the scene, was now unsupported. Naturally,
it was essential for the King to avoid all contact with Waller
until his army had been refreshed and reinforced. Bewdley
was therefore merely a ruse to obscure the King's real objective. He only stayed there two days and after sending some
cavalry in the direction of Bridgnorth, to maintain the
pretence that he was making for the northern army, Charles
doubled back to Worcester arriving in the city on 15 June.

The next day, after attending service at the cathedral, the
King left Worcester for Broadway via Evesham, where he
remained only long enough to fine the inhabitants £200 'for
their alacrity in the reception of Waller, and likewise compelled
them to deliver a thousand pair of shoes for the use of
soldiers'.[6]

Broadway was reached on the evening of the 16th where,
according to Richard Symonds, 'His Majesties lay that night
at Mr. Savage'. The next morning the Royal army pressed on
through Campden, Stow-on-the-Wold to Burford 'where his
Majestie lay that Munday night at the George Inn'.[7]

On Tuesday 17 June, 'after his Majestie had beene at church
and heard the sermon, and dyned, he marched to Witney'.[8]
Here the King received supplies and all the available forces
from Oxford. From Witney Charles marched to Woodstock
and was joined by more Royalist forces, and spent the night
at Bletchingdon. The next day he proceeded to Bicester, and
thence to Buckingham, where he rested his troops.

Waller had meanwhile realised what Charles was up to and
in his own words, 'As soon as I received assurance of His
Majesty, I rose, and leaving my foot to march gently after
with two regiments of horse to cover them, I advanced, with
the rest of my horse and dragoons after me, to Evesham'.[9]
From Evesham he marched to Tewkesbury where he received

370 musketeers and a company of dragoons sent by Massey.

By 24 June the Parliamentary army had reached Shipston on Stour and on the 26th Kineton. Here Waller received considerable reinforcements from Coventry and Warwick, together with 11 pieces of ordnance. Thus arrayed he marched towards Banbury in order to seek out his prey. On receiving this intelligence the King determined 'to give the Rebels Battel',[10] and so he too made for Banbury.

On 28 June the two armies came within sight of one another and 'upon a fair sunshine in the afternoon, after a very wet morning, both endeavoured to possess a piece of ground they well knew to be of advantage'. This was Crouch Hill, over 500 feet high and about a mile to the south-west of Banbury. Waller secured the hill first, at the foot of which he drew up his army. The Parliamentary commander was now sitting pretty, he had 'a hill at his backe, a great hedge with a deep ditch for his front and flanked about with divers hedges and ditches'.[11] But apart from a few skirmishes there was no action that day, the King having positioned his army on the opposite side of Banbury near the village of Grimsbury.

The two armies were now only a couple of miles distant from one another, separated by the river Cherwell and the town of Banbury. The King spent the night of the 28th at a yeoman's house, traditionally said to be the Grimsbury Manor House, and the next day he determined to draw Waller off from his advantageous position by marching southwards towards Daventry. As expected, Waller quit his position on Crouch Hill and followed, keeping parallel with the Royal army by marching along the Banbury-Southam road. During this march the Parliamentary army was never more than two miles distant from the King, and, because of the undulating countryside thereabouts, both armies were almost constantly in full view of each other.

Charles sent a body of dragoons on ahead to hold the bridge which crossed the Cherwell at Cropredy in order to prevent Waller from crossing it before the Royalist army was ready to give battle. At the same time he was forced to order the van of his army to hasten forward and cut off some Parliamentary reinforcements which were travelling down the Daventry road to join Waller. This last act resulted in a large and dangerous gap between the van and the rear of the Royal forces.

Waller was quick to grasp the opportunity that such a situation presented and he immediately sent 1,500 horse, together with 100 foot, and 11 guns to take Cropredy Bridge, which the Royalist Dragoons abandoned with little resistance, while another 1,000 horse under Lieutenant-General John Middleton, were ordered to cross the ford at Slat Mill, one mile south of Cropredy Bridge, and attack the Royalist rear - 'to bite the heele', which according to *Mercurius Aulicus* was a habit of Waller's.

But the King had quickly perceived Waller's plan and he ordered his van to rejoin him and the main body of the Royalist army on the high ground beyond Hays Bridge, about half a mile north of Cropredy. Waller was now caught between the Royalist rear, which had driven Middleton and his forces back across the ford at Slat Mill, and the main body of the Royalist Army at Hays Bridge. After a fierce but short engagement the Parliamentarians were forced to pull back onto the west bank of the Cherwell, leaving 11 pieces of artillery behind them on the east bank of the river.

For two days the armies remained inactive, except for occasional artillery bombardments, on opposite sides of the river. During this time the King attempted to treat with Waller, but the Parliamentary commander replied that he had no power to accept such overtures without the prior consent of both Houses of Parliament.

On Sunday 30 June, news came to the King that Parliamentary reinforcements had left London on the 24th and were then lying at Buckingham. In view of the fatigue of his soldiers and the scarcity of provisions, Charles decided to break off the engagement. And so, on 'Munday morning, about four of the clock', the Royal army marched away arriving at Moreton-in-the-Marsh on Tuesday evening. 'From thence', records Symonds, 'his Majestie with his whole army marched over the Cotswold hills, with colors flying, &c., to Broadway; thence to Evesholme that night, where he lay'.[1][2] All this in full view of Waller 'who', according to Walker, 'did not so much as attempt to fall on our Rear (no question being very well pleased to be rid of us)',[1][3] which was hardly surprising since the Parliamentarian army was tired and dispirited and was slowly disintegrating because of desertion. As Waller himself records, the city of London brigade had 'come to their old song of 'Home! Home!''; while the troops borrowed from Massey and the garrisons at Warwick and Coventry no longer felt disposed to serve under Waller. The action at Cropredy Bridge, it can hardly be graced with the appellation 'battle', was therefore indecisive, although Waller could, of course, claim that he had, as he thought, prevented the King from joining up with the northern army. The real importance of Cropredy Bridge lies in the fact that before this action the Parliamentarians had always declared that they were fighting the King's evil counsellors and not the person of Charles himself. But as the Royalists pointed out, when the King left Oxford, 'he left his Lords and Privy Counsellours,behind him, and Sir William still being commanded to fight, manifests to the World that it was not the Evil Counsellours but the good King they fought against; not to rescue him from them, but to remove him from this present world.'[14] This change in Parliament's attitude was officially confirmed early in the new year when Sir Thomas Fairfax was made Lord General of the Army and the clause calling for 'the preservation of the King's person', which had appeared in Essex's commission was omitted in Fairfax's.

Charles decided to remain at Evesham while he determined his next move. The bulk of the King's troops were billeted in and around Fladbury, which is about three miles north-west of Evesham. Richard Symonds was apparently so appalled by the palpable boorishness of an inhabitant of this Worcestershire village that he felt compelled to record her behaviour in his diary: 'The parsons wife of Fladbury, a young woman often carrying a milk-payle on her head in the street, - so far from pride'.[15]

Naturally, the presence of the Royal army at Evesham and Fladbury was felt far and wide. The daily rations of a soldier in the service of the King consisted of 'one pound of biscuit, and half a pound of cheese',[16] hence the following letter[17] written by Sir Lewis Kirke, Governor of Bridgnorth, to Sir Francis Ottley, Governor of Shrewsbury, concerning the King's request for 10 tons of cheese for his army:

Sir

His Majestie being advanced to Evesham both by his Letters from thence dated 6th Instantii Required me Speedilie to provide and send Tenn Tonne of Cheese from these parts to be delivered to the Mayor of Worcester, who shall give the owners satisfacc'on for the same according to the Markett Rates. I desire you therefore that you send in this night or soe soone after as possible you can to Bayliffe Synges House at Bridgenorth One Tonne of A good sorte of cheese whether ould or this Year's making, and there shall be an officer appoynted to Receive the same and attend itt to Worcester and to Demand and Receive the moneys for itt there, which shall upon his retourne bee speedilie paid to everie person who shall soe send in. Letting you further know, that as I have sent to his Majestie an Account how I have proceeded in his Commands by sending him a Catalogue of the names of the persons and the proportions from them required Soe I must if there be A faile in any one - signifie the same to his Majestie for my owne Excuse: I rest

Your Loveing ffreind to serve you

Bridgenorth   L. KIRKE
7th Julii 1644

The cheese was duly delivered to Kirke who paid £150 for it out of his own pocket. In view of the King's straitened circumstances it is unlikely that, even if Kirke had requested reimbursement, this would have been forthcoming.

While Charles was at Evesham he despatched a letter 'To the Lords & Commons of Parliament Assembled at Westminster' and dated 'Evesham, July 4', entreating Parliament to assist him in finding some expedient 'which by the blessing of God, may prevent the further effusion of blood, and restore the Nation to peace'.[18] But Parliament was not in a conciliatory mood and the King's overtures were ignored. In any case, Charles was not, as he thought, attempting to parley from a position of strength, for his northern army under Newcastle, Rupert, and Goring, had been annihilated at Marston Moor on 2 July, although news of this outstanding Parliamentary victory had not reached the ears of the King, or his adversaries, until after the letter had been sent by Charles and replied to by Parliament.

On 7 July Charles held a Council of War at which he was advised to move against Essex, who was now in Devon. And so, on 12 July, the Royal army marched out of Evesham, through Broadway, and back over the Cotswolds to the West

Country, while Waller, who had spent the time since Cropredy
in and around Northampton, returned 'with his broken
Army'[19] to London.

The absence of the King from Oxford gave local forces
from Northamptonshire and Warwickshire an opportunity of
retaking Banbury for Parlaiment. From such a point a strong
enough force could easily prevent Charles from regaining his
capital, Oxford, which was itself too well fortified to be taken.
There were also several other good reasons for securing
Banbury, among which was the belief that such a move would
'give liberty to trade to London from many parts'.[20]

There had already been a half-hearted attempt to seize
Banbury in the spring but, as Dugdale reports,[21] this proved
abortive:

> May 11 [1644] The Rebells from Northampton with above 200
> Horse, faced Banbury, within cannon shott of the towne, but after
> some sleight skirmish with them, wherein they lost 3 or 4 men, they
> retreited.

Parliamentary troops began moving into the area for a new
and more concerted attack on 19 July 'on which day', reports
Mercurius Aulicus, 'their horse came to Broughton, Wark-
worth, and other places thereabouts'. But there was no
positive activity until dawn on 25 August, when two companies of infantry succeeded in entering the town and gaining
possession of St. Mary's church. The church was within
range of the castle, which housed the Royalist garrison, and
in its tower cannon and musketeers were planted to draw the
enemy's fire while more troops occupied the town.

It would appear from a Parliamentarian account of this
action that the Royalists were taken completely by surprise,
'the enemy not taking alarm, untill some of our souldiers by
knocking at divers doores in the Towne to looke for Cavaliers
that lay in the houses neere the Castle, awakened them'.[22]

This same account also records that on 'Wednesday August
28 there came to our assistance Colonel Purefoys Regiment of
horse and Col. Boswels Regiment of horse, and Col. Boswels
Regiment of foot, and with them three great Guns, one
carrying 36 pound Bullet, the other two somewhat lesse,
3 Morter-pieces for Granadoes'.[23]

But in spite of these considerable reinforcements of men,

which brought the total strength of the besiegers up to 3,500, and artillery, the garrison held out, and the morale of the defenders remained high. To a request from Colonel John Fiennes, the Parliamentary commander, that the handful of Royalists in the castle should surrender, the 19-year-old garrison commander, William Compton, replied that they would 'keep the Castle for his Majestie, and as long as one man was left alive in it, will them not to expect to have it delivered'.

The besiegers then changed their tactics by placing their cannon at the bottom of North Bar, outside the main gate, an area that then consisted of open meadows. But they were still unable to effect a breach in the walls of the castle. This possibly explains the audacity of the garrison which was beginning to take the offensive by sending out raiding parties inflicting considerable damage on the enemy.

Mercurius Aulicus for Friday 30 August records that 'they [the Parliamentarians] play'd all yesterday with 2 mortar pieces, one of 9 inches diameter, the other of 6, and indeed they did but play, for there was no worke done, save what the Castle did on them, which was to such purpose, that 16 cart load of dead bodies were met one way, 5 cart load another way'.

According to the same source this prompted many of the 'Rebels men' to run away, thus following the example of the Warwickshire horse who had 'gone off' the previous Wednesday 'perhaps to send for Tinker Fox to their assistance, who', continues *Mercurius Aulicus* caustically, 'will, if he be wise, beware of Banbury'.

The Parliamentarian commander's next move was to import some miners from Bedworth who arrived on the evening of Saturday 27 September. These he ordered to tunnel their way to the walls of the castle as the Royalists had done at Lichfield Close and at Gloucester, but this had to be abandoned when the workings became flooded by underground streams. To add to Parliament's misfortune it was reported that a party of Rupert's forces were about Evesham and indicating that they intended to relieve Banbury. But this was forestalled by the despatch by Parliament of Lieutenant-General Oliver Cromwell, who was 'sent towards Banbury with 2,000 Horse to receive them if they should come that way'.[24]

Now desperate, the besiegers decided on an all-out offensive, as evidenced by the following, typically uncompromising, order:[25]

To the Constable of Roxston.

These are to charge and command you that upon sight hereof you will gather together all the ladders in your towne with an load of hay bound hard together into fardles [i.e. bundles] with thumb-ropes. And one load of good bushy faggots. And bring the said things into the church-yard in Banbury by one of the clock this day at the furthest, whence there shall be some men appointed to receive them. Hereof faile you not upon paine of death and forfeiting your whole estate. Given under my hand this 20 day of September, 1644.

John Fiennes, Col.

These preparations were, however, continually interrupted by the persistent and often successful sallies of the garrison against the lines of the besieging forces.

The offensive eventually took the form of an assault on the castle walls at five places simultaneously; the main assault being made upon the west wall which had been breached in the preliminary bombardment. But so effective was the Royalist fire that very few of the enemy even gained the inner moat. Eventually the attack had to be called off. The Parliamentarians suffered 300 casualties while the garrison claims to have suffered only nine and also to have captured 120 muskets and all the scaling ladders used in the attack.

By the end of September the Lords and Commons at Westminster were showing concern that the garrison was still in the hands of the enemy. They ordered that workmen from all the towns within 10 miles of Banbury should be impressed as pioneers and so release those soldiers employed on digging trenches for more active service.

On 1 October it was reported that the castle could be expected to surrender very shortly. Providence, however, ruled otherwise. In his western campaign Charles had routed Essex's army, after which the King was resolved to relieve the garrisons of Basing House, Donnington and Banbury Castles, all of which were under siege, and then return to his quarters at Oxford for the winter.

From Newbury the King sent the Earl of Northampton with three crack cavalry regiments to Banbury to raise the siege. Northampton was, incidentally, the elder brother of William Compton, the defender of Banbury garrison. Their father, the second Earl of Northampton was, it will be remembered, killed at the Battle of Hopton Heath. At Adderbury the earl was joined by reinforcements from Oxford, under Colonel Gage, and on Friday 25 October they advanced on Banbury.

When the commander of the Parliamentary troops that were besieging Banbury heard of Northampton's advance he sent most of his army and all the baggage away, so that when the Royalists entered the town they had little difficulty in routing what was left of the Parliamentary forces, many of whom were killed in flight between Hanwell and Edgehill. Thus the siege of Banbury was raised. It had lasted 14 weeks, during which time the garrison had withstood almost continuous bombardment and no less than 11 assaults.

As is to be expected the civilian population of Banbury suffered immeasurably, both during and after the siege. Thirty homes were destroyed, and there was an outbreak of that same endemic disease that had so afflicted nearby Oxford. Before the war, according to the Parish Registers, the death rate in Banbury never exceeded 98. The Registers for 1644, however, record 297 burials, of which less than 30 were those of soldiers. The epidemic, which raged from March until October 1644, seems to have reached its height at about the time of the siege. Out of a total of 85 burials during the months of July, August and September 1644, 60 were of those who were 'supposed to dye of the plague', and the remaining 25 burials included seven soldiers and one civilian killed as a direct result of the siege.[26]

The garrison at Banbury had lived well off the town and the surrounding countryside, which was one more reason why the Parliamentarians wished to establish a garrison of their own there. When the siege was raised the Royalist soldiers seem to have recommenced their foraging expeditions with renewed vigour, as a Parliamentary news-sheet testifies:[27]

Thursday, November 7th. It was this day certified that the enemie hath brought in very large victuall, and supplie into Banbury Castle, which they have robbed and pillaged the countrey people thereabouts of, and undone them, plundering many to the very walles, especially some honest people in Banbury.

This report was no mere piece of propaganda. The Royalists themselves admitted that this had taken place in a reference to the women of Kilsby who 'came ... to Banbury and told Sir William Compton that those 24 men (lately taken at Kilsby) belonged to them, that the 200 head of cattell and 60 horses were theirs also, desiring he will order that the cattell, horses, together with the men, might be restored unto them'. Sir William condescended on condition they would pay 'all the arrears of contribution, the horses taken to be forfeited, and some of the chief brethren for future bound to orderly payments, and never hereafter beare armes against his Majesty. This overture was refuted by the sullen brethren till at last the sisterhood began to lecture them (for others can preach as well as ladies) and they submitted. So as the arrears (which came to £300) were paid, the 60 horses [were] forfeited to Banbury, but the men, women, and cattell, returned to the place whence they came'.[28]

It is hardly surprising that the men of Kilsby showed reluctance to promise not to bear arms against the King and to agree to pay all outstanding Royalist levies, for this Northamptonshire village lay in a solidly Parliamentarian area and would therefore be paying regular contributions through the Northamptonshire Committee to Parliament, to whom it was described as being 'well-affected'.[29] And as Kilsby is a full 20 miles from Banbury this could be taken as yet another example of the range, and the depth of penetration into enemy territory, that the warring parties were prepared to effect in their efforts to levy impositions on the civilian population.

CHAPTER THIRTEEN

[1] Sir Edward Walker, *Historical Discourses upon Several Occasions* (London, 1705), p.15.

[2] Clarendon, Bk. VIII, 47.

[3] *Ibid.*, 54.

[4] *Ibid.*, 53.

[5] *Cal.S.P.Dom.* 1644, pp. 242, 244.

[6] Clarendon, Bk. VIII, 56.

[7] Symonds, *Diary of the Marches of the Royal Army*, pp. 14, 15.

[8] *Ibid.*, p.15.

[9] Hist.MSS. Comm.*Ninth Report*, Pt.II (1884) p.436.

[10] Walker, *Historical Discourses*, p.30.

[11] *Mercurius Aulicus*, 29 June 1644 Thomason Tracts E.2.

[12] Symonds, *Op.cit.*, pp. 24, 25.

[13] Walker, *Historical Discourses*, p.34.

[14] *Mercurius Aulicus*, 29 June 1644.

[15] Symonds, *Op.cit.*, p.27.

[16] *Diary of Henry Townshend of Elmley Lovett*, Vol.III, p.226.

[17] 'Ottley Papers', *Salop.Arch.Soc.Trans.*, Vol.VIII (1896), p.247.

[18] *The Letters, Speeches, and Proclamations of King Charles I*, ed. Sir Charles Petrie (London, 1935), p.145.

[19] Dugdale, *Life, Diary and Correspondence*, p.27.

[20] *A letter, being a full Relation of the Siege of Banbury Castle .. Published by Authority Sept. 4 1644.*

[21] Dugdale, *Op.cit.*, p.67.

[22] *A letter, being a full Relation of the Siege of Banbury Castle.*

[23] *Ibid.*

[24] *Perfect Diurnal*, No. 60 (1644).

[25] *Mercurius Aulicus*, 25 October 1644, Thomason Tracts E.17.

[26] 'Baptism and Burial Register of Banbury, Oxfordshire, Part I, 1558-1653', transcribed by Mrs. N. Fillmore, ed. J.S.W. Gibson, *Banbury*

Historical Society Publication, Vol.VII, 1965/66, pp.246-248.

[27] *Perfect Occurrences* No. 13 (1644).

[28] *Mercurius Aulicus,* 26 January 1645, Thomason Tracts E.270.

[29] *The Parliament Scout,* No.84 (1645), Thomason Tracts E.26.

CHAPTER FOURTEEN

SUMMER AND AUTUMN CAMPAIGNS IN THE MIDLANDS - 1644

The King's march through the west Midlands after his escape from Oxford, and the siege of Banbury were not, of course, the only incidents of bellicose activity in the region during the summer of 1644. There was also the reoccupation of Tewkesbury by Edward Massey and Lord Denbigh's unsuccessful siege of Dudley Castle; two events that have already been alluded to but which require further exposition.

Massey's success at Tewkesbury was the culmination of a systematic campaign to gain the initiative in Gloucestershire and Herefordshire, using the military supplies furnished by Westminster, and the lack of effective Royalist command in the area, to advantage. During the spring Massey had fortified Ledbury and in one operation had subsequently seized the Royalist garrisons of Westbury where 'the enemy held the Church and a strong house adjoyning',[1] Little Dean and Newnham, and destroyed three iron mills and furnaces in the Forest of Dean; all with the loss of one trooper. Massey also occupied Ross, albeit temporarily, took Beverstone Castle, while its Governor, Captain Oglethorpe, was away indulging in amorous diversions with his mistress, and effectively closed to the Royalists the direct route between Oxford and Bristol by occupying Malmesbury.

The effect of Massey's success upon the inhabitants of the areas now under his control was to say the least predictable. This was especially true in Gloucestershire, of which Corbet wrote:

> After these things many gentlemen of the county began to looke towards the Parliament, and tender their obedience, desiring protections from this government, to secure themselves from spoyle, and the souldiers violence. Nevertheless as the personall estates of all knowne delinquents within the reach of this command were seized, and the profits of their lands sequestered, so these men were not to be

ignorant or insensible of the value of their peace .[2]

Massey's next objective was Tewkesbury, which he had allowed Vavasour to occupy during the previous winter in the expectation that such an act would give the Royalist commander a false sense of security. The town had been rendered penetrable by a small commando unit which silenced the guards before the alarm could be given. Besides the Governor, Major Mynne, 'eighteen barrels of powder ... an hundred and twenty skeyns of match, two hundred new pikes, foure and thirty large hand-granadoes, good store of musket-shot, and two brasse drakes [three pound cannon]' were taken. 'But the place itselfe was the greatest consequence, and worthy of the service', wrote John Corbet, 'being now a strong frontier-town securing that side of the country, and commanding a good part of Worcestershire'.[3] The fact that Tewkesbury had now changed hands for the eighth time exemplifies the strategic importance of this town. Most of the Royalist soldiers who managed to escape when Massey occupied Tewkesbury made their way to Worcester or joined the King, who was then at Evesham.

At about the time that Massey was entering Tewkesbury, Lord Denbigh, assisted by 'Tinker' Fox, Colonel Mytton, the Parliamentary Governor of Wem, and Sir Thomas Middleton, began to lay siege to Dudley Castle, which had long been a thorn in the Parliamentary side. But Denbigh's activities were curtailed by the arrival of a Royalist force under Lord Wilmot who had been sent from Worcester by the King to relieve the garrison. Denbigh had attempted to abandon the siege and retire to Stafford before the Royalist forces reached Dudley, but he was caught unawares and a short but bitter action was fought between the armies of Wilmot and Denbigh on Tipton Green.

A brief on-the-spot account of this battle is contained in a letter written by a Parliamentary officer, Luke Lloyd, to his wife and dated 'Wassall' (Walsall) 13 June (the day after the battle). 'They [the Royalists] weare by the confession of those prisoners wee tooke, betwixt 4 or 5 thousand stronge, and we not 2,000. They fell upon our reare before we could begin to march, onely our forelorne advanced. They assaulted us a quarter of a mile this side the leager with such fury, that had not our men behaved themselves very galantly, we had bin utterly defeated, but they were encountered so sharply that they weare faine to retreate towards the Castell and weare so handsomely beaten they had no mynd to come on againe.'[4]   The Royalists then drew off towards Bewdley.

Although the Parliamentarians remained masters of the field a resumption of the siege of Dudley Castle was now out of the question, which left Denbigh and Mytton's forces free to join those of Waller who were shadowing the King's army on its march through the Midlands.

Denbigh and Mytton did not, however, remain long with Waller, as they feared that their absence might encourage the King's northern army to make inroads into their territory. Thus the next action of these two commanders, in which Tinker Fox again assisted, was the capture of the Royalist garrison at Oswestry, through which supplies travelled from North Wales to the Royal Army in the North of England.

Oswestry was assailed by Denbigh on 24 June, in answer to which the defenders gave the Parliamentarians 'a hot salute' with their artillery.   But the Royalists were unable to maintain themselves against Denbigh's onslaught in which the town gate was demolished with two shots, one of them 'striking a woman's bowels out, and wounding two or three'[5] and the soldiers were forced to relinquish the town and retreat into the castle.

In order to save time and the further effusion of Parliamentarian blood, Denbigh resolved to blow up the castle with the Royalist soldiers still in it, but before he could effect this explosive deed there met him 'a party of women of all sorts down on their knees confounding him with their Welsh howlings, that he was fain to get an interpreter'.[6]   Translated, the substance of these entreaties addressed to Denbigh was that the women might be allowed to speak to their husbands and sons who were attempting to defend the Castle and persuade them to surrender.   Denbigh agreed and after much wrangling over terms the Castle was surrendered; 'the prisoners that were taken being as many or more than those that took them, the towne and castle'.[7]   Those Royalist troops who were able to escape followed the example set by their comrades at Tewkesbury by either making their way to Worcester or joining the King at Evesham.

But this, and the other local successes of the Midland Parliamentarians during the spring and early summer of 1644, were offset by the effect of Denbigh's departure from the scene in July. The earl was summoned to London to answer certain allegations that had been laid before the Committee of Both Kingdoms concerning his possible disloyalty to the cause, and incidents of irregular conduct by both himself and his forces. These charges were based on rumours that Denbigh was considering changing sides, that he intended to betray Stafford to the Royalists, and that he raised money by his own warrant without the consent of Parliament. Denbigh's predicament was due in part to his actions being misunderstood, and to those other Midland commanders, particularly Brereton and Gell, who regarded the young peer's position with a jaundiced eye and sought by innuendoes to discredit him.

During Denbigh's absence the little co-operation that had existed between local commanders in the area under his control ceased almost completely. A request from Colonel Archer, the Governor of Campden, for assistance from Colonel Fox in confirming a garrison at Evesham met with poor response. Fox sent 60 men out of the 150 asked for, and these were not even armed, and so Archer, being unwilling 'to goe nakedly with a few foote into the towne',[8] was forced to abandon his design.

Added to the breakdown in co-operation between commanders was the gradual disintegration of Denbigh's own forces, owing to desertion and lack of funds. The Staffordshire foot, for instance, seized the opportunity presented by Denbigh's absence to desert wholesale and only the timely intervention of Major Frazer of Warwick prevented the total disbandment of Denbigh's cavalry. 'Wee your lordships poore officers', wrote Frazer to Denbigh, 'knoweing what prejudice it would be to the Parliament that such a regement should be disbanded, have engaged our horses and clothes for money to give your souldiers some satisfaccion for the present (every one accordinge to his abilitie), soe that thereby wee hope to keepe together'.[9]

The effect of Denbigh's absence on the security of those parts of the Midlands for which the earl was responsible was felt almost immediately he had left for London. This is made clear in a letter,[10] dated Oswestry, 18 July 1644, addressed to Denbigh, in which Colonel Mytton bemoans the earl's incapacity to render assistance:

> Prince Rupert is retreatinge this waie [following his defeat at Marston Moor]. Where I shall have releife I cannot imagine. I will referre all to God and defend the towne to the utmost of my power, and if the enemie gaine it I hope you shall heare that there shall be no neglect in your most humble servant,
>
> THO. MYTTON.

As it happened, Rupert assiduously avoided all contact with the enemy on his march from Yorkshire to rejoin his uncle in the west.

But local Royalists were more willing than Rupert to take advantage of the situation then prevailing in the Midlands. Colonel Lewis Chadwick, Governor of Stafford, informed Denbigh in a letter dated 28 September 1644 that Lichfield was fortifying itself strongly, and taxing the county insufferably for that purpose.[11] While 3,000 Warwickshire gentlemen complained of the enemy's plundering in their county not the least incident of which happened in late July when 'the Cavaliers from Lichfield, or Dudley Castle, about eighty of them, came to Birmingham; these Cavaliers came into the town on a sudden, and took nineteen of their horse, and plundered the market of all the beasts in the town, about an hundred and forty, and carried away the very calves; but the soldiers got away, and none were of them taken, neither durst the town offer to rise against the Cavaliers, because of the cruelties they should then have exposed themselves to, had they done it'.[12] This was in addition to a visit made by the Royalists to this unfortunate town in April which was reported as being 'the third time of plundering of Birmingham', and the report goes on to say that 'the forces under the command of Prince Rupert, Duke of Plunderland, have again lately entered Birmingham, and re-plundered it, taking away whatsoever was of any worth or value in the said town, to the utter undoing and impoverishing of the inhabitants'.[13] Thus the Warwickshire gentry considered that their county was likely to be further pillaged if the Earl of Denbigh was not soon allowed to return to his command.[14]

Another letter, dated 3 October, this time from Colonel Rugeley, who, like his superior, Chadwick, was loyal to Denbigh, speaks of the continued suffering in Staffordshire in consequence of the earl's prolonged absence. 'The enemie taking advantage of our distractions, drawe downe their forces, and dayly infest these parts ... I desire nothinge more than to heare that your enemies be vanquished and that your honour is makinge ready to returne to us, in whose presence consists our beinge and the welbeinge of our country'.[15]

But the well-being of the country had to 'consist' without Denbigh for, although the House of Lords voted that he was cleared of any suspicion of disaffection, and should return to his command, Denbigh's enemies in the Commons prevailed and succeeded in reversing the Lords' resolution. In consequence the earl was divested of his command. Also, those Midland commanders who had remained loyal to him during the investigation of his activities were purged. This was especially true of the Governor of Stafford, Colonel Chadwick, and Colonel Rugeley, without whose help the alleged betrayal of Stafford to the Royalists could not have been effected. The removal of Chadwick and Rugeley was carried out by Brereton and Gell who entered Stafford in the early morning of 3 December 1644 with 200 foot and 100 horse and arrested the two men. Chadwick was sent to Eccleshall Castle and Rugeley to London - both to await the result of an official enquiry into their activities. Officers of lesser rank and others in the town who were 'notoriously to be suspected and disliked' were either 'secured or discharged', and the residue of those officers that remained and were considered 'fit to be continued' were exchanged with men from other garrisons in the area. The Stafford garrison was then entrusted to Captain Stone, 'a man much approved by the Committee and townsmen'.[16]

If military inactivity, or at best the assumption of a defensive posture, were the order of the day in Denbigh's Midland Association, events in the areas conterminous to it provided a sharp contrast, while at the same time relieving the Association from some of the more extreme consequences of its internal distractions. In August the power of the Royalists in

North Wales was completely destroyed, largely by Brereton's
Cheshire forces and those of Colonel Mytton from Shropshire.
This prompted Roger Fenwicke and Anthony Hungerford to
lament the deplorable condition of Denbigh's own forces,
billeted on the Shropshire villages of Moreton Corbet and
Stoke-upon-Tern, who were without adequate clothing, and,
in the absence of positive direction from Denbigh, were on
the point of deserting at this propitious moment in Parliament's fortunes. For 'nowe is the time', urged Fenwicke and
Hungerford, 'of greatly advantageing the publique, the enemie
being in these parts altogether disheartned through their great
losses'.[17]

In the east Midlands Colonel Gell and Lord Grey, taking
the result of the Battle of Marston Moor as a sign that the
Royalist cause was now doomed, began to attack systematic-
ally all the Royalist garrisons in their neighbourhood in an
effort to precipitate the King's total defeat.

The chief focus of Gell and Grey's attentions was Henry
Hastings, who was a considerable source of embarrassment
to Parliament in and around Leicestershire, and who had
become more strongly linked to the King's cause by the
honour of the baronage of Loughborough, bestowed 23
October 1643. From Ashby-de-la-Zouch and other garrisons
thereabouts established by him, the forces of the newly-
elevated baron kept up a constant harrying campaign against
local Parliamentarians, in which he was wont to 'rob all the
carriers that pass to and fro in those parts',[18] beat up enemy
quarters and intercept despatch riders.

'So sad have been the sufferings of that county [of
Leicester], and Rutland, by reason of the disharmony there',
bemoaned *The Parliament Scout*. 'Poore Leicestershire!
not a county more right for the Parliament, and yet no county
so tattered and torn as it hath been ... that a few men in a
couple of noblemen's houses, Belvoir, and Ashby de la Zouch,
should waste a county as they have done.'[19]

The tide of fortune was, however, beginning to turn
against Loughborough even before Grey and Gell's concentrated offensive. On 1 July, the day before Marston Moor, a
party of 120 of Loughborough's men who were plundering
about Hinckley were set upon by '80 good horse' commanded

by Captain Babbington, which had been ordered by Lord Grey to intercept the Royalists. The action took place on Bosworth Field 'to the very place where king Richard was slain'. 'At the first charge', continues a Parliamentary report of the incident, 'the enemy fled; our men made a hot pursuit for three miles, killed six, wounded many, took 40 prisoners ... We lost not one man; captain Babbington shot in the hand ... Three-score horses taken. One hundred cattle, besides sheep and other goods in a very great proportion, rescued and restored to the owners.'[20]

This success was followed up on 6 July by a raid on Tutbury Castle, held for Hastings by Sir Andrew Kingston, in which Gell captured 58 horses, and an attack by the combined forces of Grey and Gell on one of Hastings's smaller outposts at Wilne Ferry on the Trent. This last attack was effected by the novel use of 60 or so cart-loads of hay and suchlike combustible material. The carts were first hauled to the edge of the Royalist trenches, thus providing the Parliamentarians with protection against hostile bullets, and then, the wind being favourable, they were ignited. The result was singularly dramatic; within minutes the Royalists, blinded and half suffocated by the acrid smoke, and scorched by masses of flying hay, surrendered to a man, providing the Parliamentarians with considerable quantities of arms, ammunition and valuable artillery.

The attack on Wilne Ferry was not an end in itself but simply a preliminary to the successful siege of the more important Royalist garrison at Wingfield Manor. Hastings made a futile attempt to relieve this garrison by drawing on troops from several other garrisons in the vicinity, including Ashby, Tutbury and Lichfield, for a concentrated attack of the besiegers to be mounted from Burton-upon-Trent. The following letter[21] to the Governor of Lichfield relates to this enterprise:

Colonell Bagott,

I stayd untill now in expectation to hear from Newarke, but as yet nobody is come to mee. I conceive your souldyers are weary; and, therefore, I would have you to quarter them this night at Burton; which they may doe safelie, with reasonable guards. If you have any hay ready about Salter's brydges, send out warrants to carry it to-morrow to Lichfield. Write back to mee what you doe so soon as you receive this. God willing, I will be with you this night.

So I rest,

Your assured loveing friend

Ashby, Tuesday   LOUGHBOROUGH
30th of July, 1644.
8 o'clock morninge.

Unfortunately Hasting's manoeuvre was defeated by one of
Gell's ablest cavalry officers, Major Saunders, who prevented
the proposed combination of Royal forces by beating Bagot
out of Burton and surprising another Royalist regiment under
Colonel Eyre which was resting in Boyleston Church. In this
twin engagement Saunders took no less than 300 prisoners
and a considerable quantity of military supplies, 'and all
without loss of one man on either side'.

Hastings next attempted to raise the siege of Wingfield by
attacking the Parliamentary supply line. Hearing that some
carriers lay at Leicester on their way to Derby and possibly
carrying ammunition for the use of the besiegers of Wingfield
House, 'the Grand Rob Carrier, Generall Hastings, joyning
with some other forces from Beaver, came to Belgrave, a small
town within a mile of Leicester'.[2 2] They lay there one night
and next morning'they met an honest poor man near Belgrave
and asked him whence he came; he answered, 'From Leicester',
and then they asked him where the ammunition was that was
brought from London, and who he was for, to which question
he answered as well as he could; but, the bloody villains! one
of them discharged a pistol against him, and the others cut and
hacked him so that the poor man died there most miserably'.
As it happened the man was carrying only 'plums and spice'
which were devoured on the spot by his murderers. The dead
man was, however, avenged by a company of Grey's men
from Leicester who fell upon the so aptly named 'Grand Rob
Carrier' and his band while they were still feasting on their
plunder and forced them to retreat.

To add to Hastings's misfortunes Wingfield finally surrendered on 12 August to Gell and Grey's forces, who had received
valuable assistance from the Earl of Manchester's army
returning to Lincolnshire after its triumph at Marston Moor.

Hastings, who for so long had enjoyed military supremacy
in Leicesterhsire and Derbyshire, was now on the defensive;
so much so that he felt obliged to withdraw all his men and

provisions out of the town of Ashby into the castle. His own exploits, and those of his men, became almost invariably unsuccessful and frequently contained an element of pathos. Towards the end of September a party of Hastings's men attempted to ambush a Parliamentary convoy *en route* from Leicester to Nottingham, but missed it. Undaunted, they decided to attack the empty wagon train as it passed through Costock on its return journey. The result was that 'the Leicester men, though fewer in number, beat the de la Zouchians, killed their captaine, and divers of their men, took many prisoners and horse',[23] not to mention a quantity of ammunition left behind by the remainder of his gallant band in their hasty flight. While 'the convoy returned safe to Leicester the same night with all their prisoners and prize, and were entertained with much joy and triumph'.[24]

Other exploits carried out by Hastings's men included a raid on the town from which Hastings had taken his title, Loughborough, where, according to *A Perfect Diurnal* 'on the last Lord's day, according to their accustomed prophanation of that day, rode into the church at sermon time, and would have taken away the preacher out of the pulpit, but the women of the towne, expressing more valour than their husbands dared to doe at that time, rescued him from them and disappointed their purpose'. The report continues: 'On the Lord's day before another party of them came to Roadeley, a towne neere Mount-Sorrell, and in the same manner entred the church and tooke away three men and carryed them to Ashby'.[25]

The harassment of clerics seems to have been a diversion which the Parliamentarian troops also practised, as an extract from the Royalist *Mercurius Rusticus* testifies: '... tenne or twelve troopers under the command of Captain Samuel came from Northampton to Wedon Pinkney in the same county, and comming thither at prayer time, they came into the church ... came up to the reading pew, where Master Losse parson of that parish was officiating divine service, and commanded him to leave off his pottage and ... that he must goe along with them to Northampton'. But Mr. Losse was able to secure himself in the belfry and the soldiers eventually left empty handed, but not before they had ridden up and down the length of the church 'spurring and twitching their horses purposely to endanger the people'.[26]

In October there were moves to put a stop to Hastings's activities completely. Gell and his Derbyshire forces set up a garrison at Barton Park, opposite Tutbury, while detachments from Gell's army and Grey's Leicestershire forces 'being ingrossed into one body ... advanced to besiege Ashby-de-la-Zouch, which is one of the strongest and most considerable holds that the enemy hath in those places; and', continues the 26 November edition of *The London Post*, 'the better to effect their enterprize, they are now fortifying a great house not far from it, a very defensible place of itself, which commands one of the chiefest passages thereunto'.

The 'great house' referred to was Lord Beaumont's home at Coleorton, about 30 miles north-east of 'that notorious denne of rob cariers',[27] Ashby-de-la-Zouch. *Perfect Occurrences of Parliament* for the week ending 29 November 1644 reported that the Parliamentarians 'though they do not besiege the Castle, yet they will keep them [the Royalists] in, and so secure the country from being plundered by them, and procure free trade and free passage in those parts, which will be a great comfort to them'. But the following report from *A Perfect Diurnal* for 31 December 1644, would indicate that the Parliamentary forces were not content with simply blockading Ashby:

> The Leicester forces at Cole Orton got in very well, and have lately performed a good piece of service against the enemy at Ashby-de-la-Zouch; where, entering the town, they beat the enemy into the tower, Hastings' stronghold, took divers papers and many arms.

Lichfield garrison received similar attention to that afforded to Ashby and Tutbury by the establishment, in the autumn of 1644, of a permanent Parliamentarian garrison at Burton upon Trent. Hitherto such a move had been frustrated by self-interested elements, a fact that had not entirely escaped the notice of the Earl of Essex. 'Some Staffordshire gentlemen', wrote the Lord General, 'were opposed to it, in regard of the poorness of the inhabitants there, and that the town consisteth only of clothyers and maultsters, and if that be made a garrison and shut up from trading, they would suddenly be impoverished'. But the arguments in favour of a garrison at Burton were overwhelming. 'Wee shall thereby receive the contribution of Repton and Gresley hundred, towards the maintenance thereof, from whence wee have not hitherto had any; and also be enabled to protect the inhabitants of that hundred from the daylie inroads and oppression of Ashby, Tutbury, and Lichfield garrisons',[28] reassured one advocate of the move. And so 200 horse and 100 foot from Staffordshire joined with some of Gell's Derbyshire forces to garrison Burton.

The only effective Royalist garrison remaining in the east Midlands was Newark and in December conjoint forces from Nottinghamshire and Derbyshire occupied Southwell 'to block up Newarke, on the North syde Trent'.[29] This meant that all the Royalist forces of Tutbury, Lichfield, Ashby and Newark were now effectively bottled up in their respective garrisons.

In contrast with the reverses suffered by his forces in parts of the Midlands the King was enjoying an unparalleled run of success in the West of England where he thwarted Essex's attempt to invade Cornwall. But with the advent of winter Charles was forced to return to Oxford, into which city he and his victorious army entered on 2 November.

Much had occurred at Oxford during the King's five months of absence. On 19 September the Governor was rendered incapacitated, the circumstances of which were recalled, not without a touch of humour, by Anthony Wood thus:[30]

> Sir Arthur Aston was governor of Oxon at what time it was garrison'd for the king, a testy, froward, imperious and tirannicall person, hated in Oxon and elswhere by God and man. Who kervetting on horsback in Bullington green before certaine ladies, his horse flung him and broke his legge: so that it being cut off and he therupon rendred useless for employment, one coll. Legge succeeded him. Soone after the country people comming to the market would be ever and anon asking the sentinell 'who was governor of Oxon?' They answered 'one Legge'. Then replied they:- 'A pox upon him! Is he governor still?

The Governor's unfortunate accident was followed by a great fire which, like the plague of the previous year, was directly attributable to the military occupation of the city. The fire which started on Sunday 6 October was, reported

Wood, 'such an one (for the shortness of the time wherein it burned) that all ages before could hardly paralel. It began about two of the clock in the afternoon in a little poore house on the south side of Thames street [now George Street] ... occasion'd by a foot-soldier's roasting a pigg which he had stolen'.[31]

Nehemiah Wallington, a singularly pious individual, attributed the fire to God: 'Observe that the head-quarters of those who had fired so many towns should now be visited with the most sad and wonderful fire that hath happened there many years in any part of the kingdom ... that this fire was upon the Sabbath day, to shew the just judgement of God'.[32]

Whether or not the fire which 'burnt up near a fourth part of the City',[33] and was computed by Wallington to have cost £300,000 (£3m. by today's reckoning), was providential is, of course, a matter of opinion. Less conjectural, however, was the plight of those made homeless and financially ruined. The following is an extract from a petition[34] to the King's Commissioners from the Corporation of Oxford giving reasons for the citizens non-payment of their contributions towards the maintenance of the garrison and other of the King's impositions.

> That by the late lamentable fire very many Inhabitants whose estates consisted of houses, householde Stuffe, Wares and goods, are utterly ruined, amonge which 8 common Brewhouses and 10 Bake-houses were burnt besides many malt houses, Mault, wheat, Wood and other provisions, who must be all relieved by thother Inhabitants, especially by those who are allyed and friends unto them.

On 19 November Charles celebrated his 44th birthday and while, at Oxford, the event was being observed with the customary festivities, Londoners were marvelling at a peculiar celestial phenomenon which to many possessed all the ingredients of an augury. 'On ... his Majesty's birthday', diarised John Greene, a London lawyer, 'ther was seene in the fields neere London, as is very confidently reported by divers, 3 suns and a rainbow with the ends reversed.'[35]

A fuller account appeared in the *Perfect Diurnal* for 19 November 1644. 'I cannot omit to take notice of a prodigious sign in the firmament this day, the truth whereof I have heard attested by several persons of credit, and the

more remarkable it being the king's birthday. The manner of
it was thus: There appeared three sunnes in a contrary way to
that usual, and a Rainbow with the bend towards the earth
contrarywise one of the sunnes within the bow, and the two
ends of the bow going upward butted at the end of one sun,
the other to the other.   What may be the effect of such
Prodigies I leave to others'.

William Lilly, who described himself as a 'Student of
Astrologie', was more positive in his translation of this
unearthly manifestation. In a pamphlet, published in 1645,
entitled *The Starry Messenger*[3][6] he wrote 'that such like
Prodegies, Comets, &c. do never shew themselves, but as
precursors of mischiefe ... It must according to the course of
Nature, be the Forerunner of some more than usuall accident
to Emperours, Kings, Queenes, Princes, and the Chiefest
Potentates of Europe ... and Charles is one of the prime
Monarches of Europe, and also in regard it was visible in
England, a Kingdome of his own, and of which he is rightfull
Inheritor ...   Here's many old Laws and Customes to be
abrigated; here's many ancient families to be deprived of their
Inheritances; here's election of new Customs, Laws, perhaps
a new Government ...; here's one that would rise to be greater
than his forefathers;   Ambition deludes him, and death
deprives him of all Monarchicall intents: Exit.'

CHAPTER FOURTEEN

[1] Corbet, *History of the Military Government of Gloucester*, p.87.

[2] *Ibid.*, p.89.

[3] *Ibid.*, p.95.

[4] Hist.MSS.Comm., *14th Report* (1894), Appendix, Pt.IV, p.63.

[5] *Two Great Victories; one obtained by the Earle of Denbigh at
Oswestry* [22 June]; *The other by Col. Mytton* [at Duddleston,
19 June] Thomason Tracts, E.53.

[6] *Ibid.*

[7] *Denbigh MSS.*, (Hist.MSS.Comm. *4th Rep.*), p.267.

[8] *Ibid.*, p.270.

[9] *Ibid.*, p.269.

[10] *Ibid.*

[11] *Ibid.*, p.276.

[12] *Perfect Passages*, No. 31 (1644).

[13] Wallington, *Historical Notes of Events, Vol.II, pp.216, 217.*

[14] Hist.MSS.Comm.*Sixth Report* (1877), Appendix, Pt.I, p.29.

[15] *Denbigh MSS.* (Hist.MSS.Comm. *4th Rep.*), p.270.

[16] *Cal.S.P.Dom.* 1644-1645, p.173.

[17] *Denbigh MSS.* (Hist.MSS.Comm. *4th Rep.*), p.271.

[18] Wallington, *Op.cit.*, Vol.II, p.138.

[19] *The Parliament Scout*, No. 61 (1644).

[20] *A true Relation of a Defeat given to Colonel Hastings by the Lord Gray's forces, July 1, 1644, at Bosworth Field, in the very Place where King Richard the Third was slain* (London July 6 1644); John Nichols, *The History and Antiquities of the County of Leicester* (London, 1795-1815), Vol.IV, Pt.II, p.558.

[21] Shaw, *History and Antiquities of Staffordshire*, Vol.I, p.71.

[22] *A Perfect Diurnal*, No. 54, (1644).

[23] *The Parliament Scout*, No. 66 (1644), Thomason Tracts E.12.

[24] *A Perfect Diurnal*, No. 60 (1644).

[25] *Ibid.*, No. 62 (1644).

[26] Ryves, *Mercurius Rusticus*, Part I, pp. 93, 95.

[27] *A Perfect Diurnal*, No. 69 (1644).

[28] Shaw, *History and Antiquities of Staffordshire*, Vol.I, p.70 (General History).

[29] *Ibid.*, Vol.I, p.72.

[30] *Life and Times of Anthony Wood,* p.110.

[31] *Ibid.,* p.111.

[32] Wallington, *Historical Notes of Events,* Vol.II, pp.238, 239.

[33] Bulstrode Whitelocke, *Memorials of the English Affairs* (London, 1682), p.102.

[34] *Oxford Council Acts,* 1626-1665, p.126.

[35] 'The Diary of John Greene (1635-1657)', ed. E.M. Symonds, *E.H.R.* Vol.XLIII (1928), p.601.

[36] *The Starry Messenger; or, An interpretation of that strange Apparition of three Suns seene in London, 19th Novemb. 1644, being the Birth Day of King Charles, by William Lilly, Student in Astrologie* (London, 1645).

CHAPTER FIFTEEN

NEGOTIATION, MORE INCIDENTS OF RAPINE, AND THE EMERGENCE OF A THIRD FORCE

Another year of war had passed; a year that had witnessed the demise of Royalist power in North Wales and the defeat of the King's northern army at Marston Moor, leaving, in the words of one Royalist, 'the whole of the North ... in the power and tyranny of the enemy, except some few garrisons, which like monitors in schools observe faults only in the absence of the master'.[1]

This situation brought considerable relief to the inhabitants of Derbyshire to whom the King's northern forces had, since the start of the war, been of considerable nuisance value. In May 1643 'the Earl of Newcastle sent a great force into Derbyshire to plunder the shire, which they performed, leaving no place unransacked, but ruining in inhuman and barbarous manner, neither sparing friend nor foe'. And even earlier, in October 1642, it was reported 'that Sir Francis Wortley, a Yorkshire Malignant, is come to Wirksworth, 8 miles from Derby, with two troops of horse, to pillage that country. They seize upon all the horses that come in their way; they pillaged the farm of Bakewell's House named Mr. Rellisonne; he withstood them as long as he could with his bow and arrow, but being too weak for them, they slew him'.[2]

The year had also seen the gradual emergence of Parliament's predominance in the east Midlands, and, to a lesser extent, in Gloucestershire, and also in the Welsh border counties, where Sir William Brereton, with Middleton and Mytton, acted upon the whole of the border country from the mouth of the Dee to the confluence of the .Wye and Severn with a vigour that tormented the Royalists. But Charles still controlled the west of England, and his own main field army, which now had the defeat of Essex to its credit, was still intact and wintering less than 60 miles from

London, at Oxford.

The thoughts of war-weary England during the winter of 1644/45 became centred upon the current peace negotiations being held on Parliamentary ground at Uxbridge. Nothing, however, was really expected to come of this meeting between the two parties to 'save a Nation, out of a bleeding, nay almost dying condition, which the long continuance of the War hath already brought it into'.[3]   And, 'as for any accommodation', opined John Greene, 'although a treaty be agreed unto and the Parliament acknowledged by the Kinge, yet it is in my judgement wonderful improbable, and scarce hoped for by any men of understanding'. Greene's pessimism, which reflected the general mood of the population, permeated his whole outlook: 'In the beginning of the last years [1644], as appears by my Almanacke', he wrote, 'I could foresee nothing but a long continuance of these unhappy wars. Now at the beginning of the next I am more strongly confirmed in my former opinion.'[4]

The three principal points at issue were the reform of the Church, the control of the nation's armed forces, and the future settlement of Ireland.   On church reform the Parliamentary party was itself disunited. Parliament had originally agreed to adopt the Presbyterian form of church government in deference to the Scots, who had, in return, offered Parliament military support.   This required the demise of the episcopacy in England, and, by way of declaration of intent, Parliament executed, on 10 January 1645, the instrument of Charles' religious policies, William Laud, Archbishop of Canterbury. John Vicars probably spoke for the majority of Englishmen in his appraisal of Laud: 'a most proud and hypercriticall crafty Tyrant and persecuter of Gods Saints [i.e. godly, pious persons] hee lived, and a most obdurate and marbleheaded Athiest hee also imprudently & impenitently dyed'.

But there existed in the Parliamentary party a powerful faction of 'Independents' which repudiated all forms of official church government, whether administered by bishop or presbyter and considered that the form of religious worship should be determined by individual congregations.

Because of this division Parliament was unable to present

a united front on religion, a fact that proved of little consequence anyhow because the King had no intention of abandoning episcopacy and, no doubt, saw the execution of his old friend and mentor, Laud, as a significant comment on a professed desire for peace.

Both Charles and Parliament considered that they alone should have command of the country's armed forces - Charles because, as monarch, it was his right, and Parliament because they were fearful lest the King should use the army to further his own political ends. Parliament and the Scots, who were also represented at Uxbridge, were mindful of Charles's attempts to impose the hierarchy, rites, and ceremonies of the Anglican Church or, in Nehemiah Wallington's terminology, 'Bishops, Episcopacy, Superstition and Idolatry', onto Presbyterian Scotland in 1638 by military force.

The Irish question was as intractable as those concerning the religious settlement and the control of military forces. In 1641 bands of Catholic native Irish had attacked the Protestant Anglo-Scottish settlements in Ulster 'committing horrible outrages, sparing neither man, woman, nor child'.[5] Now Parliament was demanding that the Protestants in Ireland be avenged and the power of the Catholic Church there be extirpated, for it was felt that 'as popery and treachery goe hand in hand, while popery is kept under; so popery and tyranny are inseparable companions, when popery gets the upper hand'.[6]

But the Irish 'Rebels', in the expectation that their identification with the Royalist cause would secure for them freedom to practise their religion without fear of persecution, had offered their support to the King when civil war broke out in England. And Charles, more through expediency than out of sympathy for their cause, had willingly accepted the Irish as allies, which was first evidenced at the King's ceremonial entry into Chester on 23 September 1642 when 'the Lord Dillon and another Irish Lord, a great rebel, came with his Majesty into the city'.[7]

While the peace talks ground to a standstill military activity at a local level, and the consequent effects on the population, still continued in the Midlands, even though an armistice had been agreed to during the negotiations. After all, the garrisons and small local armies still had to live and, as the inexhaustible appetite of war had rendered much of the population insolvent and unable to furnish their weekly pay, the local forces of both sides were resorting to indiscriminate plunder as a matter of policy in order to subsist. This was particularly so in the case of the Royalists who were left more to their own devices than the Parliamentarians and 'did openly profess they had little to live on but what they took from others'.[8]

In December 1644, for instance, the house of a recently deceased Shropshire Royalist, Mr. Barker, was burned to the ground by soldiers from Shrewsbury 'lest the Parliament forces should come and make a garrison of it'.[9] These same soldiers, also plundered food, furniture and fittings, amounting to 16 cart-loads, which Barker's daughters had taken from the house before it was ignited.

On 4 January 1645 'a great party of Cavaliers came into Chipping Norton, where they quartered, and, at their going thence, to show their impartiality (though there was but one Roundhead in the town) they plundered every house therein of whatsoever was of value, and took two hundred sheep, and above forty pounds from one man'.[10]

Seven days later, on 11 January, the Royalists plundered the Oxfordshire village of Culham 'most miserably, stripping from women of rank all their clothes, took from Lady Carey, an ancient lady sick in her bed, her rings from her fingers, her watch, and whatever they could carry away'. And on 23 January the King's Banbury forces were reported to have 'got into Northamptonshire ... plundered about Kilsby, where they were most inhuman, drove away sixty head of cattle, two hundred sheep, and plundered the townsmen to their very shirts upon the matter, for they left them nothing that was good'.[11]

According to a letter 'dated at Birmingham, February the 1st', that town once again paid a heavy price for its allegiance to the Parliamentary cause. For the letter reports that Colonel Leveson, the governor of Dudley Castle, took advantage of the temporary absence from the area of Colonel Fox by sending a party of 400 foot and horse, under Sergeant-Major Henningham, for yet another raid on Birmingham.

The Royalists first surrounded the town in order to keep the people in and then 'they fell to plunder very cruelly for the space of four hours, insomuch that the poor women and children did make such a lamentable cry that they might have been heard half a mile off crying "murther, murther", and yet could find no pity, but carried away all that they could lay hands on that was worth the carrying away'.

They emptied Thomas Gisborne's shop of cloth 'and plundered his house all over'. They carried away all Francis Millard's ironware and also plundered his house. 'Widow Greaves, a godly poor woman, they took all she had from her, and turned her out in the street in her bare smock, and bare-legged'. The Royalists also plundered Widow Weyman, another 'godly poor woman, that was gone that night to Coventry', William Allen, a shoemaker, Widow Simmons, whose children were pulled out of their beds, and their bedding and clothes taken from under them, and 'many more, too tedious to set down the particulars, these being the least of their cruelties'.[1][2]

In Worcestershire 'a party of the enemies went to the house of one Mr. Baker, an active man for the Parliament, at a place called Hinton upon the Green, which they totally plundered and afterwards burnt it down to the ground'.[1][3]

All these accounts emanate from a Parliamentarian source, namely from the writings of Nehemiah Wallington who, one suspects, may, in addition to his extreme piety, have possessed rather prurient inclinations, as well as a tendency to ignore the fact that certain elements of his own side were as wonton and diligent as their adversaries in their lust for murder and rapine. Even so, there must be some element of truth in these reports because later in the year the King's younger nephew, Prince Maurice, as Lieutenant-General of Worcestershire and the adjoining counties, was compelled to issue an order[1][4] to the effect that:

> Whereas I am informed it hath been a late practice by subordinate Governors and other inferior Commanders and officers, to assume a power for imprisoning and restraining the persons, and seizing the goods and Cattle of divers persons, and releasing them at their own wills; without giving any account of the same: which irregular proceedings have tended much to the grievance of the said Inhabitants of this County, and dis-service of his Majesty. For the avoiding of

such inconveniences and abuses hereafter. These are to signify to all whom it doth or may concern That I do hereby expressly forbid the Governors of all subordinate Garrisons or Forts and all other officers of what quality soever within this County, to presume or take a power to restrain or release the persons, or seize or dispose the goods or cattle of any the said Inhabitants upon any pretence whatsoever without special warrant for the same under my hand, or the like from Col. Samuel Sandys, Governor (under Me) of this Garrison and Commander in Chief of all the forces in this County. Hereby likewise authorizing all whom it may concern to deny obedience to such Committments, warrants, and orders as are not qualified as aforesaid. And that no person shall be committed to, or detained prisoner elsewhere than in the Marshalsea to this Garrison, except by special order as aforesaid. Given at Worcester under my Hand and Seal at Arms this 10th day of October 1645.

Maurice.

The Major of this Garrison is to give orders for publication of this my order.

Some idea of the extent of the misery and desolation that the Royalist forces had inflicted on the inhabitants of an area sympathetic to their cause, and the resultant state of mind of those thus afflicted, can be gained from the papers of the Worcestershire Royalist, Henry Townshend:

That the Country is fallen into such want and extremity through the number and oppression of the Horse lying upon free quarter that the people are necessitated (their Hay being spent) to feed their Horses with corn, whilst their Children are ready to starve for want of Bread.

Their exacting of free quarter, and extorting sums of money for the time of their absence from their quarters, mingled with threats of firing their Houses, their persons with death, and their goods with pillaging.

Their barbarous seizing men's persons, and compelling them to ransom themselves with very great sums of money to their undoing; and disabling them to assist his Majesty, and that without any order, or warrant; as (for instance) Mr. Foley, the two Mrs. Turvey and many others.

Their daily robberies of all Market people, killing and wounding men who resist, and stand on their own defence, their contempt of all discipline, disobedience to all orders, Quartering where they please and how, as long as they list, so it be in security, and without duty.

Their opprobious and base language of the Commissioners, intermingled with scorns and threats.

Their assaulting and seizing on the person of Sir Ralph Clare at his own house by one Major Fisher and his company without any Order; Against whom is reserved exemplary justice and reparation.

> That the quarters which were assigned to the 400 Horse belonging to this County being taken from them, and allotted to others, hath enforced some officers to give over their Commands; the rest to live upon free quarter, being disabled to recruit their shattered troops.
>
> That all the country lying between Severn and Teme, and on the banks of the Severn (which are his Majesty's only secure quarters) And also the parishes adjacent within 4 miles of the City, are by free quarter of the Horse eaten up, undone and destroyed, together with the country lying about Kidderminster and Bewdley, with their several Armies passing to and fro, which should, and could, have plentifully supplied the City with all manner of provisions against the time of a siege.
>
> That the Insolencies, oppressions, and Cruelties have already so disaffected and disheartened the people: that they are grown desperate, and are already upon the point of rising everywhere, and do not stick to say that they can find more justice, and more money, in the Enemy's quarters than in the King's.[15]

In the eastern counties of the Midlands the bottled-up Royalist garrisons were less successful in their attempts at replenishing their dwindling supplies from an area that had already suffered at the hands of the Parliamentarians themselves. Mr. Nowell of Rutland, for instance, having had to witness the firing of his own house and those of his neighbours because he refused 'to forfeit his liberty or goods to the justice of the Parliament',[16] and Master Andrewes, Rector of Boughton in Northamptonshire having 'had his benefice sequestered, his estate seized, himselfe three times imprisoned, at last banished from his parish, and then the leads were pulled off his church to be employed (as Sir Richard Samuel said) in a better service'.[17]

Mr. Nowell and Master Andrewes were obviously not Parliamentary sympathisers but, according to *Mercurius Aulicus,* the Parliamentarians were not 'perfidious only to his Majesties good subjects, but theire owne creatures are practised upon when the plundering spirit possesses them, as is manifest by Colonell Craford of Alesbury in his last weekes circle, who hath so pillaged the veryest brethren in and about Northamptonshire that if their prayers take effect heele not dye like an Englishman'.[18]

Another instance of malversation by the Parliamentarians in an area from which they normally drew considerable support occurred at Wellingborough where a party of Lord

Grey's men ransacked the town and 'What they could not carry away, they spoile, so that the losse sustained by the towne is valued at six thousand pounds'.[19]

Early in February the garrison at Ashby made a sortie to compel the country thereabouts to furnish it with hay. But while the Royalists were bringing the provender to the castle they were set upon by a detachment of Parliamentarian troops from Coleorton and 'after a little engagement, Hastings' men fled, and were routed and pursued, 40 of them taken prisoners, 60 horse, arms, and all their hay'.[20] And again, on 21 February, a party from Ashby tried to raid 'Mr. Quarles his house, a place within some two or three miles of Leicester', but this again ended in disaster for the would-be plunderers were routed by a force from Leicester and captured to a man. On 26 February apparently out of desperation, 'a party of the Royalists from Ashby attacked Cole Orton, intending to have surprised and plundered the town, but in the attempt lost seventy or eighty of their horse'.

Similar activity by the Royalist garrison at Belvoir was frustrated by the Committee of Both Kingdoms which ordered the County Committee of Leicester and Rutland 'to garrison Stonely [probably Stonesley six miles due south of Belvoir] for the better blocking up of Belvoir Castle, which we concieve will be much to the benefit of those parts if it can be effectually straitened'.[21] But, according to the Parliamentary news-sheet *Perfect Occurrences of Parliament,* this did not prevent the 'Cavaliers' from robbing 'Harborough in Leicestershire from one end of the town to the other, beginning at the sign of the Ram, and plundering all along to the Crown'. While in Northamptonshire a design by Parliamentarian troops from Northampton 'to prevent the plunderings and taxes laid by the enemy upon the county, sufficiently demonstrated in the late sad business upon that well-affected town of Kilsby', by occupying Fansley House was abandoned when 'scouts brought word the enemy was coming with more horse than his Majesty had within ten miles of Oxford, which so amazed the party that they returned back to Northampton'. It seems, however, that the Royalist horse were only 100 in number and were, in fact, on their way 'with Major Farmers corps to his mother's ... to be buried'.[22]

But by now the official truce had expired with the long expected breakdown of the negotiations at Uxbridge. Each side had accused the other of lack of sincerity in its desire for peace. 'There was one Love', recorded Clarendon, 'a young man that came from London with the commissioners, who preached, and' told his auditory, which consisted of all the people of the town [of Uxbridge] and of those who came to the market, the church being very full, that they were not to expect any good from that treaty; for that they were men of blood who were employed in it from Oxford, who intended only to amuse the people with the expectation of peace till they were able to do some notable mischief to them'.[23]

The first real 'mischief' was, however, carried out by the Parliamentarians themselves. On 21 February, the day before the expiration of the truce, by order of the Committee for Shropshire, 'there were drawn out of the garrisons of Wem, Morton Corbett, and Stoke, 250 foot and 250 horse'.[24] These were joined by 250 foot and 350 horse from Staffordshire, for an attack on Shrewsbury.

The first sally against the town was made in the early hours of the following morning by '40 troopers, dismounted, with their pistols and about as many fire-locks, who were led on by one Mr. Huson, a minister, Capt. Willars, and Lieut. Benbow'. These were followed by a larger party of foot who 'having gained the streets, part of them marched to the market-place', and 'after some exchange of shot gained the main court of guard there. The rest marched to castle-forward-gate [foregate] which within a quarter of an hour was gained, the gates opened, the draw-bridge let down, at which our horse, under the command of Colonel Mytton and Colonel Bowyer, with the gentlemen of Committee, entered. It was now about break of day ... Being thus entered, the castle and a strong out-work at Frankwell held out, but by twelve o'clock the castle was delivered upon these conditions: "That the English should march to Ludlow, but the Irish to be delivered up", which we shall hang with authority. The strong work at Frankwell was surrendered upon bare quarter'.[25]

This Parliamentarian version of the taking of Shrewsbury concludes with the customary note of piety: 'And thus it pleased God of his great goodness to deliver so strong a hold unto our hands, with the loss only of two common soldiers. We cannot be sufficiently thankful, for it is a place of great concernment. And now many honest people are delivered out of an Egyptian slavery'.[26] It was because Shrewsbury comprised so many 'honest' people, that is, those with Parliamentarian sympathies, that the town was not plundered. This affinity, as *The Moderate Intelligencer* points out, was largely engendered by the fact that many of the townspeople were 'worne out ... in their estates for want of trade with London, which it did much, and which is the great advantage of the Parliament townes, garrisoned, for they grow rich by trade with London, whereas the others generally are poorer'.[27]

Of the prisoners taken there were eight knights, including the Governor, Sir Michael Ernely (Ottley had relinquished his command and was no longer at Shrewsbury), 27 'gentlemen', including two colonels, and 200 other prisoners, of whom 49 were Irish. Also taken were 15 pieces of ordnance, and considerable quantities of arms and powder.

The authority by which the Irish were summarily hanged was an ordinance passed by Parliament on 24 October 1644, commanding that no quarter should henceforth be given to any Irishman or Papist born in Ireland, and that they should be excepted from every capitulation, and forthwith put to death.[28] Parliament felt that they were justified in taking this action because of the atrocities committed by the native Irish against the Protestant settlers in Ireland in 1641.

The taking of Shrewsbury by what was in fact a joint enterprise between Colonels Mytton and Reinking, although both claimed the entire credit, strengthened considerably Parliament's position in the border country; the town 'being (as of old) a great commander of Wales, and they that have it, have by it the Welsh much devoted to them, because of intercourse of trade'.[29]

The position of the Royalists in this area was jeopardized still further by the emergence during the winter of 1645 of a society of farmers and peasants who had banded together to redress 'the fruits of civil war', which were the indiscriminate 'robberies, ravishings and innumerable wicked actions, committed by the barbarous souldiers'[30] belonging to the many garrisons which abounded in these counties of the west

Midlands. These Clubmen, as they came to be known, had no political motives other than the extirpation of the effects of civil strife from their home territory. They carried banners on some of which was emblazened both their motto and their manifesto:

> If you offer to plunder or take our cattel,
> Be assured we will bid you battel.

Although the activities of this third force were directed against both of the contending parties in the Civil War, it was, nevertheless, the Royalists who bore the brunt of the Clubmen's discontent. In December 1644 the inhabitants of Newport and Wenlock in Shropshire refused to furnish their weekly pay to the then Royalist governor of Shrewsbury, and about Clun and Bishops Castle hundreds of country people rose in arms declaring 'themselves to be neither for the King or Parliament, but stand upon their own guard for the preservation of their lives and fortunes'. The demands of the Clubmen of Clun and Bishops Castle were the removal from the area of one of the King's more cruel and exacting officers, a Dutch colonel, Van Gare, and the demolition of two vexatious garrisons, Stokesay Castle and Leigh House.

On 5 March 1645 there was a similar revolt in Worcestershire, where, at a meeting on Woodbury Hill, between one and two thousand people declared for the inhabitants of north-west Worcestershire, 'that we, our wives and children have been exposed to utter ruin by the outrages and violence of the soldier ... are now enforced to associate ourselves in a mutual league for each other's defence ... against all murders, rapines, plunder, robberies, or violence which shall be offered by the soldier or any oppressor whatsoever'.[31] The declaration was presented to the local Sheriff, Mr. Bromley of Holt, in the hope that the King would hear of the grievances of the Worcestershire folk.

In the meantime all over the county the activities of the recalcitrant inhabitants of Worcestershire were taking effect. Parishes that had associated to become part of the Clubmen movement furnished themselves with powder and arms, and every parishioner worth £10 a year provided himself with a musket. Thus armed, Worcestershire men were able to defend their lives and property from the marauding Royalists from the local garrisons, towards the maintenance of which they no longer felt obliged to contribute their weekly pay.

'By degrees the cloud had rolled on towards Herefordshire, and burst on a sudden with violence and disorder. Oppression was their pleas: neutrality their cry.' In Herefordshire the discontent was attendent upon the brutalities of the Royalist soldiers, particularly the Irish, from the garrisons at Canon Frome and Hereford. The country folk refused to grant the Royalists free quarter, recruits or money, and threatened reprisals against any who would. And when in March 1645 the Governor of Hereford, Colonel Barnabas Scudamore, sent a company of men to exact contributions of money and fodder from the inhabitants of Broxash 'a fray occurred ... between them and the soldiers of Scudamore; some blood was shed and much threatening language employed'.[32]

Soon the whole county was up in arms. Between 15,000 and 16,000 Herefordshire men, supported by Clubmen from adjacent counties, presented themselves before the walls of Hereford, 'calling out for redress or vengeance', and 'with arms in their hands they delivered a set of demands in writing; among others was the withdrawal of this garrison of Canon Frome'.[33] According to John Corbet 'the summe of their demands were to this effect, that such as theirs as were held prisoners there, should be delivered forthwith; that satisfaction be given to the country for the losse they sustained by plunder, as also to the wives and children of those that were slaine: that the country might be freed from contribution and all manner of payment to the souldier; that since the present forces of Hereford were not able to defend the county, they forthwith quit the garrison, and leave it to be kept by the country, who are able to defend the same, and the whole country with less charge'.[34]

In his hastily drawn-up reply Scudamore promised to use his 'best endeavours for easing of their just grievances presented in an orderly way and protect them with all the strength under my command ... And I doe here offer all that Hundred of Broxashe or any other that have been alike faulty with them to forgett all that is past on their submission and protestation to pay Contribucions and in all other thinges faithfully to serve his Majesty'.[35]

When news of this rising reached Gloucester, Massey immediately saw the possibility of turning the event to Parliament's advantage. 'Herefordshire and part of Worcestershire have risen in arms and pretend to save themselves from contributing either to the King or Parliament', wrote Massey to Sir Robert Harley, and the rest of the Committee of Parliament for Gloucester at Westminster, and continued, 'a force of 15,000 or 16,000 countrymen have beaten the Governor of Hereford into his garrison and lie before the city to keep him in. Therefore I marched to Ledbury and sent unto them, but as yet they will not acknowledge the Parliament. I have written to the Committee of Both Kingdoms and I entreat you to "further" them to take the matter into their serious consideration. If we lay hold of the opportunity it may much forward the Parliament's designs, if not, it may much prejudice their proceedings.'[36]

But the rebels chose to conclude a peace with Scudamore wherewith, according to Corbet, 'these men were lost to us and to themselves also'.[37] For they had barely dispersed when Rupert and his brother Prince Maurice, who had lately been created Major-General of the counties of Worcester, Salop, Hereford and Monmouth, arrived to restore in the minds of the insurgents a respectful obedience to their King.

On 29 March at Ledbury, the princes came upon a large assembly of countryfolk, most of whom fled, except for 200 stout souls who fired on the Royalist army. But the rebels were soon overwhelmed. Massey had moved some troops from Gloucester to the Herefordshire border, 'where many of the countrey people resorted unto him, some with fire weapons, some with others; but the want of strength, especially of horse, rendered him of little capacity to preserve them. The people having good desires, but daunted with the greatness of the enemy, and the slenderness of our forces, were wholly lost'.[38]

In exacting retribution Prince Rupert's army, 'at that time the greatest in the kingdom', did 'take men's persons, spoyle their estates, disarme the countrey, reape the benefit of the late insurrection, and extract money by force and terrour from the poure people'.[39] In addition 'without exception all persons of what quality soever ... of all and every town, parish and village' in the counties of Worcester and Hereford, were ordered on pain of imprisonment, to take an oath acknowledging the power of the King and condemning Parliament and its 'adherents and Partakers', of whom the Earl of Essex, Manchester and Fairfax, Waller and Massey were referred to by name. Also, that they would 'hinder popular tumults, and risings, rendezvous, meetings, confederacies and associations of the people, towns, hundreds, counties, which are not warranted to assemble by his Majesty's express commission'; and 'that his Majesty's taking up arms for the causes by Himself so oft declared in print is just and necessary'.[40] Thus the west Midland manifestation of this peculiar but natural attendant of the Civil War died, and with it the sanguine hopes of those whom this popular movement was designed to foster.

CHAPTER FIFTEEN

[1]'Letter from Arthur Trevor to the Marquis of Ormonde, Sept. 13,' *A Collection of Original Letters and Papers,* *Vol.*I, p.61.

[2] Wallington, *Historical Notes of Events,* Vol.II, pp.163, 116.

[3] *The Letters and Speeches of Oliver Cromwell,* with elucidations by Thomas Carlyle, ed. S.C. Lomas (London, 1904), Vol.I, p.186.

[4] 'Diary of John Greene', *E.H.R.* Vol.XLIII (1928), p.602.

[5] Wallington, *Op.cit.,* Vol.I, p.295.

[6] *A Briefe Declaration of the Barberous and inhumaine dealings of the Northern Irish Rebels* (London, 1641).

[7] *A true Relation of his Majesties coming to Shrewsbury, 20 Sept., and His passage from thence, 23 Sept. to Chester, etc.,* Thomason Tracts. E.119.

[8] *Special Passages,* No. 7.

[9] Wallington, *Op.cit.,* Vol.II, p.242.

[10] *Ibid.,* p.246.

[11] *Ibid.,* pp.247, 248.

[12] *Ibid.*, pp.251, 252.

[13] *Ibid.*, p.253.

[14] *Diary of Henry Townshend of Elmley Lovett*, Vol.III, pp.237, 238.

[15] *Ibid.*, pp.239, 240.

[16] Ryves, *Mercurius Rusticus*, Part I, p.66.

[17] *Mercurius Aulicus*, 21 April 1644, Thomason Tracts E.47.

[18] *Ibid.*, 8 April 1645.

[19] Ryves, *Op.cit.*, Part I, p.57.

[20] Whitelocke, *Memorials of the English Affairs*, p.124.

[21] *Cal.S.P.Dom.* 1644-1645, p.310.

[22] *The Parliament Scout*, No. 84 (1645), Thomason Tracts E.26.

[23] Clarendon, Bk.VIII, 219.

[24] *A True and Full Relation of the Taking of the Towne and Castle of Shrewsbury* (London, 1645), Thomason Tracts, E.271.

[25] *Ibid.*

[26] *Ibid.*

[27] *The Moderate Intelligencer*, No. 1 (1645) Thomason Tracts E.271.

[28] *Denbigh MSS.* (Hist.MSS.Comm. 4th Rep.), p.271

[29] *The Moderate Intelligencer*, No. 1 (1645).

[30] Whitelocke, *Memorials of the English Affairs*, p.120.

[31] *Diary of Henry Townshend of Elmley Lovett*, Vol.III, p.222.

[32] *Military Memoir of Colonel John Birch*, ed. J. & T.W. Webb, Camden Society, N.S., Vol.VII (1873), p.112.

[33] *Ibid.*

[34] Corbet, *History of the Military Government of Gloucester*, p.129.

[35] Webb, *Memorials of the Civil War in Herefordshire,* Vol.II, Appendix XX.

[36] *Portland Manuscripts,* Vol.III, (Hist.MSS.Comm.,) 14th Report, Appendix, Part II (1894), p.137.

[37] Corbet, *Op.cit.*, p.132.

[38] *Ibid.*

[39] *Ibid.*, pp. 132, 133.

[40] *Diary of Henry Townshend of Elmley Lovett,* Vol.III, pp. 231, 232.

CHAPTER SIXTEEN

THE KING'S THIRD MARCH THROUGH THE
MIDLANDS - SUMMER, 1645

The God of all Glory and Power,
who hath created us, and given us
now more War than we expected.
He of his goodnesse send us Peace.
(I hope this is no ill Wish.)
                              Amen.
                    William Lilly

With the arrival of spring both Parliament and the King took
stock of their relative positions. In spite of their territorial
gains during 1644 the Parliamentarians were still unable to
effect an outright victory over the King. 'Whatever's the
matter?' complained one Parliamentarian. 'Two Summers
past over, and we are not saved; our victories so gallently
gotten, and (which was more pitty) so graciously bestowed,
seem to be put into a bag with holes; what we wonne one
time, we lost another; the treasure was exhausted, the
countries wasted, a Summers victory proved but a Winters
story; the game however set up at Winter, was to be new
played again the next Spring, and men's hearts failed them
with the observation of these things'.[1]

It was decided that the principal cause lay within the army
itself. Orders sent by the Committee of Both Kingdoms to
commanders in the field were, it was found, only obeyed if
they complied with the commanders' own preconceived
assessment of the situation. Essex's decision to abandon the
pursuit of Charles to Waller in June 1644, contrary to the
orders of the Committee of Both Kingdoms, typifies this
problem. Also, although the Parliamentary party at Westminster was by now displaying something of a united front,
the army was still divided; some commanders were 'too fond
of a peace, others for spinning out the War, and others so
engaged in particular feuds, that little vigor was to be expected

from such disagreeing instruments'.[2]

What Parliament needed to defeat Charles was a standing army, hitherto unknown in England, of well-disciplined professional soldiers who would, in the main, be volunteers, thus eradicating the situation that made leaves of absence a matter of private convenience. This army would require but one commander, who would carry out the wishes of Parliament without question.

By April 1645 Parliament had such an army which, at full strength, consisted of 21,000 men made up of 6,000 horse, 1,000 dragoons and 14,000 foot. The nucleus of this New Model army was provided by the remnants of the three previously existing field armies of Essex, Manchester and Waller. Pay for the army was ordered to be £44,955 per month 'to be raised by proportionable assessments throughout the Kingdom';[3] and the Captain General was Sir Thomas Fairfax.

Anyone who was a member of the House of Commons or the House of Lords was precluded from serving in the new army be a Self Denying Ordinance. Thus it was felt that commanders would have less power to 'bandy against one another', and could 'more easily be called from their Commands, and punished; and so divisions be prevented'. The Ordinance was also calculated to 'stifle the objection of the Members seeking their own profit' and allow them to 'better attend the affairs of Parliament'. In this way 'the Army moving on new wheels, will more speedily put a period to the War, which is the general desire'.[4] Significantly the commissions for the New Model Army were issued in the name of the Parliament only and not in the name of the King and Parliament as had hitherto been the case with commissions issued by Parliament.

Apart from Essex, Manchester and Waller many Midland peers and members of Parliament were forced to resign their commissions, including Lord Grey of Groby, Member of Parliament for the city of Leicester, Sir Arthur Hesilrige, the Member for the county of Leicester, John Fiennes, the Member for Oxfordshire, and Colonel Edward Leigh of Rushall, one of the two Members for Stafford. Only Oliver Cromwell, Sir William Brereton and the Commander of the

Parliament's forces in North Wales, Sir Thomas Middleton, retained both their commissions and seats in the House of Commons, partly through political ingenuity and partly through the universal recognition of their extraordinary ability as military commanders.

Meanwhile in the Royalist camp the King was becoming fired with an almost megalomaniac optimism, and with good reason. For, although considerable territory had been lost to the enemy during 1644, the main field army of the Royalists was still intact, and barely two days' march from London.

Charles's Scottish ally, James Graham, Earl of Montrose, had, during the late winter, proved himself capable of menacing the Parliamentarian Scots in their own country, thereby dissipating their effectiveness in assisting the Parliamentary party in England. While the King's straitened circumstances had been not a little assuaged by the 'acquisition' of nearly a quarter of a million pounds worth of bullion from some Spanish ships that sought shelter from the winter's storms in Bristol. But Charles's confidence was most stimulated by the recollection of his victory against Essex in Cornwall in the late summer of 1644.

To the King's feeling of assurance was added that of hatred for his enemies. Gone was the conciliatory attitude that prompted him, in July 1644, to take the initiative in sueing for peace. The execution of Archbishop Laud and the breakdown of the Uxbridge negotiations had shown Charles that those who adhered to the Parliamentary party 'were arrant rebels, and that their end must be damnation, ruin, and infamy'. In the past he was often accused of weakness and vacillation, but now he was determined to show that he was a man of strength.

Charles chose to demonstrate his resolution on Wednesday 7 May 1645 when, at 10.32 in the morning, he left Oxford for his third and final march through the Midlands. Once again a direct march on the capital was not the primary objective. This time the immediate purpose of the march was the relief of Chester, through which the Royalists maintained contact with Ireland, and which was being besieged by Sir William Brereton, and the ultimate object was the reconquest of the north.

The prospect of Charles on the move again was a grim one for Midland folk, especially for those living directly on the Royal route. The following order[5] sent from Worcester to the High Constables of the Worcestershire hundreds augured ill for many.

> Whereas the time is now approaching for his Majesty's Army to draw into the field, and his Majesty having given commands that there be great store of biscuit bread speedily provided out this County for provision for the said Army, These are to charge and command you together with the Petty Constables within your division to bring or cause to be brought into the Magazine within the City of Worcester within one week next after the date hereof - Bushels of good, sweet, sound and marketable wheat out of the towns within your division (except Hartlebury and Wolverley which are appointed to furnish Hartlebury Garrison). And these are further to command you to bring in to the City of Worcester within the time aforesaid out of your division - shovels, spades, pick axes and such like Instruments for his Majesty's marching Army. And you are to let your Divisions know that I must expect from them a very strict account of the said service.
>
> That if their backwardness therein shall happen to draw any hard pressure upon them they may be left without excuse, and thank themselves for the same. Given at Worcester under my hand this third day of April 1645.
>
> Maurice

The supplies, which amounted to 3,000 bushels of wheat, and 500 pick axes, shovels, and spades, were to be transported to the King's army as it moved through the county by 'sufficient and serviceable teams of horses, with 5 able Horses at the least, a strong and able cart, and two carters with each team',[6] requisitioned from those hundreds that had furnished the provisions.

Local Parliamentarian leaders attempted to forestall Maurice's instructions by issuing an order[7] of their own addressed 'to the Constables Thirdboroughs and all other officers and inhabitants of the County of Worcester'.

> Whereas several warrants have come unto you for the bringing in some quantities of wheat and other provisions to the City of Worcester now a Garrison of the enemy. And for providing of shovels, spades, pick axes, and other Instruments as likewise a certain number of Teams, with Horses, Carts, and Carters for the service of the Enemy. These are straitly to charge and command you in the name and by authority of the High Court of Parliament that

upon pain of imprisonment, and sequestration of lands, and goods, you forbear to execute or to do anything in order to the execution of, or that you give any obedience to the said warrants, as being immediately destructive to the true Religion, the laws and liberties of this Kingdom. Given under our Hands at the Borough of Warwick the 7th of April 1645.

Tho. Rous,	Will. Lygon,
Jo. Egiocke,	N. Lechmere,
Ed. Rous,	Jo. Fownes,
Will. Moore,	Hen. Hunt,
Jo. Gyles,	Will. Collins.

In addition to Prince Maurice's forced services, and the attendant threat from the Warwickshire Parliamentarians if they were compliant with the Royalists' demands, the inhabitants of Worcestershire were still required to make their normal contributions towards the upkeep of the local garrisons. In fact, Maurice chose this moment to issue an order against several places that were in arrears to the effect that 'collectors shall forfeat £5 apiece for every month they refuse duties herein, besides double payment of the Contribution by those who shall neglect the payment'.[8]

As the King rode out of Oxford the Court astrologer, George Wharton, announced that 'the severall positions of the heavens duly considered and compared amongst themselves ... do generally render His Majesty and his whole army unexpectedly victorious and successful in all his designs'.[9] To which Wharton's rival, William Lilly, in spite of a pronouncement that he would not 'play the Critick with this University Freshman', as he called Wharton, 'or cavill at his ignorance', replied that the prediction was 'set forth purposely by G. Wharton to advance their [the Royalists] declining condition, to impede Parliaments'; for 'God is on our side; the constellations of heaven after a while will totally appear for the Parliament, and cast terror, horrour, amazement, and frights on all those damne-blades now in armes against us'.[10]

The King's first halt, on what was later to be called his 'Leicester march', was at Woodstock where Prince Rupert detached himself from the main army and proceeded to Chipping Norton. On 8 May Charles was at Stow-on-the-Wold where he held a Council of War at which it was decided that General Goring should take a part of the Royal army,

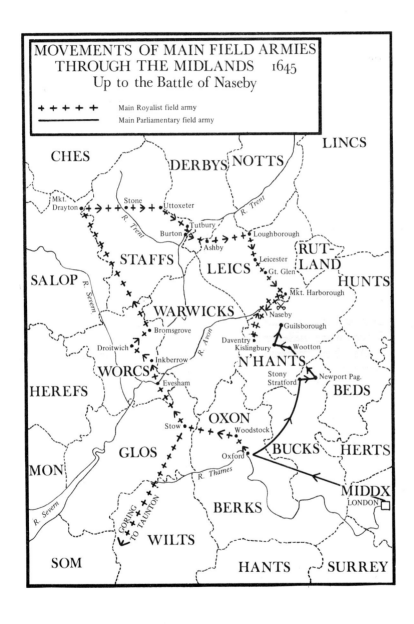

MOVEMENTS OF MAIN FIELD ARMIES
THROUGH THE MIDLANDS   1645
Up to the Battle of Naseby

+ + + + +   Main Royalist field army

——————   Main Parliamentary field army

comprising 3,000 horse and 300 foot, into the West Country. This, as stated by Clarendon, was because 'Fayrefax was then about Newbury, not in readiness to march, yet reported to be much more unready than he was, and that his design was to carry his whole army to the relief of Taunton, which was brought near to extremity; which, if he could bring to pass, would give him great reputation, and would make the Parliament near sharers with the King in the interest of the West'.[1 1]

This action echoed exactly that of Essex and Waller the year before when Essex separated his forces from those of Waller in order to pursue an independent campaign in the West. Ironically that decision too was made at Stow, and just as Essex's departure later caused regret and recrimination, so the decision to detach Goring was to give the Royalists cause 'to lament that counsel which so fately dismissed him and his forces at a time in which, (if he were born to serve his country,) his presence might have been of great use and benefit to the King'.[1 2]

On Friday 9 May the Royal army, now minus Goring's regiments, arrived at Evesham, and on the next day it was in and around Inkberrow. At the same time Rupert and his forces were billeted on Alcester.

As they travelled northwards both Rupert and the King drew men out of the surrounding Royalist garrisons in order to supplement their army which, at a little under 11,000 men, was the smallest that Charles had yet commanded. The emptied garrisons were then fired so as not to convenience the enemy. According to Wallington the King's forces, before they quit Oxford, 'burnt down divers houses between Oxford and Bristol, fearing we would make garrisons of them ... and caused other men to pull down their houses, which otherwise, they would have fired'.[1 3]

Now it was the turn of Campden House, the garrison of which was drawn out by the King on his way from Stow to Evesham, upon which the governor, Sir Henry Bard, 'took his leave of it in wantonly burning the noble structure, where we had too long inhabited, and which not many years before had cost above thirty thousand the building'.[1 4] The people living in the immediate vicinity of Campden House had little cause to regret its evacuation and subsequent destruction, for even the Royalists themselves were forced to admit that as a garrison it 'had brought no other benefit to the public than the enriching the licentious governor thereof, who exercised an illimited tyranny over the whole country'.[15]

Charles arrived at Droitwich, where he was joined by Rupert, on 11 May, and here he stayed until the 14th, while the headquarters of the Royal army was stationed on Bromsgrove. Diversionary activity was provided for some of Rupert's troops by the investment of Hawkesley House, which contained a small Parliamentarian garrison of about 120 men, commanded by Captain Gouge. On Wednesday 14 May the King left Droitwich with his guards to inspect the leaguer before Hawkesley House which 'just as his Majestie appeared in view was delivered unto the mercy of the King and his officers', for 'the soldjers would not fight when they perceived it was the King's army. After Lord Astley [whose pressed foot soldiers brought out of Herefordshire carried out the siege] had the pillage of the howse and the soldjers prisoners, the house was sett on fyre'.[16]

Meanwhile Parliament, cognisant of the King's latest peregrinations, had quickened its newly overhauled war machine. Intelligence as to the King's movements poured into Derby House, in The Strand, London, from whence the Committee of Both Kingdoms conducted military operations. On 10 May a letter was despatched to Major General Browne informing him that 'the King now being marched from Oxford, we [the Committee] think it convenient that a garrison be put into Bletchingdon House'. This was part of a plan to effect 'the straitening of Oxford',[17] and so prevent the King's return to his capital. The house had actually been taken by the Parliamentarians on 24 April 1645, when the commander of the Royalist garrison there, Colonel Windibanke, fearful for the lives of several ladies in the house, including his own wife, 'valiantly gave up the house and all his armes, besides 50 horse that came in thither for shelter; and this without a shott'. On his return to Oxford Windibanke was rewarded for his display of gallantry towards the ladies at Bletchingdon in the garden of the Castle where, after being 'condemned by a councell of war to dye', he was shot.

Another instruction from Derby House, also dated 10 May,

was addressed to Lieutenant-General Cromwell, who had been observing the King's activities since leaving Oxford. In this instruction the Committee informed Cromwell that 'we have received yours of the 9th, giving notice of the King's march. We do not think it convenient that you should follow in the King's rear, but rather to march towards Warwick, if the King should continue to march northward. Engage not unless you see apparent advantage, for thereby you will cover and preserve the Association, and be in order to the future joining of the forces now under your command with the Scottish army and the rest of the Northern forces'.[18]

The Association referred to was that of the monolithically Parliamentarian Eastern Counties of England. Cromwell commanded the Association's largest regiment which, like Sir Arthur Hesilrige's Leicestershire 'regiment of lobsters', possessed a predilection for heavy armour, for which they received the appellation 'Ironsides', a name also given to Cromwell personally. Cromwell's regiment of 'godly men' represented a physical application of the Machiavellian assertion that the sinews of war are good soldiers and not gold, and Cromwell's own concept that a few honest men are better than numbers. Universally regarded as without peer in either the Royalist or Parliamentarian armies, the Ironsides were used by Parliament as a pattern for its New Model Army.

The Ironsides had, in fact, already engaged the rear portion of the Royalist army as it passed through Burford on 8 May, taking one of the King's colours, while 'General Goring tooke forty of Cromwell's horse prisoners, and two colonels'.[19]

After the destruction of Hawkesley House the King spent the night 'at Cofton-hall, two myle off'.[20] Here he was joined by three prominent Midland Royalists with their forces; Colonel Scudamore, Governor of Hereford, Colonel Leveson, Governor of Dudley Castle, and Colonel Michael Woodhouse, Governor of Ludlow. The following morning the Royal army assembled in the grounds of Cofton Hall; and the house, being of no further use to the Royalists, was destroyed, providing yet another fiery beacon to mark the King's advance.

On Thursday 15 May, the King rested at Himley and on Friday he lay at Bushbury 'a private sweete village where Squire Gravenor (as they call him) lives',[21] while Rupert made his headquarters at Wolverhampton. The next day saw Charles at Chetwynd Hall and Rupert at Newport in Shropshire; 'and so, by easy and slow marches, they prosecuted their journey towards Chester'.[2 2]

But while he was still in Staffordshire the King learned that Brereton had abandoned the siege of Chester, leaving the Royal army free to prosecute its 'northern design' without delay. Following on the news of Chester, however, came the intelligence that Parliament had sent a strong army into the west to crush Goring and that Fairfax 'was himself and his army sat down before Oxford';[2 3] Parliament, 'having found by experience for three years last past, that the advantage of that place, situate in the heart of the Kingdom, hath enabled the enemy to have ill influences upon the City and Counties adjoining, and to infest all other parts'. The fall of Oxford was therefore considered essential in the struggle 'to put an end to the continuance of this unnatural war'.[2 4]

The King now resolved to relieve the pressure on Oxford, and possibly strike a fatal blow at Fairfax's New Model Army, before proceeding with his plan to reconquer the north. He recalled Goring from the West Country and summoned General Charles Gerard, commander of the Royalist army in South Wales, and ordered them to rendezvous with him at Leicester. And so, after spending a night at Market Drayton, Charles turned eastwards passing through Stone, Uttoxeter and so into Derbyshire.

At Marston there was, according to Symonds's Dairy, an attempt at instilling some notion of correct military conduct into the King's forces: 'a foot soldjer was tyed (with his sholders and breast naked) to a tree, and every carter of the trayne and carriages was to have a lash; for ravishing two women'.[2 5] But the effectiveness of this and similar punishments in the Royal army were negated by the inconsistency with which they were carried out.

On Whitsunday, 25 May 1645, the King lay at Tutbury Castle, and his army at Burton-on-Trent; and, travelling by way of Ashby, where it was reported that the Royal army did 'very much spoil the county and [impoverish it by] imprisoning and ransoming the men',[2 6] and Loughborough, he arrived before the Parliamentarian garrison town of

Leicester on 29 May. It was on this day that news reached
the King of Massey's successful attempt to 'add glory unto
conquest, and crown his actions with never-dying honour', as
one of the Colonel's more enthusiastic admirers put it, by
taking 'the strong-garrisoned Evesham in a storm of fire and
leaden hail'.[27] The loss of Evesham, which occurred on
20 May, was a serious blow to the Royalists, for it severed the
direct line of communication between Oxford, Worcester, and
South Wales. It may also have strengthened Charles's resolve
to attack Leicester and so deface it and to leave behind a
fearful monument to the divine vengeance of rebellion against
a lawful king.

The following day 'His Highness Prince Rupert sent a
trumpet (after he had shott two great pieces of the towne) to
summon it for his Majestie'.[28] But the commander of the
Leicester garrison, Colonel Sir Robert Pye, refused to
surrender. 'Thereupon', records Clarendon, 'the battery began
to play, and in the space of four hours made such a breach
that it was thought counsellable the same night to make a
general assault with the whole army in several places, but
principally at the breach; which was defended with great
courage and resolution, insomuch that the King's forces were
twice repulsed with great loss and slaughter, and were even
ready to draw off in despair when another party, on the other
side of the town, under the command of Colonel Page,
seconded by a body of horse that came but that day from
Newark, and, putting themselves on foot, advanced with
their swords and pistols with the other, entered the town, and
made way for their fellows to follow them: so that break of
day, the assault having continued all the night, all the King's
army entered the line'.[29]

On gaining the town the Royalists still met with considerable resistance, but eventually the garrison was forced to
capitulate 'upon Composition', the Parliamentarian John
Rushworth tells us, 'that neither clothes nor money should
be taken away from any of the soldiers of that fort ... nor any
violence offered to them'. But, continues Rushworth, 'the
King's soldiers, contrary to the articles, fell upon the soldiers,
stripped, cut, and wounded many of them'.[30]

Another Parliamentarian source spoke of the 'many ...

in the Midlands 191

bloody outrages committed, the like scarce to be paralleled', for, 'after they [the Royalists] had entered the town, they killed many that begged for quarter, and put divers women inhumanly to the sword ... they turned divers women and children out of their houses into the open streets, almost naked and succourless, and some of them they committed to prison, where they be now in great misery'. And they also 'hanged Master Raynor, an honest, religious gentleman, and one Mr. Sawer in cold blood'.[31]

This lack of adherence to the articles of surrender was confirmed by the Royalists themselves. The King's Secretary for War, Sir Edward Walker, admitted that 'the town [was] miserably sackt without regard to church or hospital',[32] and this was echoed by Clarendon: '... the conquerors pursued their advantage with the usual license of rapine and plunder, and miserably sacked the whole town, without any distinction of persons or places, churches and hospitals as well as other houses [being] made a prey to the enraged and greedy soldier'.[33] These atrocities, according to Clarendon were, nevertheless, 'to the exceeding regret of the King; who well knew that, how dissaffected soever that town was generally, there were yet many who had faithful hearts to him'.[34]

Rushworth contradicts this by saying that when one of the King's officers was seen 'rebuking some of those that did so abuse the ... Parliament soldiers, this deponent did ... hear the King reply, "I do not care if they cut them three times more, for they are mine enemies", or words to that effect; and that the King was then on horseback, in bright armour, in the said town of Leicester'.[35]

Whichever version is the correct one it is unlikely that Charles would have had much sway over the behaviour of his troops anyhow, because atrocities in the heat of action are almost bound to be committed in engagements of this nature where the Royalists 'lost three for one in the assault'.[36]

This, initially, was the attitude that *The Moderate Intelligencer* took towards the behaviour of the Royalist troops at Leicester. 'There was much hurt done in the towne its confessed', says the issue of 5 June 1645, 'but not anything to speak of more than what was done in heate ... Some women were seen dead, which was casual rather than on purpose.'

The following week's edition, however, rails at the King in Leicester and counsels him to 'call to mind, if he have time, the cruelties done to his poore subjects the weeks past, there [at Leicester], and in the counties about. Consider how ill gotten goods prosper. Let somebody tell him that his commanders, when they entred Leicester, and in particular the late governour of Campden House, gave command to ravish all, and that he brag'd he had done it the same day severall times'.[3 7]

As to the actual number of those slain at Leicester, *The Moderate Intelligencer* which, like its predecessor *The Parliament Scout,* can be relied upon for fairly accurate and balanced reporting, claimed that the defenders lost 300 men and the Royalists 400.[3 8] But *Mercurius Aulicus* refuted this figure for the Parliamentarian losses and insisted that only 120 'rebels' were slain, 'which may fully stoppe their shameful mouths that offer to talke of cruelty in his Majesties souldiers'.[3 9]

As *The Moderate Intelligencer* reported, not only Leicester itself but the entire county appears to have suffered at the hands of the Royalists, to the extent, thought Wallington, that 'the losses will not be repaired there seven years'.[4 0] For instance, 'at Wigston two miles from Leicester, they [the Royalists] ... most barbarously murdered Mistress Burrows and two of her children, her husband, a godly and religious divine, being then prisoner in Leicester, if not slain'.[4 1]

Charles and his army finally quit Leicester, leaving behind a small garrison and a new governor, on 2 June. But, as the astrologer Lilly had predicted, the constellations of heaven now appeared for the Parliament. Within a matter of days Leicester would be avenged and the Royalist cause would meet its doom. The King was not, of course, cognisant of this when he and his army, laden with plunder, turned towards Oxford.

CHAPTER SIXTEEN

[1] Joshua Sprigge, *Anglia Rediviva* (London, 1647), p.6.

[2] Rushworth, *Historical collections abridged and improved,* Vol.V, p.511.

[3] *Ibid.*

[4] *Ibid.*, p.516.

[5] *Diary of Henry Townshend of Elmley Lovett*, Vol.III, p.225.

[6] *Ibid.*, p.227.

[7] *Ibid.*, p.229.

[8] *Ibid.*, p.230.

[9] George Wharton, *An Astrological Judgement upon his Majesties Present March: Begun from Oxford, May 7 1645* (Oxford, 1645).

[10] *An Examination of an Astrologicall Judgement upon His Majesties present March, begun from Oxford 7 May 1645 being a Postscript to the Starry Messenger* (London, 1645).

[11] Clarendon, Bk. IX, 30.

[12] *Ibid.*, 31.

[13] Wallington, *Historical Notes of Events*, Vol.II, p.259.

[14] Clarendon, Bk. IX, 32.

[15] *Ibid.*

[16] Symonds, *Diary of the Marches of the Royal Army*, p.167.

[17] *Cal.S.P.Dom.* 1644-1645, pp.477, 476.

[18] *Ibid.*, p.476.

[19] Symonds, *Diary of the Marches of the Royal Army*, p.165.

[20] *Ibid.*, p.167.

[21] *Ibid.*, p.169.

[22] Clarendon, Bk. IX, 32.

[23] *Ibid.*

[24] 'Letter from the Speakers of Parliament to the Norwich Committee, 19 May 1645'. (Fairfax Correspondence), *Memorials of The Civil War*, ed. Robert Bell (London, 1849), Vol.I, pp. 225, 226.

[25] Symonds, *Diary of the Marches of the Royal Army*, p.176.

[26] *Cal.S.P.Dom.* 1644-1645, p.544.

[27] *Virtue and Valour Vindicated* (London, 1647).

[28] Symonds, *Diary of the Marches of the Royal Army*, p.179.

[29] Clarendon, Bk. IX, 33.

[30] Rushworth, *Historical collections of private passages of state* (London 1680-1701), Pt. IV, Vol.II, p.1411.

[31] *A Perfect Diurnal,* No. 97 (1645).

[32] Walker, *Historical Discourses,* p.128.

[33] Clarendon, Bk. IX, 33.

[34] *Ibid.*

[35] Rushworth, *Historical collections,* Pt. IV, Vol.II, p.1411.

[36] Walker, *Historical Discourses,* p.128.

[37] *The Moderate Intelligencer,* 14 June 1645, Thomason Tracts E.288,

[38] *Ibid.,* 5 June 1645, Thomason Tracts E.288.

[39] *Mercurius Aulicus,* 8 June 1645.

[40] Wallington, *Historical Notes of Events,* Vol.II, p.263.

[41] *A Perfect Diurnal* No. 97 (1645).

CHAPTER SEVENTEEN

THE BATTLE OF NASEBY
AND THE KING'S RETURN TO OXFORD

And now the marshalled armies who ride for
     Charles the King
Shall tighten rein and think of death as of a
     present thing
When down the lanes of battle the armoured
     Ironsides ring.

                                        Drinkwater

Parliament had been powerless to prevent the sacking of Leicester, although an order was sent from the Committee of Both Kingdoms to Sir John Gell instructing him to join his Derbyshire forces with those of Nottinghamshire 'to obstruct the King's forces in the siege of Leicester'.[1] But by the time Gell had assembled his army the King had taken the town and was again on the move.

Thus the King's progress through the Midlands remained unchecked, and the Parliamentarian garrisons that lay in the path of the enemy, such as those at Coleorton and Bagworth House in Leicestershire, Barton House in Derbyshire, and diminutive Rutland's only garrison, Burley House, were evacuated and destroyed by the late occupants themselves.

But the lack of effective opposition by these local garrisons represented tactical expediency rather than a policy of non-resistance, for Parliament was resolved to force Charles into a full-scale battle against the New Model Army before he could regain Oxford. In this confrontation it was hoped that Parliament might not only inflict retribution on the Royalists for their rape of Leicester, but also that a speedy end could be made of the war.

To this end Fairfax was ordered by the Committee of Both Kingdoms to abandon the siege of Oxford and advance with his army towards that of the King. Gell was told to

receive further reinforcements from Staffordshire and Yorkshire 'and march southward, so far as you can with safety,
upon the rear of the enemy'. Sir William Brereton was
instructed to remain in Cheshire 'for the better defence of and
preservation of those parts', but to send a proportion of his
forces to Gell. Cromwell and the forces of the Eastern
Association received orders to rendezvous with Fairfax at
Bedford. The Earl of Leven, Commander of the Scots army,
was requested 'to march southward toward Sir Thomas
Fairfax'; while the Parliamentarian Scoutmaster General,
Sir Samuel Luke, was urged to 'communicate daily or oftener
with the Committee and Sir Thomas Fairfax, both regarding
the motions and strength of the enemy'.[2]

The King, meanwhile, had resumed his march, which took
him through Great Glen to Market Harborough. Here a review
of the Royal army revealed how much it had been weakened
by the recent action at Leicester 'by the loss of those who
were killed and wounded in the storm, by the absence of those
who were left behind in the garrison, and by the running
away of very many with their plunder',[3] the town of Leicester
having been 'full of wealth which the countries had brought
in for safety'.[4]

Walker computed that the number of the King's remaining
foot was less than 3,500, 'which', observed Clarendon, 'was
not a body sufficient to fight a battle for a crown',[5] particularly as 'the Northern horse were all discontented, and could
hardly be kept from disbanding or returning home in disorder.
But with much ado', continues Walker, 'they being appeased
we continued our march, and the next day at Harborow had
news that Fairfax was drawn off from Oxford ... and ... that
he was marched towards Buckingham. This was not welcome
news, yet such as obliged us rather to make towards him and
hazard a battel, than to march Northwards and be met in the
face with the Scots, and have him in our rear'.[6]

From Market Harborough the Royal army marched to
Daventry, 'and there stayed five days, both to mark the
motion of Fairfax and to receive some provision from
Oxford'.[7] Charles lodged in the town at *The Wheatsheaf,*
while the infantry were stationed in the field and the cavalry
at Staverton and the adjacent villages.

The following Thursday the King was hunting deer in Fawsley Park, about three miles south of Daventry, when he learned of the approach of the Parliamentary army, and 'upon the 13th of June the King received intelligence that Fayrefax was advanced to Northampton with a strong army, much superior to the numbers he had formerly been advised of'.[8] Whereupon Charles pulled his army back some 18 miles to Market Harborough intending to return to Leicester whence he could draw on the garrison at Newark, and where he could await the expected reinforcements from the west of England in comparative safety.

That night Charles is reported to have been visited by an eve-of-battle apparition in the true Shakespearian manner. The spectre, that of Lord Strafford, whose demise the King had sanctioned out of political expediency four years earlier, told Charles that he was come to return good for evil by warning him that in the Parliamentarian army was one whom the King would never conquer by arms and that if he did fight he would be undone.

But the decision whether or not to fight was taken out of the King's hands when, in the early hours of Saturday 14 June, it was reported that Fairfax had moved to within a few miles of the Royalist camp. The Parliamentarian commander had quitted Northampton on 12 June, when he learned of the King's withdrawal to Market Harborough. By 13 June he had gained Kislingbury where, to the shouts of 'Ironsides is here to head us', Lieutenant-General Oliver Cromwell, accompanied by his regiment of mounted Ironsides, cheered the whole army by joining Fairfax as Commander of the Parliamentary horse. On the night of 13 June Fairfax entered Guilsborough while his vanguard had advanced a further four miles to the village of Naseby, where they surprised and captured 20 of Rupert's horsemen playing quoits, and a party of 'Cavaliers' supping at a long table in the inn. The table is now preserved in the north aisle of Naseby parish church.

As a battle with Fairfax was now inevitable, the Royalist Council of War decided that 'they would not stay to expect his coming, but would go back to meet him'.[9] And so, Walker informs us, 'in the morning early, being Saturday the 14th of June, all the army was drawn up, upon a rising ground of very great advantage, about a mile from Harborough, which was left on our back, and there put in order and disposed to give or receive the charge'.[10]

The Royal army arrayed against Fairfax comprised only 3,600 horse and 4,000 foot while Fairfax himself commanded an army of just under 14,000 men, which was 3,000 or 4,000 below the established strength. Other deviations from the tenets on which the New Model Army was founded included the fact that more than half of Fairfax's infantry were impressed men, and intoxication among the Parliamentarian soldiery appears to have been rife. 'I think these new modelles kneads all their doe with ale, for I never saw soe many drunke in my life in soe short a tyme', observed Sir Samuel Luke.

In spite of this, only by the arrival of Goring's forces from the west, or the application of the most consummate generalship, could the King hold his own against such overwhelmingly superior numbers. But Goring had sent a letter to the King announcing the impossibility of his leaving the west, and urging Charles to postpone a confrontation with the enemy until he was able to join him. Unfortunately for Charles this vital dispatch was intercepted by Fairfax, who now became even more convinced that victory was within his grasp. As for generalship, the decision taken at Stow-on-the-Wold to detach Goring's forces from the main Royalist army is evidence enough of the competence of the King and his military commanders.

The Royalist army awaiting the Parliamentary onslaught on Borough Hill, soon grew restive as the morning wore on and there was no imminence of action. Rupert was therefore sent with a body of horse towards Naseby to ascertain the whereabouts of the enemy. From a vantage point near the village of Clipston, which is situated about three miles north-east of Naseby, the Prince witnessed the Parliamentarians in what he fancied was a full retreat. In fact, they were merely retiring to a more advantageous position. But Rupert in his usual heedless impetuosity saw this as the moment to strike and advised that the Royal army should advance to a flat ridge, called Dust Hill, about a mile south of Sibbertoft.

Fairfax replied by moving his troops onto Mill Hill in a line parallel with the King's army, so that the two armies faced each other across Broad Moor at a distance of about three-quarters of a mile. The King's foot was commanded by Sergeant-Major-General Lord Astley, and the cavalry by Brigadier-General Sir Marmaduke Langdale. Major-General Philip Skippon commanded the Parliamentarian infantry, and the horse was commanded by Lieutenant-General Oliver Cromwell and Commissary-General Henry Ireton.

Cromwell later said of Naseby: 'When I saw the enemy draw up and march in gallant order towards us, and we a company of poor ignorant men, to seek how to order our battle ... I could not (riding alone about my business) but smile out to God in praises, in assurance of victory'. An eye witness afterwards recalled that just before the battle a fit of laughter seized Oliver.

As they were the weaker army it behoved the Royalists to let the Parliamentarians attack first, but 'the heat of Prince Rupert, and his opinion they durst not stand him, engaged us before we had either turned our cannon or chosen fit ground to fight on',[11] complained Walker. This initial engagement was effected at about 10 a.m., during which Rupert's horse swept Ireton and his cavalry from the field. By placing the inexperienced Ireton against Rupert, Cromwell, as cavalry commander, had shown his true military genius, for, as expected, immediately Rupert's horse had despatched Ireton they proceeded to the Parliamentary baggage train, *en route* to which they met with a destructive volley from 1,000 dragoons that had been placed behind Sulby Hedges.

Cromwell had meanwhile charged Langdale's horse, throwing them into disorder. He then led a detachment off to deal with the Royalist foot. At this point in the battle Lord Carnworth, fearing for his master's safety, seized the bridle of the King's horse and led horse and rider off the field. Demoralised by the apparent desertion of their King the entire reserve of Royalist cavalry quitted the field leaving the infantry exposed to attack in front, flank and rear. Realising the hopelessness of their position, they threw down their arms and obtained quarter. The fleeing Royalist horse was pursued and slaughtered almost to the gates of Leicester.

Rupert followed the precedent which he had set at Edgehill of returning to the field when the battle was over. Again, as

at Edgehill, there was little left for him to do. He could only
survey the scene set out before him in Broad Moor valley
depicting the total destruction of the main Royalist field
army, and perhaps ponder on what was, in effect, the end of
his uncle's reign.

Robert Baillie, the vociferous Principal of the College of
Glasgow, summed up the course of the battle thus:

> Rupert, on the King's right wing carried doune the Parliament's
> left wing, and made the Independent Collonells Pickering and
> Montague flee lyke men; but Cromwell, on our right wing, carried
> doune Prince Maurice; and while Rupert, in his furie, pursues too
> farr, Cromwell comes on the back of the King's foot, and Fairfax on
> their face, and quicklie makes them lay doune their armes. Rupert,
> with difficultie, did charge through our armie. The King, in persone,
> did rally againe the body of his horse; but they were again put to
> flight. The victory was entire. [12]

The Parliamentarian losses in this action, which Symonds
quaintly described as 'this battaile of Naseby, in the Navel of
the Kingdome',[13] are not known. John Vicars's fanciful
report that 'the slain in our part, in the most memorable
fight, was not in all full 200, and not one above Captain',[14]
must be regarded as nothing more than crude propaganda.
More reliable figures exist for the Royalist casualties, however,
900 of the King's men were killed of which there were 'above
one hundred and fifty officers, and gentlemen of prime
quality'[15] and 5,000, including 500 officers, taken prisoner.

Treatment of a special nature was meeted out to what
Vicars described as the 'whores and camp-sluts that attended
that wicked army'.[16] About a hundred of them of Irish birth
and possessing 'cruel countenances' were slaughtered in cold
blood, while their English counter-parts received permanent
facial scars to render them perpetually hideous. Walker, however, claimed that not all those slaughtered and mutilated
were prostitutes but that a number were 'souldiers wives, and
some of them of quality'.[17]

Also taken were the complete train of Royalist artillery,
40 barrels of powder, arms for 8,000 men and the King's
personal effects containing a cabinet of secret papers of which,
complained Clarendon, 'they [the Parliamentarians] shortly
after made that barbarous use as was agreeable to their natures,
and published them in print'.[18]

The surrounding countryside payed the usual price for entertaining the two armies, both before and after the battle. A letter from Derby House dated 11 June informed the Committee of Northampton that 'Sir Thomas Fairfax being now advanced towards the enemy, with whom it is probable they may be speedily engaged, you are requested to use all diligence in furnishing provisions for the army. This we expect from you as a necessary service, both in relation to your own security and the kingdoms safety'.[19] And a letter from Sir Samuel Luke to his father, dated 12 June, spoke of captured Royalist soldiers being in possession of considerable quantities of plunder and money; one sergeant having £20.[20]

After the battle the scattered and confused Royalist forces, reduced as they were to a starving and desperate condition, would not in their attempts to gain sustenance, baulk at taking the lives of those who frustrated their attempts to sate their hunger. A contrary incident, however, occurred in the Leicestershire village of Ravenstone where an exhausted straggler from the defeated Royalist army filched a loaf from a farmhouse, whereupon a stout maid-servant slew the miscreant upon the dunghill in the yard with the 'muddle' she was using to stir her washing.

At Naseby the New Model Army, universally apparelled in scarlet, and in part armed with a new flint-lock musket, received its first test in the crucible of battle, and had not been found wanting. Its success proved conclusively Parliament's military superiority, a fact already evidenced by the existence of three other powerful Parliamentary field armies besides that of Fairfax. There were the Scots, whose army was just entering the Midlands as the struggle at Naseby was being played out, and arrived too late to take a hand; there was Parliament's northern army commanded by Colonel-General Sydenham Poyntz, and the army of the newly created Western Association, commanded by Massey, who had been replaced as Governor of Gloucester in May 1645, and promoted Major-General.

The King possessed three small field armies, one in Cheshire, commanded by Lord Byron, progenitor of the celebrated 19th-century poet, another in the West of England, commanded by Goring, and Gerard's 3,000 strong force in South Wales.

But Sir William Brereton and Sir Thomas Middleton, respective commanders of Parliament's Cheshire and North Wales forces, had Byron effectively contained in Cheshire, while Massey had hemmed Goring in Taunton. This left Gerard's army as the only immediately effective military force still available to the King.

And so on fleeing the field Charles resolved to lead his broken army to Hereford 'with', remarked Clarendon, 'some disjointed imagination that he might, with those forces under Gerard, (who was General in South Wales,) who was indeed upon his march with a body of two thousand horse and foot, be able to have raised another army'.[21]

'Towards night this dismall Satterday', recorded Symonds, 'his Majestie, after the wounded were taken care for in Leicester, and that the two princes were come safe to him, and had taken order with that garrison, had left two regiments of horse there ... he marched that night to Ashby.'[22]

The following morning the King left Ashby for Lichfield, continuing thence to Wolverhampton, Kidderminster, Bewdley, where he slept at the *Angel Inn* in Load Street, and Bromyard, arriving at Hereford on Thursday 19 June, completing a march of some 120 miles in only five days. Charles remained at Hereford until 1 July, and then continued into South Wales, from where he made an attempt to join up with his Scottish ally Montrose.

Meanwhile Charles's enemies had not been idle. Fairfax invested Leicester which fell to him on 18 June, after which he joined Massey in his efforts to crush Goring's army in the west, while the pursuit of Charles was left to Lord Leven, who commanded the Scots army which had reached Mansfield on 18 June.

Leven rested at Nottingham for several days, during which time his army was considerably increased in both numbers and quality by the arrival of Sir John Gell's Derbyshire forces, bringing the total strength up to 7,000 men, plus 4,000 followers, mainly wives and children. This motley horde moved ponderously out of Nottinghamshire, across the southern tip of Derbyshire, through Staffordshire and into Warwickshire, arriving at Alcester on 8 July. Leven travelled thence to Pershore and on to the River Severn at Upton, but the Scots commander considered the bridge too weak to support his army and so he returned to Alcester. From Alcester Leven moved on to Droitwich, and, passing within a few miles of the Royalist garrison at Worcester, which prudently made no effort to interfere with his progress, he crossed the Severn at Bewdley. The Scots then marched to Tenbury and, 'as they passed by they took Canon Frome by assault, slew Barnard the governor, and put most of the garrison to the sword'.[23] They then moved on to Hereford.

The Royalists capitalised on the effect that the moving mass that was Leven's army had on those Midland shires through which it passed. The Scots 'art of perfect plundering', reported *Mercurius Aulicus,* 'makes their brethren never invite them to stay two nights together, particularly at Nottingham [where] the very Presbyterians were ready to petition against their insolent pillageing ... Nay, Burmingham in Warwickshire would not confide in them, but after one night acquaintance extolled Tinker Fox for a very small plunderer ... No wonder, therefore, that the Committees of Warwicke and other counties met at Alcester to consult about the Scots'.[24]

What this meant in purely financial terms can be judged from the fact that to just one small hamlet alone, Shilton, which is about five miles north-east of Coventry, the Warwickshire Committee paid out a total of £31 17s. as compensation for 'free quartering and plunders taken and done by the armies of the Scots ... in September 1645'. This figure included £8 13s. 4d. paid to John Glass for free quartering, and the loss of a horse and seven wethers; £6 paid to John Lee for free quartering, two colts, four sheep and other provisions and implements; £1 5s. paid to Abell Lee for five sheep, and also for the loss of some ready money; 17s. paid to Margaret Overton for one sheep and ready money; £1 paid to Elizabeth Smith for the loss of a bible and some woollens and linen; £1 10s. paid to John Large for wearing apparell, linen, 'and other things', and 13s. paid to William Smith for the loss of ready money 'and other goods'.[25]

On its arrival at Hereford Leven's army commenced a six-weeks' siege of the city which resisted all attempts to take it. The memoirs of Colonel John Birch, who later became Parliamentary Governor of Hereford, tell us that a Committee had been appointed to supply Leven's forces with provisions, but in this engagement it failed. This forced the Scots 'to seek their subsistence where they could find it', continue the memoirs; 'they employed their horse in collecting provisions, and sometimes money, through all the parishes: their varacity was almost proverbial: the common people on many occasions turned upon them - even the females, individually, helped to join in the resistance'.[26] It must be said, however, that there are no recorded instances of rape or attacks on human life perpetrated by the Scots soldiers in this particular action.

While the Scots were busily investing Hereford the King had marched as far as Doncaster. Here Charles abandoned his journey to Scotland and decided instead on a circuitous march of the Midlands. On 1 September Leven received intelligence that the King was advancing to the relief of Hereford from the direction of Worcester, 'like the sunne to the meridian', rhapsodised Barnabas Scudamore, the governor of Hereford. And so 'this Scottish mist', continued Scudamore, 'beganne to disperse, and the next morning vanished out of sight'.[27] The Scots, in fact, removed themselves to Gloucester, where the sight of these ferocious and ill-clad 'foreigners' caused almost as much trepidation among the civilian population as it had at Hereford.

At the arrival of the King it was reported that 'Hereford and the whole county were transported with exaltation and triumph',[28] a condition that was, no doubt, short-lived for Wallington tells us that the Royal army immediately 'fell to their wonted course of plundering the country, and some of the houses where the Scots quartered they pulled down, others they burnt down, but plundered them all. Honest men, that had never so little showed themselves for the Parliament, were fain to fly, and their wives and children turned out of all'.[29]

The King spent the following three months in South Wales and the north east Midlands, during which time he decimated Gerard's army by despatching it to Chester in a vain attempt to relieve Byron. He also attempted to raise recruits and rekindle the flame of hope in those who saw only too clearly that their monarch's cause was now hopelessly lost. On 10 July Fairfax and Massey had put a period to Goring's

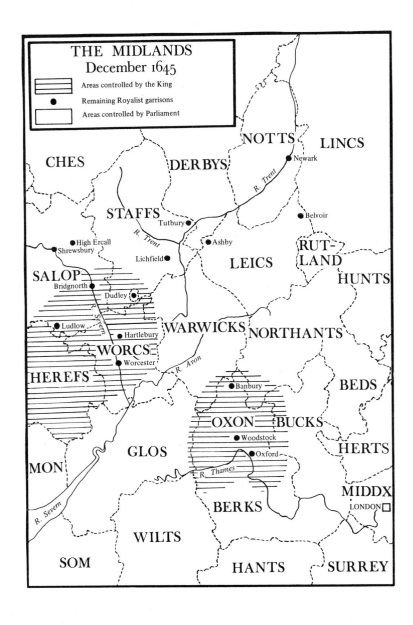

THE MIDLANDS
December 1645

Areas controlled by the King
Remaining Royalist garrisons
Areas controlled by Parliament

CHES
DERBYS
NOTTS
LINCS
Newark
R. Trent
STAFFS
Tutbury
Belvoir
R. Trent
High Ercall
Shrewsbury
Ashby
Lichfield
LEICS
RUT-
LAND
HUNTS
SALOP
Bridgnorth
Dudley
WARWICKS
NORTHANTS
Ludlow
Hartlebury
WORCS
Worcester
R. Avon
HEREFS
Banbury
BEDS
OXON
BUCKS
HERTS
GLOS
Woodstock
Oxford
MON
R. Thames
MIDDX
LONDON
R. Severn
BERKS
WILTS
SOM
HANTS
SURREY

military potential by inflicting a demoralising defeat on the King's Western army at Langport, which Fairfax followed up on 10 September by taking Bristol from Rupert, who had been despatched thence by his uncle from Hereford to take command of its defence. For failing to hold this valuable port the Prince was relieved of his command and his regiment cashiered.

On 5 November the King returned to his winter quarters at Oxford, having finished, as Clarendon relates, 'the most tedious, and greivous march, that ever king was exercised in, having been almost in perpetual motion from the losse of the battle of Naseby to this hour, with such a variety of dismal accidents as must have broken the spirits of any man who had not been the most magnanimous person in the world'.[30] In fact, the net success of Charles's peregrinations around Wales and the Midlands during 1645 was the relief of Hereford. Without doubt this, the last campaign of the ill-starred monarch, was the most disastrous.

CHAPTER SEVENTEEN

[1] *Cal. S.P.Dom.* 1644-1645, p.548.

[2] *Ibid.*, pp.571-573.

[3] Clarendon, Bk.IX, 35.

[4] *A Perfect Relation of the taking of Leciester* (London, 1645), Thomason Tracts E.288.

[5] Clarendon, Bk. IX, 35.

[6] Walker, *Historical Discourses*, p.129.

[7] *Ibid.*

[8] Clarendon, Bk. IX, 37.

[9] *Ibid.*

[10] Walker, *Historical Discourses*, pp.129, 130.

[11] *Ibid*, p.130.

[12] *The Letters and Journals of Robert Baillie,* ed. David Laing, (Edinburgh 1841-1842), Vol.II, pp.286, 287.

[13] Symonds, *Diary of the Marches of the Royal Army, p.193.*

[14] Vicars, *Magnalia Dei Anglicana,* Part IV, p.164.

[15] Clarendon, Bk.IX, 42.

[16] Vicars, *Op.cit.,* Part IV, p.164.

[17] Walker, *Historical Discourses,* p.115.

[18] Clarendon, Bk.IX, 41.

[19] *Cal.S.P.Dom.* 1644-1645, p.587.

[20] *The Letter Books (1644-45) of Sir Samuel Luke,* ed. H.G. Tibbutt (London, 1963), p.316.

[21] Clarendon, Bk.IX, 43.

[22] Symonds, *Op.cit.,* p.194.

[23] *Military Memoir of Colonel John Birch,* p.113.

[24] *Mercurius Aulicus,* 18 July 1645.

[25] Commonwealth Exchequer Papers - Assessments, loans, and contributions - Accounts and schedules - Warwickshire (S.P. 28/182).

[26] *Military Memoir of Colonel John Birch,* pp.113, 114.

[27] 'Letter from Barnabas Scudamore to Lord Digby': Webb, *Memorials of the Civil War in Herefordshire,* Vol.II, Appendix XXVI.

[28] *Military Memoir of Colonel John Birch,* p.113.

[29] Wallington, *Historical Notes of Events,* Vol.II, p.270.

[30] Clarendon Bk.IX, 132.

CHAPTER EIGHTEEN

NEMESIS

During his winter sojourn at Oxford the King fancied that victory might still be achieved, if not by feat of arms at least by creating a split between the two main religious factions in the Parliamentary party, the Presbyterians and the Independents. But events were moving too swiftly in Parliament's favour. The published contents of the King's cabinet had revealed that Charles had intended introducing foreign mercenary armies into the struggle, and that he was prepared to abolish the laws against Papists.

This caused considerable disquiet among many of the King's followers who, being cognisant of the obviously declining fortunes of their master, began to consider that perhaps their loyalties were now misplaced, and that a public disalignment from the King's cause at this time would protect them from post-war recriminations and retribution. The stream of Royalists compounding for their estates became a veritable flood, and soldiers deserted the remaining Royalist forces by the score, and some actually joined the Parliamentary armies.

The King's few remaining strongholds also began, one by one, to capitulate. Since Naseby several Midland garrisons had fallen to Parliament besides that of Canon Frome. In Shropshire, Stokesay Castle, described by Vicars as a place 'of great strength and importance in those parts',[1] capitulated on 28 June, followed by Dawley during August, 'so that now', reported *The Perfect Occurrences of Parliament* for 22-29 August 1645, 'the King hath no more garrisons than only Ludlow, Bridgenorth, and High Arcall' in the county of Salop.

By the autumn and winter the Royalist garrisons were falling to Parliament like ninepins, the event of each capitulation being recorded by Vicars in unrestrained verbosity.

In November General Poyntz assailed the Nottinghamshire garrison of Shelford House, the defenders of which, according to Vicars, 'chose rather to die in their obstinance than to aske for quarter, upon which their desperate pertinacy (there being about 180 of them in the house) most of them suffered by the edge of the sword'.[2]

Vicars also records that on 18 December Hereford was 'surprised and taken by a brave stratagem'.[3] But according to another report, 'here the killing of a sentry or two at the gate, a few shots upon scattered soldiers, or from inhabitants at windows, by which not many lives were lost, made up the sum of execution'.[4] The story is continued by a contemporary pamphlet: 'the garrison thus by policy and force surprised without remedy was plundered, neither could the commanders rhetoricke or threat prevail with the souldiers to keepe their hands from pillage'.[5]

The royalist garrisons continued to capitulate throughout the winter and into the New Year. In February 1646 Vicars recorded that Belvoir Castle in Leicestershire, 'being one of the strongest and fairest buildings in the Kingdome ... is reduced to the obedience of the Parliament, Sir Jarvis Lucas, the Governor thereof, withall the Commanders, Officers and Souldiers therein, having permission to march away to Lichfield, upon more honorable termes, indeed, than they deserved'.[6]

Another Leicestershire garrison, Ashby Castle, was invested during the following month. The garrison commander, Henry Hastings, offered to surrender on condition that he, and his brother, Colonel Perkins, should have their estates unsequestered, protection for their persons, and be granted passes to go beyond the sea. 'Too good Conditions indeed', complained Vicars, 'for such a desperate and wicked Rob-Carryer as Hastings was, but that the Kingdome might be glad to be rid of such wretches'. The surrender was made on 2 March 1646, after which the garrison was demolished, which Vicars saw as 'a great mercy and mightie preservation of the peace and tranquility of all adjacent parts about it, for which let God have all the due praise and glory'.[7] Vicars's vilification of this particular garrison and its commander was justified for, as we have already seen, the very name Hastings was synonymous with terror and rapine.

On 21 March the Shropshire Parliamentarians followed up their successful attack on High Ercall, made earlier in the month, by taking the town of Bridgnorth. The castle, however, held out a little longer, during which time the beleaguered Royalists set fire to the town in an attempt to drive out the Parliamentarians. But this only succeeded in inflicting £60,000 worth of damage on the inhabitants of Bridgnorth, many of whom were forced to seek shelter in the fields round the town, in woods, and under rocks.

The garrison, which included the late governor of Shrewsbury, Sir Francis Ottley and his wife, eventually surrendered early in April 'upon faire conditions and articles of accord, the Common Souldiers therein to march away with their hands in their Pockets, and the Officers also with their swords'.[8]

Fairfax had meanwhile taken Woodstock House, the last of the ring of garrisons that had protected the King's capital, and was laying siege to Oxford itself. This was the final blow for, in February, Byron had surrendered to Brereton, in Cheshire, and Lord Hopton, who had replaced Goring as Commander of the King's Western army, surrendered a month later.

On 21 March Lord Astley, marching from Worcester to join the King at Oxford with 3,000 men, 'being set upon near Stow on the Wolds in Gloucestershire, by Raynsborough, Fleetwood and Sir William Brereton, was so much overpowered by their conjunct strength; that he with all his men, after a sharp dispute and some loss were made Prisoners; this', continues Dugdale, 'being the last encounter that the Royallists were able to make with those insolent Rebels',[9] to which chain of disasters was added the King's failure to solicit military support from France. And so 'his Majesty observing at Oxford the ill Posture of his Affairs, resolved to betake himself to the Scotch Army before Newarke'.[10]

Charles quitted Oxford in the early hours of 27 April, disguised as Harry, the servant of a Master Ashburnham. The King's party of three passed through the Parliamentarian lines with the aid of a counterfeit warrant, and on 5 May Charles arrived among the Scots at Newark, from whom he expected to wring better conditions of surrender than from the English Parliamentarians.

As soon as Newark had fallen to them on 8 May the Scots immediately struck camp and transported themselves and the King to Newcastle-upon-Tyne while negotiations as to who should make the final settlement with Charles were made.

During the King's journey to Newcastle and his sojourn there, the last vestiges of Royalist military power in the Midlands were fading out. 'The torrent of Rebellion thus violently bearing all down before it, what garrisons remained were necessitated soon also to submit', observed Dugdale.[11]

At the end of April the plague-ridden garrison of Tutbury, which had existed for so long at the expense of the inhabitants of south-west Derbyshire, and the Needwood Forest area of Staffordshire, finally surrendered. The garrison had been besieged with varying degrees of intensity for several months by forces from Derbyshire, but they were unable to maintain the siege, and the Derby Committee was compelled to call upon the assistance of Sir William Brereton and the Committee of Stafford to 'joyn with us for the reducing of that garrison upon some reasonable Conditions for the good of both Counties'.[12]

The deterioration of the military effectiveness of the Derbyshire forces at Tutbury was due to their involvement with Parliament's Scottish allies in the siege of Newark, and to the necessity of keeping these same allies in check for, complained the Committee of Derby, 'part of the Scottish horse ... are here amongst us to the exceeding damage of our poore Countie'. Also, the considerable trepidation caused by the existence of fever in the area had tended to reduce enthusiasm for the siege. 'The plague encroached at Tutbury', observed the Derby Committee, 'one Towne of our Countie is alreadie infected from thence, our forces and other Townes in exceeding great danger of that infection which may prove the utter ruin of many'.[13]

On 9 May Banbury garrison, described by Vicars in his usual vitriolic style as a 'most pestilent, pernicious, and vexatious den of Theeves and Royall Robbers ... and especially most vexatious and pernicious to the Inhabitants of North-amptonshire, its next neighbour',[14] also surrendered. As in the case of Ashby, Vicars was perfectly justified in forming this opinion, which is borne out by a report in the *Perfect Diurnal* dated 15 September 1645, concerning 'the late sufferings of a worthy and honest gentleman in Northampton-shire by the enemy; in short, thus: the King's forces at Banbury did lately carry loads of straw into the house of Mr. Cartwright at Aynho-on-the-Hill, in Northamptonshire, four miles off Banbury, and set the straw on fire, and burnt down, not only his own dwelling house, being a very fair, goodly building, wherein the King himself lodged after the battle of Edgehill, but also burnt all the barns, stables, and out-houses belonging to it, lest it should be made a garrison by the Parliament'.[15]

Now it was the turn of Dudley Castle, before the walls of which Sir William Brereton had appeared on 27 April. In a letter to two members of the Staffordshire Committee Brereton described the garrison as 'one of the strongest houldes both by situation and fortification that wee have seene in this kingdome, not to bee approached, nor I believe undermined, nor scaled, nor battered and noe advantage was omitted for the further Strengthening thereof'.[16]

Nevertheless the garrison offered little resistance and surrendered within 16 days of Brereton's arrival, the occupants being allowed to march away, leaving behind 'neere twelve monethes provision of victualls, twentie barrells of powder and neere 400 armes'.[17] In true Puritan fashion Brereton ascribed this victory to divine providence: 'They were well furnished with beare, and plentifullie with water. Soe as if that God (which by the sounding of rammes hornes and seaven tymes compassinge the walles of Jericho brought downe those strong walles) had not also taken away their courage and divided them amongst themselves, this might have been a tedious and expensive worke and one of the last reduced garrisons in the kingdome'.[18]

The capitulation of Dudley Castle on 13 May 1646, was followed almost immediately by the collapse of the Stafford-shire garrison of Hartlebury, which surrendered to Colonel Morgan on 16 May. Four days later on 20 May the King's last stronghold in Shropshire, Ludlow, fell to Parliament.

Now only three Midland garrisons of any importance remained, Lichfield, Worcester, and Oxford, and it was to the commanders of these garrisons, specifically mentioned, and to 'all other Commanders of any other Townes, Castles, or Forts within the Kingdome of England or Dominion of Wales', that Charles addressed the following order:[19]

CHARLES REX

Having resolved to comply with the designs of the PARLIAMENT in every thing that may be for the good of the Subjects and leave no meanes unassayed for removing the differences betwixt us; Therefore we have thought fit the more to evidence the reality of our intentions of settling a happie and firme peace, to require you, upon honourable terms conditions to quit those TOWNES, CASTLES, and FORTS intrusted by you to us, and to disband all the forces under your severall commands.

NEWCASTLE the 10 June 1646

After much haggling over terms the garrison at Oxford finally complied with the King's order on Wednesday 25 June, on which day it capitulated to Fairfax, the Princes Rupert and Maurice who had been ensconced therein being allowed safe conduct on condition that they quitted the country. The departure of the main body of Royalists from the city was conterminous with what to some was a singularly portentious event. At that moment, wrote Vicars, 'there fell a very bitter and violent storme of raine which held for about an houre (some lesser showers we had besides likewise that day) but suddenly after the enemy were marched forth, and ours about to enter Oxford the stormes ceased, and the rest of day very cleare and faire, and this by the way some doe observe very remarkable'.[20]

Stories relating to the miseries inflicted on the inhabitants of Oxford, and even on visitors to the city, while the Royalists were in residence are legion. Most of the recorded incidents seem to have occurred during Sir Arthur Aston's governorship. On 26 April 1644, Nehemiah Wallington recorded that 'Sir Arthur Aston, the Governor of Oxford, a grand papist, doth so tyranize over the inhabitants of Oxford, misusing the Mayor and Aldermen, and all the Protestants in the town'.

Wallington then enumerated a number of actual cases, beginning with 'a gentleman that was in Oxford at a tavern, where he called for a pint of sack, enquiring about some in the town, to whom he came about monies due to him. The vintner asked him from whence he came; he answered from London. The said vintner gave notice thereof to Sir Arthur Aston, who caused him to be apprehended, and the next day to be racked, and examined upon the rack; he made it appear that his business was about monies due to him, and produced a note, and nothing could be suspected justly by him but fair; yet, nevertheless, such was the Governor's cruelty, that after he had racked him, he caused him the next day to be hanged upon the gallows; but he died cheerfully, only he said it grieved him to part with his wife and two children, whom he left at London. And after they had hanged him, they stripped him of his very shirt and buried him naked .

There was also another hanged because he came from London, though nothing proved against him; and Prince Charles had got a pardon for the prisoner that was going to execution, and brought the pardon himself for him; and when he heard that the prince was coming with a pardon, Sir Arthur with his foot turned the ladder himself, the prisoner being then upon it; and when the pardon came, he was so far gone that he could not be recovered.'

Another such incident involved 'a poor Brewer at Oxford that sued to have his drink drunk before his face off his cart; who for putting by a soldier that came with his cane to drink out of a vessel, was so beaten for it that he died'.

And 'one Mary Brook, servant to Mr. Church, an Inn Keeper in Oxford, sweeping of the door, said that was the dirt of the papist horses' feet, and wished they were all hanged; at which time Sir Arthur himself riding by heard her, and called for her, and caused her to be fettered and manacled with irons, and sent to prison, and from thence to the gallows and hanged. But she having a brother that is page of his Majesty's Buttery, he did petition for her to his Majesty, who called for her, and discharged her; since which she hath made an escape, and is now in London, and affirms the same'.[2][1]

An issue of *A Diary, or Exact Journal,* dated 9 August 1644, continued the list of atrocities committed by the seemingly psychopathic governor of Oxford, by publishing a letter sent by Colonel King to his friend: 'Noble friend, we are so tormented with this ill conditioned Governor Colonel Aston, that we know not what course to take. You know the cruelty that he hath offered from time to time, concerning Master Martin; and Sir William Rane was plundered upon his death-bed, his ring taken off his finger; the cutting off the Leiutenant's hand at Towcaster, which is since dead, the beating Barnardo Davis, High Constable of Oxford, kicking his wife, beating a gentleman of quality that had like to have run him through for his labour, the imprisoning of his fellow Malignants that did not bring their corn in as they were appointed, had they not been prevented by the Parliament forces. How many poor coachmen have been undone by this Governor Aston, they know themselves best; as for William Bight, in Vinegar Yard, Richard Beard, Henry Richman, Robert Harts in Fuller's Rents; some of them kept in prison, some having four horses and a coach taken away from them'.

The theme was taken up by *Perfect Occurrences* for the week ending 3 January 1645 in an effort to belie the genuineness of the Royalist terms during the peace negotiations of 1644/5. It made much of the 'experience of those inhabitants of Oxford who are sensible of the misery of the peace of the Cavaliers, insomuch that in that city there are many hundreds that have been exceedingly abused by them, when the Cavaliers in a mad humour have broken open one man's doore, ... cut and wounded others that have crossed them, plundered, imprisoned, and cruelly handled them, who have been great malignants ... It was fitter for a second Book of Martyrs to reckon up a catalogue of all their cruelties in, than so short a toome as this paper can afford'.

In spite of the King's instructions the remaining garrisons continued to resist, even though they were heavily besieged and were without hope of relief. At Lichfield Brereton had already been forced to take drastic measures in an effort to dislodge the garrison there. He had erected a battery on a mound near to the Cathedral Close, 'and', in Brereton's own words, 'plaid four or five days freely uppon their highest spire steeple ... The effect whereof was almost like that of Sampsons pulling downe the house (which did great execution) at his death. Soe here the fall of this spire did mightie execution as well, uppon the chauncell, wherein was their quire service and organs placed, as alsoe on the other syde of

the steeple upon that parte of the body of the Minster
wherein the pulpitt stood, into both which there was great
breaches as though the Lord were purposed to reckon for
that hypocrisie, prophanesse and ignorance which had been
therein nourished and practised. This spire was the greatest
ornament of that grose structure which now looketh very
nakedly and bare'. Brereton concluded, 'that this downefall
would alsoe humble their loftie proud spiritts in the Close'. [22]

In September 1650 the artilleryman responsible for the
destruction of the steeple met his end in circumstances of
peculiar violence. Dugdale reported this unfortunate individual's demise as if it were providential: 'The gunner that shott
downe Lichfield steeple in the seige (of 1646) this month in
shooting of a cannon at Stafford, for triumph upon Major
General Harrison his coming thither, was kild by the breach
thereof; his chin and one arme being torne off. He lived a
day or two'. [23]

During the siege of Lichfield it had been the humane
practice of the Governor to permit Parliamentarian prisoners
within the Close to be visited by their wives who had taken up
residence in the city. But Brereton, in an effort to exert
further pressure upon the garrison, ordered, on 26 May, that
'a list bee taken of the names of all the wives of those that
are in the Close that they may bee speedily sent into the close
to their Husbands and not permitted to come out againe and
if they or any shall dare to come out of the close the officers
of the guard are required to shoote them or otherwise to bee
answerable for the same at a Counsell of Warre'.

This prompted the following plaintive, but vain, plea[24] to
Brereton on behalf of the unfortunate women:

> That by Reason of your strict Command last night given to thrust
> us out of our Habitations uppon the Garrison of the Close of Litch,
> and the vyolent Carriage of your Soldyers to the great endangering
> of our Lives, Wee are enforced to Lodge in the Cold open Ayre, and
> there likelie to perish for want of Releife to sustaine nature, which
> all the Garrison absolutely denying us either admittance, sustenance
> or other necessaries to defend us from the Cold or hunger; whereby
> some of us are already much endangered in our healthes and likely
> to Come to some untymely and miserable end, if not otherwise
> Remedyed and helped.
>
> May it therefore please you out of your Christian Charitie to give
> us (Relying only uppon your mercie) leave to Repaire into the

Countrey to prevent perishing for lacke of food and Lodging, that soe our Innocent blood may not untymelie bee taken away by this lingring kind of death and most greivous suffering.

And wee shall ever pray for your health and. happinesse.

Ursula Hill
Anne Pyddocke
Anne Cowsie
Elisabeth Baker
Judith Ballard
Katherine Bazbry
Frances Sute
Elizabeth Stubes

The garrison's reply to this treatment took the form of a letter 'signed by the generall consent of the whole garrison' and shot into the ranks of the besiegers. The letter rated Brereton 'that not being able in a manly way to prevayle against us, hee hath betaken himselfe to barbarous and inhumane attempts, and such as hath never yett been practiced by Christians, bloodily thrusting poore innocent women and children (noe way engaged in the quarrell) uppon that danger which they dare not looke uppon themselves, exposeing them to famine or their mercilesse swords'.

Apart from revealing that the Parliamentarians had offended the Royalists' sense of chivalry (even though the Royalists had themselves denied the women succour) the letter, which was dated 27 May, also disclosed that the garrison knew nothing of the King's surrender to the Scots on 5 May. In an outburst of pathetic optimism the garrison declared, through the letter, that 'wee doe hereby desire the countrey to take notice that the king is nowe at the head of a very powerfull army consisting of 30,000 men, which by Gods assistance may resettle him and all his loyall subjects in their rights and wee doubt not but will speedilie redeme us'.[25]

It was some time before the garrison commander was finally convinced that the King no longer possessed an army with which to relieve the garrison, but he did eventually capitulate, upon 'honourable terms of surrender', on 10 July.

Major-General Whalley, a kinsman of Cromwell's, commenced the investment of Worcester on 21 May, frequent and daring sallies against the town being made by raiding

218

parties headed by a drunken Captain Hodgskins, 'called Wicked Will for his desperateness and valor'. But it was not until news reached the garrison that Fairfax had taken Oxford and was marching on Worcester that its commander, Colonel Henry Washington, finally agreed to surrender. The formalities were entered into at the Round Mount on Rainbow Hill during the afternoon of 23 July, and the victorious Parliamentarians entered the last major garrison in England to hold out for the King at 5 p.m. the same day.

The ending of hostilities brought with it the unmourned demise of the military garrisons of both sides that had proliferated throughout the Midlands during the war. Colonel Birch's military memoirs tell us that 'according to the dispositions of the governor they proved too often the misery rather than the protection of the neighbourhood, and were liable to be commanded by strangers or foreigners who had no sympathy with the surrounding country. A large amount of public and private suffering was occasioned by these intruders, whose exactions and insolencies became odious, and whose fortified abodes were often converted into scenes of contention and rapine'.[26]

CHAPTER EIGHTEEN

[1] Vicars, *Magnalia Dei Anglicana*, Pt.IV, p.177.

[2] *Ibid.*, Pt.IV, p.313.

[3] *Ibid.*, Pt.IV, p.330.

[4] *Military Memoir of Colonel John Birch*, p.118.

[5] *A New Tricke to take Townes or The just and perfect relation of the sudden surprisall of Hereford, taken December 18, 1645* (London 1645); *Military Memoir of Colonel John Birch*, Appendix XVI.

[6] Vicars, *Op.cit*, Part IV, p.361.

[7] *Ibid.*, p.378.

[8] *Ibid.*, p.413.

[9] Dugdale, *A Short View of the Late Troubles in England*, pp. 202, 203.

[10] Rushworth, *Historical collections abridged and improved*, Vol. VI, p.1.

[11] Dugdale, *Op.cit.*, p.257.

[12] 'Letter from the Committee of Derby to Sir William Brereton and the Committee of Stafford', Letter Book of Sir William Brereton, p.46, Birmingham Reference Library.

[13] *Ibid.*

[14] Vicars, *Op.cit.*, Part IV, p.421.

[15] *A Perfect Diurnal*, No. 112 (1645).

[16] Letter Book of Sir William Brereton, p.190.

[17] *Ibid.*

[18] 'Letter from Sir William Brereton to Mr. Ashurst and Mr. Swinfen touching the surrender of Dudley Castle, May 13th 1646', Letter Book of Sir William Brereton, p.191.

[19] Vicars, *Op.cit.*, Part IV, p.444.

[20] *Ibid.*, p.446.

[21] Wallington, *Historical Notes of Events*, Vol.II, pp.217, 218.

[22] 'Letter to Mr. Ashurst & Mr. Swinfen & to London touching batteringe downe the greatest of the three steeples of the Minster of Litchfield', Letter Book of Sir Wm. Brereton, pp.250-1.

[23] Dugdale, *Life, Diary and Correspondence*, pp. 97, 98.

[24] Letter Book of Sir William Brereton, p.258.

[25] 'Letter written by Sir Thomas Tyldesley his owne hand and shott with an Arrowe into the Towne', Letter Book of Sir William Brereton, p.260.

[26] *Military Memoir of Colonel John Birch*, p.111.

CHAPTER NINETEEN

THE SECOND CIVIL WAR, EXECUTION OF THE KING, AND THE COMMITTEE FOR INDEMNITY

Within nine months of his surrender Charles was handed over to the English Parliament by the Scots on payment of £200,000 in hand, and security for a similar sum to be paid at a later date. With their 30 pieces of silver secured the the Scots marched back into their homeland, while the King, now a prisoner of Parliament, was conveyed to Holdenby House in Northamptonshire.

Meanwhile the energies of the Parliamentary party were almost exclusively devoted to a struggle for supremacy between the Presbyterians, led by Denzil Holles, and the Independents, led by Sir Henry Vane and Oliver Cromwell, and backed up by the army. And one manifestation of this struggle was the abduction of Charles from Holdenby House by the army in June 1647. Two months later the Independent faction, or rather the army, had gained control and although Cromwell did his best to come to some sort of settlement with Charles the majority in the army was less concerned with seeking a just peace with the King than furthering its own ideal of what Robert Baillie, a rabid Presbyterian, saw as 'a horrible liberty', in pursuit of which there were some who were more than anxious 'to abolish the monarchy and settle themselves in a new kind of popular government'.[1]

Cromwell's problem was further exacerbated by the difficulties of negotiating with a king whose sense of reality was obscured by doctrinaire views of divine right. This was glaringly apparent from his persistence in over-stating his own power, and his inability to comprehend fully the danger of his situation.

In November 1647 Charles escaped from custody and fled to the Isle of Wight from where he entered into a covenant with those very subjects of his who had entertained that 'infamous contract' of 'selling' him to Parliament, the Scots. In exchange for Charles's embracement of Presbyterianism the Scots agreed to invade England and rescue their King.

But a letter from Charles advising the Queen 'that he was now counted by both the Scotch presbyterians, and the army ... but he thought he should close with the Scots sooner than the other',[2] is popularly supposed to have fallen into Cromwell's hands. Picking up 2,500 pairs of shoes from Northampton, some Coventry-made stockings at Leicester and reinforcements from local contingents of Leicestershire, Nottinghamshire, and Derbyshire at Nottingham, Cromwell joined Major General John Lambert and marched against the invading Scots who were led by the Duke of Hamilton. Cromwell's and Lambert's forces, who were out-numbered two to one, hammered the enemy in a running battle that began at Preston in Lancashire on 17 August 1648 and ended with the surrender of what was left of the Scottish foot at Warwick and finally the horse at Uttoxeter on 25 August.

Thus ended the Scots invasion, which, together with a few small conterminous risings by Royalists in the West of England, Kent and Essex, constituted what became known as the Second Civil War. During this renewal of hostilities the Midlands experienced the usual effects consequential to military activity in the region, even though the main action took place elsewhere. A typical example of this is provided by the petition[3] for compensation of Richard Richardson, a farmer from Bramshall in Staffordshire:

> Wheras the Parliament armie in the pursute of the Scots to Uttoxater, and resting at Bramshall aforsaid two dayes and nightes, the greater part of the company being setled in the church and in the house of this your petitioner, and their horses feeding in, and spoyling, the closes of corne, pease, and hay of this said petitioner, the losse amounting to the valew of about six powndes, as it is judged by the inhabitantes, which corne, pease and hay was all the hope of this your petitioner for the sustenance of himselfe, his wife and family this yeare following, which grownd he rented at a hard rate, and in regard of his great losse: This your petitioner humbly prayeth this Honourable Bench to take his said great losse into consideration and to give order for some reliefe towards the sustenance of himselfe and his familie, for which this your petitioner shall remaine ever thankfull and humbly pray &c.

October 2 1648

The truth herof, we whose names are subscribed doe testifie:

Jo: Creeke, minister.   Rogger Baggeley
Tho: Warner   George Taylor
Andrew Ebson

The invasion was regarded by Parliament as rebellion against lawful authority rather than civil war. In consequence Scottish prisoners of war did not receive the usual consideration afforded to the soldiers of a defeated enemy. William Dugdale recorded in his diary how the Scots prisoners, who were dispersed throughout the Midlands and maintained at the cost of local authorities, were 'miserably used. The Moorelanders rose upon the Scots and stript some of them ... They were for hunger, some of them exposed to eate cabage leaves in Ridgley, carrot tops in Coleshill'.[4]

At Chapel-en-le-Frith in Derbyshire a vast number of Scottish prisoners were crowded into the church with little or no thought for their material comfort. A record of the incident and its consequences appears in the parish register thus:

> 1648 Sept: 11. There came to this town of Scots army, led by the Duke of Hambleton and squandered by Colonell Lord Cromwell sent hither prisoners from Stopford under the conduct of Marshall Edward Matthews, said to be 1,500 in number put into the church Sept: 14. They went away Sept: 30 following. There were buried of them before the rest went away 44 persons, and more buried Oct. 2 who were not able to march, and the same that died by the way befoɪe they came to Cheshire 10 and more.

If the account of the loss of the despatch implicating the King in the Scottish attempt to invade England is authentic, it can justifiably be regarded as one of those instances in history by which momentous results follow on the interception of correspondence. Henceforth many were of the opinion that only by ridding themselves and the country of Charles could a recrudescence of war be averted. 'We immediately, from that time forward, resolved his ruin',[5] Cromwell is reported to have said of the King.

A special court was convened to try the King for high treason, the charge being that he, Charles Stuart, 'out of a wicked design to erect and uphold an unlimited and tyrannical power, to rule according to his will, and to overthrow the rights and libertys of the people ... has traitorously and malicously levy'd war against the present Parliament, and the people therein represented ... and therein guilty of all the Treasons, Murders, Rapings, Burnings, Spoils, Desolations and mischiefs to this Nation in the said Wars, or occasioned thereby'.[6]

Then followed a list of 13 dates and places when and where the alleged crime was perpetrated. Almost half of the places cited were, significantly, in the Midlands, and included Nottingham where, on or about 24 August 1642, the King set up his Standard of War; Edgehill or 'Kynton-Field' in the county of Warwick, on or about 23 October 1642; Gloucester on or about 30 October 1643; Cropredy Bridge in Oxford-shire, on or about 31 July 1644; Leicester, on or about 8 June 1645; and Naseby in Northamptonshire on 14 June 1645. Of the remaining seven incidents, two, those of the first and second battles of Newbury, took place sufficiently close to the Midlands to have had some effect on the inhabitants of that region.

The legality of both the court and its indictments were at the time considered suspect in many quarters. The regular judiciary considered 'that because of their Oaths, they could not advise in this business, being it was an alteration of the Government of the Kingdom'. And the House of Lords rejected the Commons' ordinance 'that it was Treason in the King to levy war against the Parliament'.[7]

But the Commons answered opposition by turning them-selves into a Grand Committee to consider the power of the Commons in Parliament, and the Committee voted:

1. That the people under God, are the original of all just power.

2. That the Commons of England assembled in the Parliament, being chosen by, and representing the people, have the Supream Authority of this Nation.

3. That whatsoever is enacted and declared for Law, by the Commons in Parliament, hath the force of Law, and all the people of this Nation, are included thereby, although the consent and con-currence of the King, and House of Peers, be not had thereunto.

Whitelocke records that 'these being reported to the House, were upon the question all passed without a negative

Voice to any of them'.[8]

And so what was now 'the Supreme Authority of this Nation, the Commons of England assembled in Parliament', tried and condemned the King 'for notorious Treasons, Tyrannys, and Murders',[9] for which he was put to death on 30 January 1649.

Elias Ashmole, the Lichfield-born antiquarian, noted a number of portentous events that coincided with the King's death. Those in the Midlands included an outbreak of the plague at Syston in Leicestershire, the sudden appearance of blood upon cloths in Gloucestershire, and a more lengthy report 'of the maide at Alcester who was cured of the Kings Evill [scrofula] who had extreame paine that very houre & minute that the King was beheaded, that her cloths were taken of, and one drop of blood yssued from that place where her sore was'.[10]

In truth Charles had sinned and sinned greatly, perhaps not with the transgressions for which he was tried but with those of arrogance and duplicity. These are not necessarily crimes in ordinary men but in Charles they were sufficient to contribute substantially to his tragic demise.

The sense of proportion, generally developed in more ordinary human beings by the rough and tumble of every-day existence, was denied to Charles. Thus, he attempted to rule as his medieval forbears had done, but ignored the fact that in so doing he was rendering himself as prone as they were to the violent overthrow of his regime, and the usurpation of his throne. He believed, and continued to believe, that he possessed an indefeasible right to rule which no amount of adverse circumstances could lessen or destroy.

In this respect it could be said that Charles displayed an intellectual honesty of singular consistency, but unfortunately for him the outlook of his enemies was more practical. To them God spake through the arbitrement of war. Charles's divine right had been clearly condemned, and the divine justness of Parliament's cause upheld on the field of battle. 'I desire the whole honour and glory may bee ascribed to God with whom it is as easie to deliver upp the strongest as the weakest houlds', wrote Sir William Brereton when referring to the surrender of Dudley Castle.[11]   And of the Battle of Naseby Oliver Cromwell said, 'this is none other but the hand of God; and to Him alone belongs the glory, wherein none are to share with Him'.[1][2]

These same sentiments were also applied to the execution of Charles, an event which prompted Wallington to comment that 'whatever may be unjust with men, God is righteous and just in whatever he doth'.[1][3]

Providential interpretation apart the trial and execution of the King must be seen as the victor exercising his right to wreak his vengeance on a vanquished enemy, and the need to liquidate an embarrassing obstacle to future political aims. In this respect the fate of Charles can be likened to that of the 24 defendants at the International Military Tribunal at Nuremberg three centuries later.

Perhaps the most suitable epitaph for Charles is that which came from the pen of William Lilly: 'For my part I doe beleeve he was not the worst, but the most unfortunate of Kings'.[1][4]

After the Civil War a Committee for Indemnity was set up. This Committee served to legalise the sequestration of Royalists' property and the exaction of impositions, which, according to English Common Law, were illegal. It also exonerated those Parliamentary agents who used military force to exact illegal taxes. But the bulk of the Committee's work seems to have involved the hearing of petitions from those seeking redress of charges wrongfully brought against them arising out of their activities during the war.

One of the petitioners to the Committee for Indemnity was Thomas Sharpe, a Parliamentary soldier stationed at Warwick Castle. The case also involved one William Greene, a collarmaker of Stratford-upon-Avon, whom Sharpe described as 'an inveterate Malignant who hath sevralle tymes raysed the rabble people of the said towne against the Parliament souldiers'. In his testimony Sharpe informed the Committee that 'your petitioner comeing into the said towne, the said Greene haveing notice thereof, through his intolerable malice to all the Parliament party, runneth from his house with a great clubb in his hand and unexpectedly to your petitioner, and without any provocation, assaulted your petitioner in the streete, cryeing, "have at you Parliament Rogue". Whereupon your petitioner, defending himselfe, gave the said Greene some slight wounds, whereof hee is recovered, for which your petitioner was bound over to the assizes by recognizance of £40, with suretyes to answere the same to his great concern and expense. And besides is threatened to be sued by the said Greene therefore'. Sharpe concluded: 'Your petitioner humbly prayes consideration of the premisses, and that your honours will bee pleased to order the said Greene to appeare before this Committee to answere the premisses. And that the said recognizance may bee cancelled and hee bee indemnified, and have such damages for his unjust molestation as to your honors shall seeme meete.'[15]

Another petition involved William Pullen and Richard Woodlake, who, at the time of the Scots army's siege of Hereford in 1645, were petty constables of Bosbury in Herefordshire. Upon receipt of several warrants from the Scots officers for provisions Pullen and Woodlake did, in pursuance of their duties, 'accordingly by vertue of the said orders take upp sevrall provisions of the inhabitants of the said parish, and likewise did, in affection to the Parliament, buy with theire owne money, and take upp upon theire creditt, sevrall cattle, bedding and provision for the use aforesaid, upon promise of being reimbursed their monyes by a genrall tax laid upon the inhabitants. Yet', complained the petitioners, 'John Allen the younger, Thomas Simonds, Thomas Collcombe, and diverse other of the inhabitants ... doe not only refuse to contribute towards the ingagements and disbursements of the petitioners, but doe sue them, both in lawe and in chauncery, for what the petitioners tooke upp of them by vertue of the said warrants for provision for the souldiery as aforesaid. The petitioners pray releife against the said suites, by vertue of the Ordinances for Indemnity, and that they may have reparation for their damages suffered thereby'.[16]

Other cases concerned persons who considered that they had been wrongfully accused of displaying sympathy towards the Royalist party, and had thus been rendered delinquents, and liable to a fine or sequestration. One such party was Mr. Hunt, the parson of Kibworth in Leicestershire. Hunt had been charged with having ridden in company with the

King's forces in their flight after the battle of Naseby. The
parson's defence was that he could not avoid it for, by an
unfortunate coincidence, he had chosen the afternoon of the
battle to ride towards Leicester and, continued Hunt, 'the
King's forces were then so scattered that they rode up and
down the country about Kibworth, so that a man could ride
no way, but he must needs ride in their company'.

There were other instances of a similar nature affecting a
number of inhabitants of Oswestry in Shropshire. John Davies
was accused of being with the King's forces at their siege of
Oswestry. His plea to the Committee for Indemnity was that
'I was at the seige but not in armes. I was commanded as the
rest of my neighbours to appear, and bring in provisions upon
penalty of imprisonment, my habitation being about a small
mile distant'.[17]

Roger Williams was charged with being 'in armes against
the Parliament' at the siege of Lichfield Close, and, 'that in
the yeare 1644, a little before the towne of Oswestry was
taken by the Parliament's forces, the said Williams was in
armes there for the King and did perswade others to do the
like'. Williams pleaded for indemnity on the grounds that
'I was att Litchfield Close, but not in armes. I was forced to
goe theire upon speciall occasions that did concearne my
estate ... To the second I answer I was not in armes in
Oswestry before the towne was taken'.[18]

These sort of charges were usually brought by private
individuals, which gave ample scope to those who wished to
settle an old score with a neighbour. The charges against
Davies and Williams might conceivably have belonged to this
category as they were preferred by a fellow townsman, John
Pugh, who also laid similar charges against four other inhabitants of Oswestry, Silvanus Jones, Nathanial Roberts,
Thomas Roberts, and John Payne. Thus the Committee for
Indemnity probably investigated more cases resulting from
the desire of someone to exact retribution for a personal
injury or injustice, or from the machinations of those affected
by jaundice, than resulted from positive malignancy.

CHAPTER NINETEEN
[1] *The Letters and Journals of Robert Baillie,* Vol.II, pp.383, 392.

[2] Thomas Morrice, *A Collection of State Letters of the Rt. Hon. Roger Boyle, first Earl of Orrery .... Together with ... the Life of the Earl of Orrery* (London, 1742), p.15.

[3] Document No. Q/SR.M.1648, f 6, in the Staffordshire County Record Office.

[4] Dugdale, *Life, Diary and Correspondence*, p.96.

[5] Morrice, *A Collection of State Letters*, etc., p.16.

[6] Rushworth, *Historical collections, abridged and improved*, Vol.VI, p.575.

[7] Whitelockc, *Memorials of the English Affairs*, pp.367, 361.

[8] *Ibid.*, p.361.

[9] Rushworth, *Op.cit.*, Vol.VI, pp.602, 605.

[10] *Elias Ashmole (1617-1692), His Autobiographical and Historical Notes, his Correspondence, and Other Contemporary Sources Relating to his Life and Work*, ed. C.H. Jostin (Oxford, 1966), Vol.II, pp.485, 486.

[11] 'Letter from Sir William Brereton to Mr. Ashurst & Mr. Swinfen touching the surrender of Dudley Castle, 13 May 1646', Letter Book of Sir William Brereton, p.191.

[12] Letter from Oliver Cromwell to Honourable William Lenthall, Speaker of the Commons House of Parliament, *Letters and Speeches of Oliver Cromwell*, Vol.I, p.205.

[13] Wallington, *Op.cit.*, Vol.II, p.279.

[14] William Lilly, *Monarchy or no monarchy in England* (London, 1651), p.119.

[15] Committee and Commissioners for Indemnity - Sharpe v. Greene, (S.P. 24/75).

[16] Committee and Commissioners for Indemnity - Pullen and Woodlake v. John Allen the younger and Others (S.P. 24/70).

[17] *Ibid.*, - Pugh v. Davies and Others (S.P. 24/70).

[18] *Ibid.*

CHAPTER TWENTY

THE NEW JERUSALEM,
CHARLES II AND THE THIRD CIVIL WAR

With the execution of Charles I the office of King was extirpated from the constitution, and it was further decreed a treasonable act, punishable by death, to presume to proclaim, or any way promote, the late King's son, or any other to be King of England 'by color of Inheritance or any other Claim, without the free Consent of the People in Parliament'.[1] The Commonwealth of England and Ireland was then established. But the new republic was destined for a stormy existence. The various factions that had united to form the Parliamentary Party in the struggle against the King now began to exert pressure for the realisation of the individual aims for which they had fought.

Among these factions were the Fifth Monarchy men, who were to find a champion in Major-General Thomas Harrison, the son of a Newcastle-under-Lyme butcher. These men were the imbibers of a peculiar kind of apocalyptic thought that thrives during moments of acute social crisis, which are seen as a sign of Christ's second coming. To the Fifth Monarchists the four monarchies of Babylon, Persia, Greece and Rome had all passed into history and the fifth monarchy, the monarchy of Christ, was now imminent. Their conviction grew as the fortunes of war went against the King, and when, in 1649, the monarchy was finally overthrown, they saw it as a positive, divinely-inspired presage of the second advent of Christ, and the establishment of His thousand years' rule upon earth. During the period of preparation for this outstanding event the Millenarians believed that England should be ruled by an interim government of saintly men chosen by the churches and exercising the minimum of direct political power. A system of free elections was rejected for it was considered that this might produce a Parliament of sinners who might conceivably hinder the Millenium.

Another sect, the Levellers, constituted one of the largest factions of the Parliamentary Party. Drawn, in the main, from the ranks of the Anabaptists, the Levellers envisaged the destruction of the old social, political and economic order and the establishment of a more egalitarian regime based on the communistic principles of the primitive Christians.

The political aims of the Fifth Monarchists, the Levellers, and other such radical sects caused considerable trepidation among the majority of the Members of Parliament whose liberal outlook was more or less confined to questions of religion. In secular politics their principal concern was the protection of property, the maintenance of law and order, and the retention of their own places in the government of the country; all of which would be forfeited if the anarchical tendencies of the Fifth Monarchists, and the egalitarianism of the Levellers, were given their head.

The ruling faction deemed it necessary, therefore, to deal severely with these radicals, and as the Levellers, led by 'Free-born' John Lilburne, were the most active and the most dangerous, it was they who received most attention. Throughout 1649 the Levellers had, according to the government, 'endeavoured to seduce the army, with too much success', and the Council of State felt that it was in their best interests to advise the Lord General of the Army, field commanders, and the commanders of the remaining garrisons that 'we desire that a watchful eye be kept by the officers of the regiments upon their soldiers, that they may not be wrought upon by malignant insinuations to engage in any undertaking against the Parliament' and to 'prevent or suppress the first stirrings towards insurrections'.[2]

One of the most serious manifestations of this occurred in May 1649 when 12,000 Leveller deserters from various regiments banded together for a march on London where they hoped to secure the release of their leader, Lilburne, who was being held in the Tower. But Lilburne's would-be deliverers were surprised at Burford by a strong force commanded by Cromwell. What little resistance there was took place in the centre of the town where Sheep Street joins the High Street and in this one man was killed and two were wounded. Although most of the mutineers were able to escape, some 400 were nevertheless taken prisoner and these were incarcerated for a while in Burford Church and later marched out and forced to witness the execution, by firing squad, of three of their number against the west wall of the churchyard.

But again, in September 1649, there was another Leveller uprising, this time at Oxford. Here the mutineers rounded up their officers and confined them to New College and set about securing the garrison from outside attack. They then awaited a universal uprising which would provide the Levellers cause with an offensive field army with which to establish its particular manifestation of a post-war New Jerusalem.

The Midlands was the main centre from whence the mutineers expected to find supporters, particularly from Northamptonshire, Leicestershire and Derbyshire. In the last named county 12,000 miners did actually rise against their employer, the Earl of Rutland. But the ardour of the mutineers in Oxford, who were cut off from the outside world and from the personal influence of Lilburne and his 'seditious scribbling', soon cooled and the rebellion fizzled out. Examples were made of seven civilians, who were handed over to the civil courts, and two soldiers, who were executed outside the city near the castle on the morning of Tuesday 11 September. Their source of inspiration gone the Derbyshire miners also capitulated.

In spite of the Oxford *débâcle* sporadic disturbances by the Levellers continued. 'Every day', wrote the Council of State to the Attorney-General on 17 September 1649, 'we have new information that consultations are held by the party that oppose the present government'.[3] But there were more than Levellers who opposed the government; in fact, all did who saw the new order as a manifest denial of that which they had expected the war and the destruction of monarchical institutions to bring about.

It was while this atmosphere of social and political discontent prevailed that the dead King's son chose his moment to return from exile in France and claim his lost kingdoms. He landed in Scotland on 1 July 1650 to the acclamation of a nation groaning under the tyranny of the Marquis of Argyle

and the Presbyterian Church and threatened with invasion
and annexation by England. The Scots were not, of course,
legally bound by any statute passed by the English Parliament,
and at the time of Charles I's trial it was reported 'that the
Ministers of the Kirk preach against the army in England,
and their proceedings against the King, saying they are bound
by their Covenant to preserve Monarchy, and that in the
Race of the present King'.[4] And so, at the end of the year,
King Charles II of Scotland was crowned at Scone and put at
the head of the Scottish army.

But on the day of Charles's coronation Scotland's capital,
Edinburgh, was already in the hands of the English, the New
Model Army having crossed the border on 22 July 1650, after
which, on 3 September, they effected a brilliant victory over
the Scots at Dunbar.

For the first half of 1651 the English army did nothing,
mainly because its commander, Oliver Cromwell, was ill for
much of the time. This gave Charles sufficient time in which
to prepare his army for an ambitious plan to march on
London and claim the throne of England. Even so, with half
of his Scottish kingdom in the hands of the English, and
famine and disease sweeping the remainder, the King's affairs
were far from hopeful. But Charles had inherited his father's
megalomaniacal optimism, and in July, at the head of a 16,000
strong army, which included the Duke of Hamilton, he slipped
past Cromwell's army and crossed the border into England.

When he heard of Charles's move southwards Cromwell
sent Major-General John Lambert with some horse to overtake
the enemy and harry them on their march, while Cromwell
himself followed at a more leisurely pace. Lambert was
joined by Major-General Thomas Harrison and his forces
somewhere between Preston and Blackburn, and by forces
from Lancashire, Cheshire and Staffordshire at Bolton. Thus
reinforced Lambert was able to play his part to good effect.
'After a long and terrible march', wrote Sir Richard Bulstrode,
'wherein several engagements, with different success, the
English being in the rear, and on all sides of the Scots; so that
most of the engagements were to the King's disadvantage, who
at last arrived at Worcester with his shattered army.'

Charles chose Worcester as the springboard for his attack

on London for several good reasons. It was the nearest safe point to his objective, that was not garrisoned by Parliamentarian troops. Also, 'Worcester', wrote Clarendon, 'had always been a place very well affected in itself, and most of the gentlemen of that county had been engaged for the King in the former war'; it was 'seated almost in the middle of the kingdom', continued Clarendon, 'and in as fruitful a country as any part of it; a good city, served by the noble river of Severn from all the adjacent counties; Wales behind it, from whence levies might be made of great numbers of stout men: it was a place whither the King's friends might repair if they had the affections they pretended to have'.[5]

But no Welsh levies came and few Englishmen flocked to the Royal standard, which had, ironically, been raised at Worcester on 22 August, exactly nine years to the day after Charles I had raised his at another Midland town, Nottingham.

One man who did join the King was the Presbyterian, Edward Massey, who had fled England when the Independents gained control of Parliament and the country in 1647. And a few officers at Shrewsbury made a half-hearted attempt to seize the city in the name of the new King, for which one of them, Lieutenant Benbow, who had distinguished himself at the taking of Shrewsbury from the Royalists in 1645, was later court-martialled and executed in the cabbage garden outside the town walls.

Those who might have supported Charles now either preferred the rule of an unpopular regime to a recrudescence of outright civil strife, or regarded as hopeless this attempt to restore the English crown to their dead King's son. 'The Success of Cromwell at Dumbarre and afterwards', observed Richard Baxter, 'had put a Fear upon all Men, and the manner of the Scots, coming away, persuaded all Men that Necessity forced them, and they were look'd upon rather as flying than as marching into England; and few Men will put themselves into a flying Army which is pursued by the conquering enemy.' Even so 'the King's Army of Scots was excellently well governed (in comparison of what his Fathers was wont to be): Not a Souldier durst wrong any Man of the worth of a Penny; which much drew the Affections of the People towards them'.[6]

Within days of the Royal army's entry into Worcester
Parliament had the city completely surrounded. But this was
not the only problem facing Charles. Massey, the only general
of ability in the Royal army, had been seriously injured by
his former comrades in arms. This occurred while the intrepid
commander was attempting to destroy the bridge over the
Severn at Upton, in order to afford more protection for the
Royalist forces at Worcester. And the Scots, many of whom
had fought bravely against the English in their own country,
now felt, after the hammering that they had already received
from the troops of Lambert and Harrison, less inclined to
assist their King in what to them was a foreign adventure.

When, on 3 September 1651, the Parliamentary army made
its three-pronged attack on Worcester, the Scots, who were
drawn up in battle order about a mile outside the city, at the
confluence of the Teme and the Severn, offered little
resistance. Most of the foot surrendered at the first charge.
But the Parliamentarian attack possessed such impetus that
both the surrendered Scottish infantry and the cavalry were
pushed headlong into and through the city. Charles, riding
from his lodgings in the Corn Market towards the battle, 'met
the whole body of his horse running in so great fear that he
could not stop them, though he used all the means he could,
and called to many officers by their names, and hardly
preserved himself, by letting them pass by, from being overthrown and overrun by them'.[7]

Only when the main body of the Royalist army found
itself bottled up in the north end of the city was there any
resistance, and then the battle became, in Cromwell's own
words, 'as stiff a contest ... as I have ever seen',[8] before the
Royalists were finally beaten.

About 7,000 prisoners, including Hamilton, were taken,
many of whom were 'penned in the Cathedral, with sad
outlooks'.[9] For those who escaped the corpse-strewn streets
of Worcester fresh terrors lay in store. Many were intercepted
by those troops 'that lay, through Providence, at Bewdley, and
in Shropshire and Staffordshire'.[10] Richard Baxter, who at
the time of the battle was living in Kidderminster, recorded[11]
an incident concerning some of the fugitive army and those
troops that had been providentially placed to cut off their

retreat:

> Kiderminster being but eleven Miles from Worcester, the flying
> Army past some of them through the Town, and some by it: I was
> newly gone to Bed when the Noise of the flying Horse acquainted
> us of the Overthrow: and a piece of one of Cromwell's Troops that
> Guarded Bewdley-Bridge having tidings of it, came into our Streets,
> and stood in the open Market-place before my Door, to surprise
> those that past by: And so when many hundreds of the flying Army
> came together, when the 30 Troopers cryed stand, and fired at them,
> they either hasted away, or cryed Quarter, not knowing in the Dark
> what Number it was that charged them: And so as many were taken
> there, as so few Men could lay hold on: And till Midnight the Bullets
> flying towards my Door and Windows, and the sorrowful Fugitives
> hasting by for their Lives, did tell me the Calamitousness of War.

But Parliamentarian soldiers were not the only danger that faced the defeated Royalists. Of the 'fleeing Enemy', Cromwell wrote, 'I hear the Country riseth upon them everywhere'.[12] This was confirmed, in more explicit terms, by Clarendon who recorded that 'very many of those who ran away were every day knocked in the head by the country people, and used with their barbarity'.[13]

The would-be King Charles II of England was also a fugitive. He had returned to his lodgings when it was apparent that all was lost and, according to local tradition, escaped by the back door as one of the Parliamentary commanders, Colonel Cobbett, entered by the front. Charles then passed through the northern part of the city, where minutes later his fleeing army was to make its involuntary stand, and slipped out by the St. Martin's Gate.

Thus Charles fled the city that had afforded him the same loyal support as it had done his father. According to Clarendon, 'the city opened their gates, and received the King with all the demonstration of affection and duty that could be expressed; and made provision for the army that it wanted nothing that it could desire, the mayor taking care for the present provision of shoes and stockings, the want whereof in so long a march was very apparent and grievous'.[14]

In financial terms the cost of this, and the city's continued loyalty to the Royalist cause throughout the whole period of the war, was computed at £7,885 13s. 7d. in disbursements, a loss to the citizens in money and goods of £80,000 due to plunder, £100,000 due to the destruction of the suburbs, hospitals, city lands, and citizens' estates, £180 per month for four years towards maintaining the city's fortifications, besides free quarter, contributions, personal service, servants, and fuel for the guards.[15] And, after the battle of Worcester the city, Baxter tells us, 'was much plundered by Cromwell's Souldiers'.[16] Truly Worcester had, as its motto claims, been 'Faithful in Peace and in War'.

Having effected his escape from Worcester Charles, accompanied by his servants and all the principal Royalist commanders who had survived the battle, headed north and spent the night a few miles outside Kidderminster.

Still travelling north Charles and his 60-strong *entourage* passed through Stourbridge, then moved to Whiteladies House on the Shropshire/Staffordshire border. This particular venue possessed certain unique advantages. It was relatively isolated, lying, as it did, deep in Brewood Forest, and it presented the attractive possibility of an escape into Wales. Also, the owner of the house, Charles Giffard, was riding in the Royal party and, like the principal tenants of his estate, the Penderels, he practised a proscribed religion, Catholicism, and was therefore well-versed in the art of subterfuge.

At Whiteladies Charles managed to shake off most of his embarrassingly large *entourage*. It was reported that a large Scottish force was about Tong Castle on its way back to Scotland and Charles's followers were persuaded to join them. This left the King free to pursue his own course, which was to make for London in a suitable disguise and take advantage of the anonymity afforded by the capital.

The disguise chosen by Charles was described to Samuel Pepys by the King himself in 1680. It was 'a country-fellow's habit, with a pair of ordinary gray-cloth breeches, a leathern doublet, and a green jerkin, which I took in the house of White Ladys. I also cut my hair very short, and flung my cloaths into a privy-house, that nobody might see that anybody had been stripping themselves'.[17] Thus arrayed Charles left Whiteladies for London, accompanied only by Richard Penderel and, according to the King's narration, 'aquainting none with my resolution of goeing to London but my Lord Wilmot'.[18]

But Charles never actually reached the capital. For a week

he wandered about the Midlands in an effort to avoid capture by soldiers and government agents whose enthusiasm for the chase was heightened by the considerable price which the government had placed on the head of 'Charles Stuart, Son of the late Tyrant'. The fugitives' sanctuaries included a barn and 'in a manner sufficiently declared to the World',[19] an oak in Spring Coppice on the Boscobel estate. But the private residences of those sympathetic to the King's cause provided the most cover. These were the home of Francis Woolf of Madeley in Shropshire, the home of Charles's companion, Richard Penderel, Hobbal Grange, the Giffard family seat at Boscobel House, also in Shropshire, and Moseley Hall, just north of Wolverhampton.

Charles in his narration recalled that at Moseley 'I changed my cloaths into a little better habit, like a serving-man, being a kind of gray-cloath suit'.[20] The master of the house was Colonel Lane, and his sister, Jane, volunteered to accompany Charles on the next leg of his journey to Bentley Hall, Stratford-upon-Avon, and Long Marston in Warwickshire, and then to Cirencester in Gloucestershire, and finally to Bristol.

Those Midland families who had, at the risk of their lives, assisted in the King's 'miraculous deliverance' received their rewards at the Restoration in the form of handsome pensions to be paid in perpetuity. Charles Giffard received a pension of £300 a year, Colonel Lane was granted £500 a year and his sister, Jane, £1,000. The Penderels were also handsomely rewarded, as was the family of one of Charles Giffard's servants, Francis Yates, who guided the King to Whiteladies, and was subsequently executed at Oxford by the government for refusing to say what he knew of the King's movements. Mr. Whitgreave of Moseley Hall also received recognition, and so did a certain papist priest, Father Huddleston, who was residing at the Hall at the time of Charles's clandestine visit. But the plea of Thomas Cock, an unsuccessful medical student from Worcester, for acknowledgement of his contribution to Charles's escape was denied, although his audacity must have evoked some admiration, even from a Stuart. Cock had been arrested during the battle of Worcester in mistake for the King, and, as compensation for his sufferings in the King's

cause, he petitioned for a Royal writ to the University of
Oxford to grant him the Degree of Doctor öf Medicine.
After leaving Bristol Charles spent a further five weeks
searching the south coast for a boat to take him to the
Continent, while in London 'Cromwell returned in triumph,
and was received with a universal joy and acclamation, as if
he had destroyed the enemy of the nation, and for ever
secured the liberty and happiness of the people'.[2][1]
A boat to take the King into exile was eventually com-
mandeered at Shoreham in Sussex, from whence Charles
sailed to join his mother, Henrietta Maria, in Paris. Here the
dispossessed King quickly learned duplicity and secrecy, and
became increasingly self-centred, while his vanity was nursed
by the recollection of his late sufferings. It was indeed a bad
training for a prince.

CHAPTER TWENTY

[1] Rushworth, *Historical collections abridged and improved*, Vol.VI,
p.606.

[2] *Cal.S.P.Dom.* 1649-1650, pp. 303, 304.

[3] *Ibid.*, p.312.

[4] Rushworth, *Op.cit.*, Vol.VI, p.604.

[5] Clarendon, Bk. XIII, 64, 65.

[6] *Reliquiae Baxterianae: or, Mr. Richard Baxter's Narrative of The Most
Memorable Passages of his Life and Times* (London, 1696), Lib.I,
Pt.I, pp.69, 68.

[7] Clarendon, Bk.XIII, 75.

[8] 'Letter from Oliver Cromwell to the Honourable William Lenthall,
Esquire, Speaker of the Parliament of England, Sept. 3 1651', *Oliver
Cromwell's Letters and Speeches:* with elucidations by Thomas Carlyle
(London, 1871), Vol.III, p.156.

[9] *Ibid.*, p.159.

[10] *Ibid.*, p.157.

[11] *Reliquiae Baxterianae,* Lib.I, Pt.I, p.69.

[12] 'Letter from Oliver Cromwell to William Lenthall, Sept. 4 1651', *Op.cit.,* p.157.

[13] Clarendon, Bk. XIII, 78.

[14] *Ibid.,* 64.

[15] Webb, *Civil War in Herefordshire,* Vol.II, p.276, f.n.i.

[16] *Reliquiae Baxterianae,* p.69.

[17] *An Account of the Preservation of King Charles II after the Battle of Worcester, drawn up by Himself,* ed. Sir David Dalrymple (Glasgow, 1766), p.9.

[18] *Ibid.,* pp. 9, 10.

[19] *Reliquiae Baxterianae,* p.69.

[20] *An Account of the Preservation of King Charles II,* pp. 29, 30.

[21] Clarendon, Bk.XIII, 82.

CHAPTER TWENTY-ONE

CONCLUSION

After almost a decade of intermittent internal strife England was once more at peace. But the new republic born out of the Civil War was not destined for longevity. By 1653 the great 17th-century truth had dawned, that the only alternative to absolutism was anarchy. Executive power was placed in the hands of an introspective and strangely magnanimous squire from East Anglia, who had become the greatest soldier of his age, Oliver Cromwell. 'The young Commonwealth being headless ... a governor there must be, and who should be thought fitter',[1] observed Richard Baxter. After Protector Oliver's death in 1658 the fear of further internal strife created an atmosphere sympathetic to the return of the Stuart dynasty and Charles II was restored to his kingdoms.

In spite of the relatively short duration and seeming lack of intensity of the war, its impact on Midland folk was, as we have seen, considerable. There are some, however, who dispute this, claiming that natural disasters such as harvest failure, disease, and fire, had a greater and more permanent effect upon the community than the sporadic outbursts of fighting that constituted the English Civil War.

Richard Gough, a native of Myddle in Shropshire, would disagree. Gough, who was a schoolboy at the time of the Civil War, recalled that 'King Charles the 1st sett up his standard at Nottingham, A.D.1642, and because few there resorted to him, he removed thence to Shrewsbury about the later end of Summer 1642, in hopes that this country and Wales would soone furnish him with an army, and he was not disappointed in his expectation, for multitudes came to him dayly. And of these three towns, Myddle, Marton, and Newton [they were, in effect, only hamlets of a few dozen families apiece], there went noe less than twenty men, of which number thirteen were kill'd in the warrs ... And if soe many dyed out of these 3 townes, we may reasonably guesse that many thousands dyed in England in that warre'.[2]

It is questionable whether the disasters of a more providential nature, to which these three villages were also subject, in any way minimised the impact of this great loss of life, any more than the effects of the Great War were minimised by the death rate of the 1919 influenza epidemic. In 17th-century England plague and famine were, in any case, ever prevalent possibilities to which people had become accustomed. The same could not be said about the ravages of civil war.

It has also been suggested that considerable material benefits accrued to many from the Civil War, and that because of it the staple industries of several Midland towns were developed and even established. But more families were ruined than were made during this period. Royalist and Parliamentarian families alike, and even those of no particular persuasion, had to endure the excesses of the plundering soldiery, while at the same time being forced to display their loyalty to one cause or the other, or to both, in coin and in kind. The drain on financial resources continued for the Royalists throughout the Commonwealth and Protectorate through fines and sequestration, for which very few received recompense at the Restoration.

The war brought little benefit to towns like Shrewsbury whose inhabitants were 'worne out ... in their estates, for want of trade with London'.[3] The same could not, of course, be said about such places as Northampton, Coventry, and Leicester, who were able to maintain their contact with London. But neither this, nor the fact that they secured contracts to supply the Parliamentary armies with shoes and stockings, which were probably not paid for in full, would hardly compensate for the general loss of trade that their already-established industries sustained because of the war, or for the universal hardships sustained in maintaining large garrisons in these towns.

At Northampton, in November 1643, the master shoe-makers were constrained to petition Parliament in London to the effect 'that their prentices and journeymen that have put themselves into the Parliament service, being about an hundred and fifty, might be discharged, in respect there can be none, or, very few, gotten to worke and uphold that trade, by which meanes many are likely to be impoverished, with their wives and families, it being the greatest trade practiced in that towne'.[4]

The burdens involved in 'entertaining' garrisons were not entirely financial, as we have seen from the Oxford experience. Coventry, despite the monolithic Parliamentarianism of its inhabitants, and presumably of its visitors also, could, it seems, be just as ill-used by the Parliamentary soldiery as those of the Royalist persuasion. Mr. John Byker while on a visit to Coventry 'received some rude affronts from a souldier of that garrison. He being a very civill man of good moderation, and, it seems, well instructed not to answer the foole in his folly ... withdrew himself from the place to decline the insolent madnesse of the souldier and free himself from his provocations. Being come into the streets, secure, as he thought, from violence, he was suddenly run through the body, falling downe, dyed instantly.' According to this Royalist report, 'his offence was (for as yet we can heare of no others) that he was a parsons sonne, so inveterate malice to that function and all depending on it, do these rebels leave'.[5]

Leicester must have suffered all these privations, added to which was the calamity that the town sustained at the hands of Charles I's army in the late spring of 1645, an event that moved Wallington to remark that 'in the ruins of Leicester you may behold a large map of misery, the townsmen, from the richest to the poorest, being all of them despoiled of their goods'.[6]

It should, however, be emphasised that trade and industry did not fall into irremediable decay, and as soon as there was universal peace people more or less resumed their pre-war pattern of life. Writing from Shrewsbury in 1655, Major-General James Berry observed that 'our ministers of religion are bad, our magistrates idle, and the people all asleep: only these present actings have a little awakened them'.

From this it would appear that although the immediate physical impact of the Civil War on the inhabitants of the

Midlands was considerable, it was, nevertheless, short-lived. The same could be said of the effects of the spate of political, social, and theological speculation that the war had released. What became of those minds that had been stirred up as they had not been before? What became of those discordant elements which were confusedly blended to devastate society; those elements that had imbibed the Calvinistic doctrine of just resistance to secular authority? 'It were a nation miserable indeed, not worth the name of a nation, but a race of idiots, whose happiness and welfare depended upon one man',[7] propounded their poet, John Milton.

Included in the phrenetic intellectual speculation of the period were the concepts of a more universal suffrage and 'the career open to talents', or equality of opportunity. The realisation of the latter was made possible, albeit temporarily, by the war. New men, sometimes of singularly low origin and humble calling, rose to eminence, 'Tinker' Fox provides an example of this, as does Colonel John Birch, the Parliamentary governor of Hereford, who before the war was a carter. While the humble origin of Major-General Richard Browne who, it will be remembered, took Bletchingdon House for Parliament in 1645, is recorded for posterity by Browne's detractors who dubbed him 'The Faggot Monger', and 'Sergeant Major of the wood-yard'. And two more illustrations are provided by the above mentioned Major-General James Berry who, Baxter tells us, 'had formerly lived as a Servant (a Clark of Iron-works)',[8] and Oliver Cromwell of the gentry class who attained military status hitherto reserved for the aristocracy.

None of these democratic ideals survived the Restoration. The Monarchy was restored without much thought for the security of the Nation's liberties. The franchise was never extended, even during the Commonwealth and Protectorate. The meteoric rise of so many new men also ceased at the Restoration and must, therefore, be considered a consequence of violent political and military agitation. In all cases of this nature, in which the talents and passions of men are exercised with unusual force, there will always be some whose powers will raise them to eminence. In addition, those who had brought the revolution about were subsequently impeached and held up to public obloquy in official histories, in the press, on the stage, and in the novel. While their antagonists acquired a glamorous reputation which, as we have seen, was quite unjustified.

There is no single reason for the demise of these democratic ideals. The peculiarly Laodicean attitude of the English, self-interest (always a powerful counsellor), and a preference for amelioration gained through evolution reather than revolution, were all contributory factors. Also, the anomalous and often contradictory nature of the elements that comprised the Parliamentary Party rendered a positive settlement impossible. Those who viewed the war in strictly religious terms like the Fifth Monarchists and those who saw the Royalists as merely attempting 'to square the Church of England with the Church of Rome', could find little in common with the Levellers and other sects of a more political nature.

But the radical notions that were begotten of the English Civil War did not perish completely. In 1685 Colonel Richard Rumbold was executed for his implication in a plot to assassinate Charles II and his brother James two years earlier. On the scaffold Rumbold, who had served as a Lieutenant under Cromwell, declared 'I am sure there was no man born marked of God above another; for none comes into the world with a saddle on his back, neither any booted and spurred to ride him'.[9] The spirit of 40 years before was in these words, and the political creed of the majority of those who fought for Parliament could not have been better expressed.

If the social and political aspirations of those who fought the English Civil War were deferred the power of the institution whose conflict with the monarchy precipitated the War was not. It has, since the Civil War, increased its powers of sovereignty until it now possesses more authority than any single monarch in this country's history, including Charles I. Because of this, and the absence of a genuine and independent guardian of the people's constitutional·liberties, Englishmen may, in the future, be compelled to impose on Parliament the same restraint that they imposed on Charles I three centuries ago, but with the remembrance that 'there is no victory in civill warre that can bring the conqueror a perfect triumph'.[10]

CHAPTER TWENTY-ONE.

[1] *Reliquiae Baxterianae,* Lib.I, Pt.I, p.70.

[2] Richard Gough, *The Antiquities and Memoirs of the Parish of Myddle, County of Salop* (Shrewsbury, 1875).

[3] *The Moderate Intelligencer,* No. 1 (1645) Thomason Tracts E.271.

[4] *Mercurius Aulicus,* 14 November 1643.

[5] Ryves, *Mercurius Rusticus,* Part I, p.49.

[6] Wallington, *Historical Notes of Events,* Vol.II, p.263.

[7] *The Prose Works of John Milton,* ed. J.A. St. John (London, 1848), Vol.I, pp.454, 455.

[8] *Reliquiae Baxterianae,* p.97.

[9] Proceedings against Richard Rumbold, for High Treason, A.D.1685; *A Complete Collection of State Trials,* compiled by T.B. Howell (London, 1811), p.881.

[10] *A True Relation of the Late Expedition of His Excellency, Robert Earle of Essex, for the Relief of Gloucester* (London, 1643); Bibliotheca Gloucestrensis, Pt.I, p.249.

BIBLIOGRAPHY

A. *Manuscript Sources*

Birmingham Reference Library:

Letter Book of Sir William Brereton Referring to The Time of the Leaguers at Dudley and Tutbury Castles, and Lichfield Close, 4 April to 29 May 1646, (Document No. 595611).

Gloucester City Library:

An order signed at Gloucester by Edward Massey, giving John Smith safe conduct between Bristol and Nibley, (Document No. 16069(5)).

Public Record Office:

S.P. 23's Committee for Compounding with Delinquents.
S.P. 24's Committee and Commissioners for Indemnity.
S.P. 28's Commonwealth Exchequer Papers - Army Accounts and Assessments, loans, and Contributions.

Staffordshire County Record Office:

Petition of Richard Richardson, (Document No. Q/SR.M.1648, f.6)

B. *Contemporary Pamphlets and Newspapers*

Birmingham Reference Library.

British Museum:
Thomason Tracts.

University Library, Cambridge.

N.B. The majority of those pamphlets and newspapers to which no place of origin is attached are in the University Library, Cambridge.

C. *Other Contemporary Printed Matter.*

A Collection of all the publicke Orders and Ordinances and Declarations of both Houses of Parliament, from the Ninth of March 1642 untill December 1646
(London, 1646)

Baxter, Richard

Reliquiae Baxterianae: or, Mr. Richard Baxter's Narrative of the Most Memorable Passages of his Life and Times
(London, 1696)

Corbet, John

A true and impartiall History of the Military Government of the Citie of Gloucester (London, 1647)

Dugdale, Sir William

A Short View of the Late Troubles in England (Oxford, 1681)

Lilly, William

Monarchy or no monarchy in England (London, 1651)

May, Thomas

The History of the Parliament of England (London, 1647)

Rushworth, John

Historical collections of private passages of state (London, 1680-1701)

Rushworth, John

Historical collections abridged and improved (London, 1703-1708)

Ryves, B.

Mercurius Rusticus: or, the countries complaint of the barbarous out-rages committed by the sectaries of the late flourishing kingdome (Oxford, 1646)

Sprigge, Joshua

Anglia Rediviva (London, 1647)

Vicars, John

God in the Mount, Or, England's remembrancer (London, 1642)

Vicars, John

Magnalia Dei Anglicana, Or, Englands Parliamentary-chronicle (London 1644-1646)

Walker, Sir Edward   *Historical Discourses upon Several Occasions* (London, 1705)

Whitelocke, Bulstrode   *Memorials of the English Affairs* (London, 1682)

D. *Later Publications of Contemporary Diaries, Correspondence, Histories, Memoirs, Official Documents, Records, and other Works.*

                                     Acts and Ordinances of the Interregnum, 1642-1660, ed. C. H. Firth and R. S. Rait (London, 1911)

Ashmole, Elias   *His Autobiographical and Historical Notes, his Correspondence, and Other Contemporary Sources Relating to his Life and Work, (1617-1692),* ed. C.H. Jostin (Oxford, 1966)

Atkyns, Richard   *The Vindication of, Military Memoirs of the Civil War* ed. P. Young and N. Tucker, (London, 1967)

Aubery, John   *Brief Lives and other Selected Writings,* ed. A. Powell (London, 1949)

Baillie, Robert   *The Letters and Journals of,* ed. David Laing (Edinburgh, 1841, 1842)

                                     Banbury, Oxfordshire, Baptism and Burial Register of, Part I (1558-1653), transcribed by Mrs. N. Fillmore, ed. J.S.W. Gibson (The Banbury Historical Society, 1965/66)

                                     Bibliotheca Gloucestrensis, ed. John Washbourn (London, 1823, 1825)

Birch, Colonel John   *Military Memoir of,* ed. J. & T. W. Webb (*Camden Society,* N.S. Vol. VII, 1873)

                                     The Calendar of State Papers:

	Domestic Series 1641-1643; 1644; 1644-1645; 1649-1650.
Charles I	*The Letters, Speeches and Proclamations of,* ed. Sir Charles Petrie (London, 1935)
Charles II	*An Account of the Preservation of, after the Battle of Worcester, drawn by Himslef,* ed. Sir David Dalrymple (Glasgow, 1766)
Clarendon, Edward, Earl of	*The History of the Rebellion and Civil Wars in England,* ed. W. Dunn Macray (Oxford, 1888)
	A Collection of Original Letters and Papers, Concerning the Affairs of England, 1641-1660, ed. Thomas Carte (London, 1739)
	Commons, Journals of the House of
Cromwell, Oliver	*Letters and Speeches:* with elucidations by Thomas Carlyle (London, 1871)
Cromwell, Oliver	*Letters and Speeches:* with elucidations by Thomas Carlyle, ed. S. C. Lomas (London, 1904)
	Denbigh Manuscripts, Historical Manuscripts Commission, Fourth Report (1874)
	Denbigh Manuscripts, Part V, Historical Manuscripts Commission (1911)
Dugdale, William	*The Life, Diary and Correspondence of,* ed. William Hamper (London, 1827)
	Dunrobin Manuscript, transcribed by D.E.A. Horne, *Collections for a History of Staffordshire* (The Staffordshire Record Society, 1936)
	Epistolary Curiosities, ed. Rebecca

Warner (London, 1818)

Fairfax Correspondence - Memorials of the Civil War, ed. Robert Bell (London, 1849)

Gough, Richard

The Antiquities and Memoirs of the Parish of Myddle, County Salop (Shrewsbury, 1875)

Greene, John

The Diary of, (1635-1657). by E.M. Symonds, *English Historical Review,* Vol.XLIII (1928)

Hastings' Manuscripts, Vol.II, *Historical Manuscripts Commission* (1933)

Historical Manuscripts Commission Sixth Report (1877)
Seventh Report (1879)
Ninth Report (1884)
Fourteenth Report (1894)

Hobbes, Thomas

Behemoth, or the Long Parliament, ed. Ferdinand Tönnes (London, 1889)

Hutchinson, Lucy

Memoirs of Colonel Hutchinson, ed. Rev. Julius Hutchinson (Everyman Library Edition, London, 1908)

Leicester, Records of the Borough of, ed. Helen Stocks (Cambridge, 1923)

Lords, Journals of the House of

Ludlow, Edmund

The Memoirs of, 1625-1672, ed. C.H. Firth (London, 1894)

Luke, Sir Samuel

Journal of, ed. I.G. Philip (The Oxfordshire Record Society, 1947)

Luke, Sir Samuel

The Letter Books (1644-45) of, ed. H.G. Tibbutt (London, 1963)

Milton, John

The Prose Works of, ed. J.A. St. John (London, 1848)

Morrice, Thomas	*A Collection of State Letters of the Rt. Hon. Roger Boyle, first Earl of Orrery ... Together with ... the Life of the Earl of Orrery.* (London, 1742)
Ottley, Sir Francis	*The Papers of,* ed. W. Phillips, *Shropshire Archaeological Society's Transactions,* 2nd Series, Vols. VI, VII, VIII (1894, 1895, 1896)
	Oxford Council Acts, 1626-1665 ed. M.G. Hobson and H.E. Salter (Oxford Historical Society, 1933)
Petty, Sir William	*The Economic Writings of,* ed. C.A. Hull (Cambridge, 1899)
	Portland Manuscripts, Vol.III, Historical Manuscripts Commission, Fourteenth Report, Appendix, Part II (1894)
Rupert, Prince	*The Journal of Prince Rupert's Marches, 5 Sept. 1642 to 4 July 1646,* ed. C.H. Firth, *English Historical Review,* Vol.XIII (1898)
	Sidney Papers (Letters and Memorials of State), ed. Arthur Collins (London, 1746)
	The Committee at Stafford 1643-1645, (The Order Book of the Staffordshire County Committee), ed. D.H. Pennington and I.A. Rootes (Manchester, 1957)
	Staffordshire and the Great Rebellion, ed. D.A. Johnson and D.G. Vaisey (Stafford, 1964)
Symonds, Richard	*Diary of the Marches of the Royal Army During the Great Civil War,* ed. C.E. Long *(Camden Society* Vol.LXXXIV, 1859)

Townshend, Henry   *Diary of, 1640-1663,* ed. J.W. Willis
of Elmley Lovett,   Bund (Worcester, 1916)

Wallington, Nehemiah *Historical Notes of Events Occurring
                      Chiefly in the Reign of Charles I*
                      (London, 1869)

Wharton, Nehemiah   'Letters from a Subaltern Officer in
                      the Earl of Essex's Army, written in
                      the Summer and Autumn of 1642,'
                      *Archaeologia, or, Miscellaneous
                      Tracts relating to Antiquity,* pub-
                      lished by the Society of Antiquaries
                      of London, Vol.XXXV (1853)

Wood, Anthony   *The Life and Times of,* ed. A. Clark,
                      (The Oxford Historical Society.
                      1891-1900)

E.   *Secondary and General Sources*

Ashley, M.   *Cromwell's Generals* (London, 1954)

Boase, C.W.   *Oxford,* (Historic Towns Series,
                      London, 1887)

Beesley, A.   *The History of Banbury: including
                      copious historical and antiquarian
                      notices of the neighbourhood* (Lon-
                      don, 1842)

Bond, W.G.   *The Wanderings of Charles I and his
                      Army in the Midlands in the Years
                      1642-1644-1645*
                      (Birmingham, 1927)

Burne, A.H. and   *The Great Civil War, 1642-1646*
Young, P.   (London, 1959)

Burton, J.R.   *A History of Bewdley; with concise
                      accounts of some neighbouring
                      parishes* (London, 1883)

Drinkwater, John   *Cromwell and Other Poems* (Lon-
                      don, 1913), for *The Gathering of the
                      Ironsides.*

Everitt, A.M.   *The Local Community and The
                      Great Rebellion* (Historical Assoc-

iation Pamphlet - General Series
No. 70, 1969)

Firth, C.H.	*Cromwell's Army* (London, 1902)
Fletcher, The Rev. Carteret J.H.	*A History of the Church of St. Martin (Carfax) Oxford* (Oxford, 1896)
Fox, Levi	*The Borough Town of Stratford-upon-Avon* (Stratford-upon-Avon, 1953)
Gardiner, S.R.	*History of the Great Civil War, 1642-1649* (London, 1886-1901)
Guttery, D.R.	*The Great Civil War in Midland Parishes* (Birmingham, 1951)
Hall, A.R.	*Ballistics in the Seventeenth Century* (Cambridge, 1952)
Hutton, William	*An History of Birmingham* (Birmingham, 1781)
James, M.	*Social Problems and Policy During the Puritan Revolution, 1640-1660* (London, 1930)
Kenyon, R. Lloyd	'History of the Shrewsbury Mint, with an account of the Coins struck there', *Shropshire Archaeological Transactions 2nd Series, Vol.X (1898)*
Leland, John	*The Itinerary of, in or about the years 1535-1543*, ed. Lucy Toulmin Smith (London, 1907-1910)
Manning, B.S.	*Neutrals and Neutralism in the English Civil War, 1642-1646* (Unpublished D.Phil. thesis deposited in the Bodleian Library, Oxford, (1957)
Nichols, John	*The History and Antiquities of the County of Leicester* (London, 1795-1815)
Ollard, Richard	*The Escape of Charles II* (London, 1966)

Phillips, J.R.

Memoirs of the Civil War in Wales and the Marches, 1642-1646 (London, 1874)

Rogers, H.C.B.

Battles and Generals of the Civil Wars, 1642-1651 (London, 1968)

Shaw, Stebbing

The History and Antiquities of Staffordshire (London, 1798, 1801)

State Trials, A Complete Collection of, Vol.XI, 1680-1688, compiled by T.B. Howell (London, 1811)

Sutton Town and Chase, Tales of, collected by Thomas A. Vaughton (Birmingham, 1904)

Toynbee, M.R. and Leeming, J.J.

'Cropredy Bridge', *Oxoniensia, Vol. III* (1938)

Varley, F.J.

The Siege of Oxford (Oxford, 1932)

Willis Bund, J.W.

The Civil War in Worcestershire (Birmingham, 1905)

Webb, J. & T.W.

Memorials of the Civil War in Herefordshire (London, 1879)

Wedgwood, C.V.

The King's War, 1641-1647 (London, 1958)

Wood, A.C.

Nottinghamshire in the Civil War (Oxford, 1937)

Woolrych, A.

Battles of the English Civil War (London, 1961)

Young, P.

Edgehill 1642 (The Campaign and the Battle) (Kineton, 1967)

INDEX OF PLACES

INDEX OF PERSONS

GENERAL INDEX